Scala for Data Science

Leverage the power of Scala to build scalable, robust
data science applications

Pascal Bugnion

[PACKT] open source
PUBLISHING
community experience distilled

BIRMINGHAM - MUMBAI

Scala for Data Science

First published: January 2016

Production reference: 1220116

Published by Packt Publishing Ltd.
Livery Place
35 Livery Street
Birmingham B3 2PB, UK.

ISBN 978-1-78528-137-2

www.packtpub.com

Credits

Author
Pascal Bugnion

Reviewers
Umanga Bista
Radek Ostrowski
Yuanhang Wang

Commissioning Editor
Veena Pagare

Acquisition Editor
Sonali Vernekar

Content Development Editor
Shali Deeraj

Technical Editor
Suwarna Patil

Copy Editor
Tasneem Fatehi

Project Coordinator
Sanchita Mandal

Proofreader
Safis Editing

Indexer
Monica Ajmera Mehta

Graphics
Disha Haria

Production Coordinator
Arvindkumar Gupta

Cover Work
Arvindkumar Gupta

About the Author

Pascal Bugnion is a data engineer at the ASI, a consultancy offering bespoke data science services. Previously, he was the head of data engineering at SCL Elections. He holds a PhD in computational physics from Cambridge University.

Besides Scala, Pascal is a keen Python developer. He has contributed to NumPy, matplotlib and IPython. He also maintains scikit-monaco, an open source library for Monte Carlo integration. He currently lives in London, UK.

I owe a huge debt of gratitude to my parents and my partner for supporting me in this, as well as my employer for encouraging me to pursue this project. I also thank the reviewers, Umanga Bista, Yuanhang Wang, and Radek Ostrowski for their tireless efforts, as well as the entire team at Packt for their support, advice, and hard work carrying this book to completion.

About the Reviewers

Umanga Bista is machine learning and real-time analytics enthusiast from Kathmandu. He completed his bachelors in computer engineering in September, 2013. Since then, he has been working at LogPoint, a SEIM product and company. He primarily works on building statistical plugins and real time, scalable, and fault tolerant architecture to process multiterabyte scale log data streams for security analytics, intelligence, and compliance.

Radek Ostrowski is a freelance big data engineer with an educational background in high-performance computing. He specializes in building scalable real-time data collection and predictive analytics platforms. He has worked at EPCC, University of Edinburgh in data-related projects for many years. Additionally, he has contributed to the success of a game's startup—deltaDNA, co-built super-scalable backend for PlayStation 4 at Sony, helped to improve data processes at Expedia, and started a Docker revolution at Tesco Bank. He is currently working with Spark and Scala for Max2 Inc, an NYC-based startup that is building a community-powered venue discovery platform, offering personalized recommendations, curated and real-time information.

Yuanhang Wang is a data scientist with primary focus on DSL design. He has dabbled in several functional programming languages. He is particularly interested in machine learning and programming language theory. He is currently a data scientist at China Mobile Research Center, working on typed data processing engine and optimizer that is built on top of several big-data platforms.

Yuanhang Wang describes himself as an enthusiast of purely functional programming and neural networks. He obtained his master's degrees both in Harbin Institute of Technology, China and University of Pavia, Italy.

www.PacktPub.com

Support files, eBooks, discount offers, and more

For support files and downloads related to your book, please visit www.PacktPub.com.

Did you know that Packt offers eBook versions of every book published, with PDF and ePub files available? You can upgrade to the eBook version at www.PacktPub.com and as a print book customer, you are entitled to a discount on the eBook copy. Get in touch with us at service@packtpub.com for more details.

At www.PacktPub.com, you can also read a collection of free technical articles, sign up for a range of free newsletters and receive exclusive discounts and offers on Packt books and eBooks.

https://www2.packtpub.com/books/subscription/packtlib

Do you need instant solutions to your IT questions? PacktLib is Packt's online digital book library. Here, you can search, access, and read Packt's entire library of books.

Why subscribe?

- Fully searchable across every book published by Packt
- Copy and paste, print, and bookmark content
- On demand and accessible via a web browser

Free access for Packt account holders

If you have an account with Packt at www.PacktPub.com, you can use this to access PacktLib today and view 9 entirely free books. Simply use your login credentials for immediate access.

To my parents.

To Jessica and to my friends.

Table of Contents

Preface

Data science is fashionable. Data science startups are sprouting across the globe and established companies are scrambling to assemble data science teams. The ability to analyze large datasets is also becoming increasingly important in the academic and research world.

Why this explosion in demand for data scientists? Our view is that the emergence of data science can be viewed as the serendipitous collusion of several interlinked factors. The first is data availability. Over the last fifteen years, the amount of data collected by companies has exploded. In the world of research, cheap gene sequencing techniques have drastically increased the amount of genomic data available. Social and professional networking sites have built huge graphs interlinking a significant fraction of the people living on the planet. At the same time, the development of the World Wide Web makes accessing this wealth of data possible from almost anywhere in the world.

The increased availability of data has resulted in an increase in data awareness. It is no longer acceptable for decision makers to trust their experience and "gut feeling" alone. Increasingly, one expects business decisions to be driven by data.

Finally, the tools for efficiently making sense of and extracting insights from huge data sets are starting to mature: one doesn't need to be an expert in distributed computing to analyze a large data set any more. Apache Spark, for instance, greatly eases writing distributed data analysis applications. The explosion of cloud infrastructure facilitates scaling computing needs to cope with variable data amounts.

Scala is a popular language for data science. By emphasizing immutability and functional constructs, Scala lends itself well to the construction of robust libraries for concurrency and big data analysis. A rich ecosystem of tools for data science has therefore developed around Scala, including libraries for accessing SQL and NoSQL databases, frameworks for building distributed applications like Apache Spark and libraries for linear algebra and numerical algorithms. We will explore this rich and growing ecosystem in the fourteen chapters of this book.

What this book covers

We aim to give you a flavor for what is possible with Scala, and to get you started using libraries that are useful for building data science applications. We do not aim to provide an entirely comprehensive overview of any of these topics. This is best left to online documentation or to reference books. What we will teach you is how to combine these tools to build efficient, scalable programs, and have fun along the way.

Chapter 1, Scala and Data Science, is a brief description of data science, and of Scala's place in the data scientist's tool-belt. We describe why Scala is becoming increasingly popular in data science, and how it compares to alternative languages such as Python.

Chapter 2, Manipulating Data with Breeze, introduces Breeze, a library providing support for numerical algorithms in Scala. We learn how to perform linear algebra and optimization, and solve a simple machine learning problem using logistic regression.

Chapter 3, Plotting with breeze-viz, introduces the breeze-viz library for plotting two-dimensional graphs and histograms.

Chapter 4, Parallel Collections and Futures, describes basic concurrency constructs. We will learn to parallelize simple problems by distributing them over several threads using parallel collections, and apply what we have learned to build a parallel cross-validation pipeline. We then describe how to wrap computation in a future to execute it asynchronously. We apply this pattern to query a web API, sending several requests in parallel.

Chapter 5, Scala and SQL through JDBC, looks at interacting with SQL databases in a functional manner. We learn how to use common Scala patterns to wrap the Java interface exposed by JDBC. Besides learning about JDBC, this chapter introduces type classes, the loan pattern, implicit conversions, and other patterns that are frequently leveraged in libraries and existing Scala code.

Chapter 6, Slick - A Functional Interface for SQL, describes the Slick library for mapping data in SQL tables to Scala objects.

Chapter 7, Web APIs, describes how to query web APIs in a concurrent, fault-tolerant manner using futures. We learn to parse JSON responses and formulate complex HTTP requests with authentication. We walk through querying the GitHub API to obtain information about GitHub users programmatically.

Chapter 8, Scala and MongoDB, walks the reader through interacting with MongoDB, a leading NoSQL database. We build a pipeline that fetches user data from the GitHub API and stores it in a MongoDB database.

Chapter 9, Concurrency with Akka, introduces the Akka framework for building concurrent applications with actors. We use Akka to build a scalable crawler that explores the GitHub follower graph.

Chapter 10, Distributed Batch Processing with Spark, explores the Apache Spark framework for building distributed applications. We learn how to construct and manipulate distributed datasets in memory. We touch briefly on the internals of Spark, learning how the architecture allows for distributed, fault-tolerant computation.

Chapter 11, Spark SQL and DataFrames, describes DataFrames, one of the more powerful features of Spark for the manipulation of structured data. We learn how to load JSON and Parquet files into DataFrames.

Chapter 12, Distributed Machine Learning with MLlib, explores how to build distributed machine learning pipelines with MLlib, a library built on top of Apache Spark. We use the library to train a spam filter.

Chapter 13, Web APIs with Play, describes how to use the Play framework to build web APIs. We describe the architecture of modern web applications, and how these fit into the data science pipeline. We build a simple web API that returns JSON.

Chapter 14, Visualization with D3 and the Play Framework, builds on the previous chapter to program a fully fledged web application with Play and D3. We describe how to integrate JavaScript into a Play framework application.

Appendix, Pattern Matching and Extractors, describes how pattern matching provides the programmer with a powerful construct for control flow.

What you need for this book

The examples provided in this book require that you have a working Scala installation and SBT, the *Simple Build Tool,* a command line utility for compiling and running Scala code. We will walk you through how to install these in the next sections.

We do not require a specific IDE. The code examples can be written in your favorite text editor or IDE.

Installing the JDK

Scala code is compiled to Java byte code. To run the byte code, you must have the Java Virtual Machine (JVM) installed, which comes as part of a Java Development Kit (JDK). There are several JDK implementations and, for the purpose of this book, it does not matter which one you choose. You may already have a JDK installed on your computer. To check this, enter the following in a terminal:

```
$ java -version
java version "1.8.0_66"
Java(TM) SE Runtime Environment (build 1.8.0_66-b17)
Java HotSpot(TM) 64-Bit Server VM (build 25.66-b17, mixed mode)
```

If you do not have a JDK installed, you will get an error stating that the java command does not exist.

If you do have a JDK installed, you should still verify that you are running a sufficiently recent version. The number that matters is the minor version number: the 8 in 1.8.0_66. Versions 1.8.xx of Java are commonly referred to as Java 8. For the first twelve chapters of this book, Java 7 will be sufficient (your version number should be something like 1.7.xx or newer). However, you will need Java 8 for the last two chapters, since the Play framework requires it. We therefore recommend that you install Java 8.

On Mac, the easiest way to install a JDK is using Homebrew:

```
$ brew install java
```

This will install Java 8, specifically the Java Standard Edition Development Kit, from Oracle.

Homebrew is a package manager for Mac OS X. If you are not familiar with Homebrew, I highly recommend using it to install development tools. You can find installation instructions for Homebrew on: http://brew.sh.

To install a JDK on Windows, go to http://www.oracle.com/technetwork/java/javase/downloads/index.html (or, if this URL does not exist, to the Oracle website, then click on Downloads and download **Java Platform, Standard Edition**). Select Windows x86 for 32-bit Windows, or Windows x64 for 64 bit. This will download an installer, which you can run to install the JDK.

To install a JDK on Ubuntu, install OpenJDK with the package manager for your distribution:

```
$ sudo apt-get install openjdk-8-jdk
```

If you are running a sufficiently old version of Ubuntu (14.04 or earlier), this package will not be available. In this case, either fall back to openjdk-7-jdk, which will let you run examples in the first twelve chapters, or install the Java Standard Edition Development Kit from Oracle through a PPA (a non-standard package archive):

```
$ sudo add-apt-repository ppa:webupd8team/java
$ sudo apt-get update
$ sudo apt-get install oracle-java8-installer
```

You then need to tell Ubuntu to prefer Java 8 with:

```
$ sudo update-java-alternatives -s java-8-oracle
```

Installing and using SBT

The Simple Build Tool (SBT) is a command line tool for managing dependencies and building and running Scala code. It is the de facto build tool for Scala. To install SBT, follow the instructions on the SBT website (http://www.scala-sbt.org/0.13/tutorial/Setup.html).

When you start a new SBT project, SBT downloads a specific version of Scala for you. You, therefore, do not need to install Scala directly on your computer. Managing the entire dependency suite from SBT, including Scala itself, is powerful: you do not have to worry about developers working on the same project having different versions of Scala or of the libraries used.

Since we will use SBT extensively in this book, let's create a simple test project. If you have used SBT previously, do skip this section.

Create a new directory called sbt-example and navigate to it. Inside this directory, create a file called build.sbt. This file encodes all the dependencies for the project. Write the following in build.sbt:

```
// build.sbt

scalaVersion := "2.11.7"
```

This specifies which version of Scala we want to use for the project. Open a terminal in the sbt-example directory and type:

```
$ sbt
```

This starts an interactive shell. Let's open a Scala console:

```
> console
```

This gives you access to a Scala console in the context of your project:

```
scala> println("Scala is running!")
Scala is running!
```

Besides running code in the console, we will also write Scala programs. Open an editor in the `sbt-example` directory and enter a basic "hello, world" program. Name the file `HelloWorld.scala`:

```
// HelloWorld.scala

object HelloWorld extends App {
  println("Hello, world!")
}
```

Return to SBT and type:

```
> run
```

This will compile the source files and run the executable, printing `"Hello, world!"`.

Besides compiling and running your Scala code, SBT also manages Scala dependencies. Let's specify a dependency on Breeze, a library for numerical algorithms. Modify the `build.sbt` file as follows:

```
// build.sbt

scalaVersion := "2.11.7"

libraryDependencies ++= Seq(
  "org.scalanlp" %% "breeze" % "0.11.2",
  "org.scalanlp" %% "breeze-natives" % "0.11.2"
)
```

SBT requires that statements be separated by empty lines, so make sure that you leave an empty line between `scalaVersion` and `libraryDependencies`. In this example, we have specified a dependency on Breeze version `"0.11.2"`. How did we know to use these coordinates for Breeze? Most Scala packages will quote the exact SBT string to get the latest version in their documentation.

If this is not the case, or you are specifying a dependency on a Java library, head to the Maven Central website (http://mvnrepository.com) and search for the package of interest, for example "Breeze". The website provides a list of packages, including several named breeze_2.xx packages. The number after the underscore indicates the version of Scala the package was compiled for. Click on "breeze_2.11" to get a list of the different Breeze versions available. Choose "0.11.2". You will be presented with a list of package managers to choose from (Maven, Ivy, Leiningen, and so on). Choose SBT. This will print a line like:

```
libraryDependencies += "org.scalanlp" % "breeze_2.11" % "0.11.2"
```

These are the coordinates that you will want to copy to the build.sbt file. Note that we just specified "breeze", rather than "breeze_2.11". By preceding the package name with two percentage signs, %%, SBT automatically resolves to the correct Scala version. Thus, specifying %% "breeze" is identical to % "breeze_2.11".

Now return to your SBT console and run:

```
> reload
```

This will fetch the Breeze jars from Maven Central. You can now import Breeze in either the console or your scripts (within the context of this Scala project). Let's test this in the console:

```
> console
scala> import breeze.linalg._
import breeze.linalg._


scala> import breeze.numerics._
import breeze.numerics._


scala> val vec = linspace(-2.0, 2.0, 100)
vec: breeze.linalg.DenseVector[Double] = DenseVector(-2.0,
-1.9595959595959596, ...


scala> sigmoid(vec)
breeze.linalg.DenseVector[Double] = DenseVector(0.11920292202211755,
0.12351078065 ...
```

You should now be able to compile, run and specify dependencies for your Scala scripts.

Who this book is for

This book introduces the data science ecosystem for people who already know some Scala. If you are a data scientist, or data engineer, or if you want to enter data science, this book will give you all the tools you need to implement data science solutions in Scala.

For the avoidance of doubt, let me also clarify what this book is not:

- This is not an introduction to Scala. We assume that you already have a working knowledge of the language. If you do not, we recommend *Programming in Scala* by *Martin Odersky, Lex Spoon,* and *Bill Venners.*

- This is not a book about machine learning in Scala. We will use machine learning to illustrate the examples, but the aim is not to teach you how to write your own gradient-boosted tree class. Machine learning is just one (important) part of data science, and this book aims to cover the full pipeline, from data acquisition to data visualization. If you are interested more specifically in how to implement machine learning solutions in Scala, I recommend *Scala for machine learning,* by *Patrick R. Nicolas.*

Conventions

In this book, you will find a number of text styles that distinguish between different kinds of information. Here are some examples of these styles and an explanation of their meaning.

Code words in text, database table names, folder names, filenames, file extensions, pathnames, dummy URLs, and user input are shown as follows: "We can import modules with the `import` statement."

A block of code is set as follows:

```scala
def occurrencesOf[A](elem:A, collection:List[A]):List[Int] = {
  for {
    (currentElem, index) <- collection.zipWithIndex
    if (currentElem == elem)
  } yield index
}
```

When we wish to draw your attention to a particular part of a code block, the relevant lines or items are set in bold:

```scala
def occurrencesOf[A](elem:A, collection:List[A]):List[Int] = {
  for {
    (currentElem, index) <- collection.zipWithIndex
    if (currentElem == elem)
  } yield index
}
```

Any command-line input or output is written as follows:

```scala
scala> val nTosses = 100
nTosses: Int = 100


scala> def trial = (0 until nTosses).count { i =>
  util.Random.nextBoolean() // count the number of heads
}
trial: Int
```

New terms and **important words** are shown in bold. Words that you see on the screen, for example, in menus or dialog boxes, appear in the text like this: "Clicking the **Next** button moves you to the next screen."

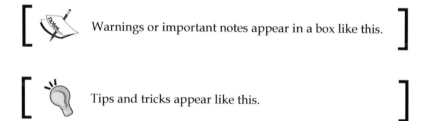

Warnings or important notes appear in a box like this.

Tips and tricks appear like this.

Reader feedback

Feedback from our readers is always welcome. Let us know what you think about this book—what you liked or disliked. Reader feedback is important for us as it helps us develop titles that you will really get the most out of.

To send us general feedback, simply e-mail feedback@packtpub.com, and mention the book's title in the subject of your message.

If there is a topic that you have expertise in and you are interested in either writing or contributing to a book, see our author guide at www.packtpub.com/authors.

Customer support

Now that you are the proud owner of a Packt book, we have a number of things to help you to get the most from your purchase.

Downloading the example code

You can download the example code files from your account at `http://www.packtpub.com` for all the Packt Publishing books you have purchased. If you purchased this book elsewhere, you can visit `http://www.packtpub.com/support` and register to have the files e-mailed directly to you.

The code examples are also available on GitHub at `www.github.com/pbugnion/s4ds`.

Errata

Although we have taken every care to ensure the accuracy of our content, mistakes do happen. If you find a mistake in one of our books—maybe a mistake in the text or the code—we would be grateful if you could report this to us. By doing so, you can save other readers from frustration and help us improve subsequent versions of this book. If you find any errata, please report them by visiting `http://www.packtpub.com/submit-errata`, selecting your book, clicking on the **Errata Submission Form** link, and entering the details of your errata. Once your errata are verified, your submission will be accepted and the errata will be uploaded to our website or added to any list of existing errata under the Errata section of that title.

To view the previously submitted errata, go to `https://www.packtpub.com/books/content/support` and enter the name of the book in the search field. The required information will appear under the **Errata** section.

Piracy

Piracy of copyrighted material on the Internet is an ongoing problem across all media. At Packt, we take the protection of our copyright and licenses very seriously. If you come across any illegal copies of our works in any form on the Internet, please provide us with the location address or website name immediately so that we can pursue a remedy.

Please contact us at `copyright@packtpub.com` with a link to the suspected pirated material.

We appreciate your help in protecting our authors and our ability to bring you valuable content.

eBooks, discount offers, and more

Did you know that Packt offers eBook versions of every book published, with PDF and ePub files available? You can upgrade to the eBook version at www.PacktPub. com and as a print book customer, you are entitled to a discount on the eBook copy. Get in touch with us at customercare@packtpub.com for more details.

At www.PacktPub.com, you can also read a collection of free technical articles, sign up for a range of free newsletters, and receive exclusive discounts and offers on Packt books and eBooks.

Questions

If you have a problem with any aspect of this book, you can contact us at questions@packtpub.com, and we will do our best to address the problem.

1
Scala and Data Science

The second half of the 20th century was the age of silicon. In fifty years, computing power went from extremely scarce to entirely mundane. The first half of the 21st century is the age of the Internet. The last 20 years have seen the rise of giants such as Google, Twitter, and Facebook—giants that have forever changed the way we view knowledge.

The Internet is a vast nexus of information. Ninety percent of the data generated by humanity has been generated in the last 18 months. The programmers, statisticians, and scientists who can harness this glut of data to derive real understanding will have an ever greater influence on how businesses, governments, and charities make decisions.

This book strives to introduce some of the tools that you will need to synthesize the avalanche of data to produce true insight.

Data science

Data science is the process of extracting useful information from data. As a discipline, it remains somewhat ill-defined, with nearly as many definitions as there are experts. Rather than add yet another definition, I will follow *Drew Conway's* description (http://drewconway.com/zia/2013/3/26/the-data-science-venn-diagram). He describes data science as the culmination of three orthogonal sets of skills:

- Data scientists must have *hacking skills*. Data is stored and transmitted through computers. Computers, programming languages, and libraries are the hammers and chisels of data scientists; they must wield them with confidence and accuracy to sculpt the data as they please. This is where Scala comes in: it's a powerful tool to have in your programming toolkit.

- Data scientists must have a sound understanding of *statistics and numerical algorithms*. Good data scientists will understand how machine learning algorithms function and how to interpret results. They will not be fooled by misleading metrics, deceptive statistics, or misinterpreted causal links.

- A good data scientist must have a sound understanding of the *problem domain*. The data science process involves building and discovering knowledge about the problem domain in a scientifically rigorous manner. The data scientist must, therefore, ask the right questions, be aware of previous results, and understand how the data science effort fits in the wider business or research context.

Drew Conway summarizes this elegantly with a Venn diagram showing data science at the intersection of hacking skills, maths and statistics knowledge, and substantive expertise:

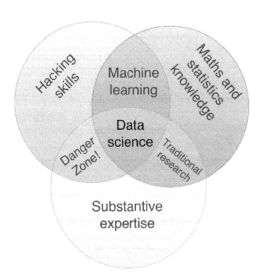

It is, of course, rare for people to be experts in more than one of these areas. Data scientists often work in cross-functional teams, with different members providing the expertise for different areas. To function effectively, every member of the team must nevertheless have a general working knowledge of all three areas.

To give a more concrete overview of the workflow in a data science project, let's imagine that we are trying to write an application that analyzes the public perception of a political campaign. This is what the data science pipeline might look like:

- **Obtaining data**: This might involve extracting information from text files, polling a sensor network or querying a web API. We could, for instance, query the Twitter API to obtain lists of tweets with the relevant hashtags.

- **Data ingestion**: Data often comes from many different sources and might be unstructured or semi-structured. Data ingestion involves moving data from the data source, processing it to extract structured information, and storing this information in a database. For tweets, for instance, we might extract the username, the names of other users mentioned in the tweet, the hashtags, text of the tweet, and whether the tweet contains certain keywords.

- **Exploring data**: We often have a clear idea of what information we want to extract from the data but very little idea how. For instance, let's imagine that we have ingested thousands of tweets containing hashtags relevant to our political campaign. There is no clear path to go from our database of tweets to the end goal: insight into the overall public perception of our campaign. Data exploration involves mapping out how we are going to get there. This step will often uncover new questions or sources of data, which requires going back to the first step of the pipeline. For our tweet database, we might, for instance, decide that we need to have a human manually label a thousand or more tweets as expressing "positive" or "negative" sentiments toward the political campaign. We could then use these tweets as a training set to construct a model.

- **Feature building**: A machine learning algorithm is only as good as the features that enter it. A significant fraction of a data scientist's time involves transforming and combining existing features to create new features more closely related to the problem that we are trying to solve. For instance, we might construct a new feature corresponding to the number of "positive" sounding words or pairs of words in a tweet.

- **Model construction and training**: Having built the features that enter the model, the data scientist can now train machine learning algorithms on their datasets. This will often involve trying different algorithms and optimizing model **hyperparameters**. We might, for instance, settle on using a random forest algorithm to decide whether a tweet is "positive" or "negative" about the campaign. Constructing the model involves choosing the right number of trees and how to calculate impurity measures. A sound understanding of statistics and the problem domain will help inform these decisions.

- **Model extrapolation and prediction**: The data scientists can now use their new model to try and infer information about previously unseen data points. They might pass a new tweet through their model to ascertain whether it speaks positively or negatively of the political campaign.

- **Distillation of intelligence and insight from the model**: The data scientists combine the outcome of the data analysis process with knowledge of the business domain to inform business decisions. They might discover that specific messages resonate better with the target audience, or with specific segments of the target audience, leading to more accurate targeting. A key part of informing stakeholders involves data visualization and presentation: data scientists create graphs, visualizations, and reports to help make the insights derived clear and compelling.

This is far from a linear pipeline. Often, insights gained at one stage will require the data scientists to backtrack to a previous stage of the pipeline. Indeed, the generation of business insights from raw data is normally an iterative process: the data scientists might do a rapid first pass to verify the premise of the problem and then gradually refine the approach by adding new data sources or new features or trying new machine learning algorithms.

In this book, you will learn how to deal with each step of the pipeline in Scala, leveraging existing libraries to build robust applications.

Programming in data science

This book is not a book about data science. It is a book about how to use Scala, a programming language, for data science. So, where does programming come in when processing data?

Computers are involved at every step of the data science pipeline, but not necessarily in the same manner. The style of programs that we build will be drastically different if we are just writing throwaway scripts to explore data or trying to build a scalable application that pushes data through a well-understood pipeline to continuously deliver business intelligence.

Let's imagine that we work for a company making games for mobile phones in which you can purchase in-game benefits. The majority of users never buy anything, but a small fraction is likely to spend a lot of money. We want to build a model that recognizes big spenders based on their play patterns.

The first step is to explore data, find the right features, and build a model based on a subset of the data. In this exploration phase, we have a clear goal in mind but little idea of how to get there. We want a light, flexible language with strong libraries to get us a working model as soon as possible.

Once we have a working model, we need to deploy it on our gaming platform to analyze the usage patterns of all the current users. This is a very different problem: we have a relatively clear understanding of the goals of the program and of how to get there. The challenge comes in designing software that will scale out to handle all the users and be robust to future changes in usage patterns.

In practice, the type of software that we write typically lies on a spectrum ranging from a single throwaway script to production-level code that must be proof against future expansion and load increases. Before writing any code, the data scientist must understand where their software lies on this spectrum. Let's call this the **permanence spectrum**.

Why Scala?

You want to write a program that handles data. Which language should you choose?

There are a few different options. You might choose a dynamic language such as Python or R or a more traditional object-oriented language such as Java. In this section, we will explore how Scala differs from these languages and when it might make sense to use it.

When choosing a language, the architect's trade-off lies in a balance of provable correctness versus development speed. Which of these aspects you need to emphasize will depend on the application requirements and where on the permanence spectrum your program lies. Is this a short script that will be used by a few people who can easily fix any problems that arise? If so, you can probably permit a certain number of bugs in rarely used code paths: when a developer hits a snag, they can just fix the problem as it arises. By contrast, if you are developing a database engine that you plan on releasing to the wider world, you will, in all likelihood, favor correctness over rapid development. The SQLite database engine, for instance, is famous for its extensive test suite, with 800 times as much testing code as application code (`https://www.sqlite.org/testing.html`).

What matters, when estimating the *correctness* of a program, is not the perceived absence of bugs, it is the degree to which you can prove that certain bugs are absent.

There are several ways of proving the absence of bugs before the code has even run:

- Static type checking occurs at compile time in statically typed languages, but this can also be used in strongly typed dynamic languages that support type annotations or type hints. Type checking helps verify that we are using functions and classes as intended.

- Static analyzers and linters that check for undefined variables or suspicious behavior (such as parts of the code that can never be reached).

- Declaring some attributes as immutable or constant in compiled languages.

- Unit testing to demonstrate the absence of bugs along particular code paths.

There are several more ways of checking for the absence of some bugs at runtime:

- Dynamic type checking in both statically typed and dynamic languages

- Assertions verifying supposed program invariants or expected contracts

In the next sections, we will examine how Scala compares to other languages in data science.

Static typing and type inference

Scala's static typing system is very versatile. A lot of information as to the program's behavior can be encoded in types, allowing the compiler to guarantee a certain level of correctness. This is particularly useful for code paths that are rarely used. A dynamic language cannot catch errors until a particular branch of execution runs, so a bug can persist for a long time until the program runs into it. In a statically typed language, any bug that can be caught by the compiler will be caught at compile time, before the program has even started running.

Statically typed object-oriented languages have often been criticized for being needlessly verbose. Consider the initialization of an instance of the Example class in Java:

```
Example myInstance = new Example() ;
```

We have to repeat the class name twice—once to define the compile-time type of the myInstance variable and once to construct the instance itself. This feels like unnecessary work: the compiler knows that the type of myInstance is Example (or a superclass of Example) as we are binding a value of the Example type.

Scala, like most functional languages, uses type inference to allow the compiler to infer the type of variables from the instances bound to them. We would write the equivalent line in Scala as follows:

```
val myInstance = new Example()
```

The Scala compiler infers that myInstance has the Example type at compile time. A lot of the time, it is enough to specify the types of the arguments and of the return value of a function. The compiler can then infer types for all the variables defined in the body of the function. Scala code is usually much more concise and readable than the equivalent Java code, without compromising any of the type safety.

Scala encourages immutability

Scala encourages the use of immutable objects. In Scala, it is very easy to define an attribute as immutable:

```
val amountSpent = 200
```

The default collections are immutable:

```
val clientIds = List("123", "456") // List is immutable
clientIds(1) = "589" // Compile-time error
```

Having immutable objects removes a common source of bugs. Knowing that some objects cannot be changed once instantiated reduces the number of places bugs can creep in. Instead of considering the lifetime of the object, we can narrow in on the constructor.

Scala and functional programs

Scala encourages functional code. A lot of Scala code consists of using higher-order functions to transform collections. You, as a programmer, do not have to deal with the details of iterating over the collection. Let's write an occurrencesOf function that returns the indices at which an element occurs in a list:

```
def occurrencesOf[A](elem:A, collection:List[A]):List[Int] = {
  for {
    (currentElem, index) <- collection.zipWithIndex
    if (currentElem == elem)
  } yield index
}
```

How does this work? We first declare a new list, collection.zipWithIndex, whose elements are (collection(0), 0), (collection(1), 1), and so on: pairs of the collection's elements and their indexes.

We then tell Scala that we want to iterate over this collection, binding the currentElem variable to the current element and index to the index. We apply a filter on the iteration, selecting only those elements for which currentElem == elem. We then tell Scala to just return the index variable.

We did not need to deal with the details of the iteration process in Scala. The syntax is very declarative: we tell the compiler that we want the index of every element equal to elem in collection and let the compiler worry about how to iterate over collection.

Consider the equivalent in Java:

```
static <T> List<Integer> occurrencesOf(T elem, List<T> collection) {
  List<Integer> occurrences = new ArrayList<Integer>() ;
  for (int i=0; i<collection.size(); i++) {
    if (collection.get(i).equals(elem)) {
      occurrences.add(i) ;
    }
  }
  return occurrences ;
}
```

In Java, you start by defining a (mutable) list in which to put occurrences as you find them. You then iterate over the collection by defining a counter, considering each element in turn and adding its index to the list of occurrences, if need be. There are many more moving parts that we need to get right for this method to work. These moving parts exist because we must tell Java how to iterate over the collection, and they represent a common source of bugs.

Furthermore, as a lot of code is taken up by the iteration mechanism, the line that defines the logic of the function is harder to find:

```
static <T> List<Integer> occurrencesOf(T elem, List<T> collection) {
  List<Integer> occurences = new ArrayList<Integer>() ;
  for (int i=0; i<collection.size(); i++) {
    if (collection.get(i).equals(elem)) {
      occurrences.add(i) ;
    }
  }
  return occurrences ;
}
```

Note that this is not meant as an attack on Java. In fact, Java 8 adds a slew of functional constructs, such as lambda expressions, the Optional type that mirrors Scala's Option, or stream processing. Rather, it is meant to demonstrate the benefit of functional approaches in minimizing the potential for errors and maximizing clarity.

Null pointer uncertainty

We often need to represent the possible absence of a value. For instance, imagine that we are reading a list of usernames from a CSV file. The CSV file contains name and e-mail information. However, some users have declined to enter their e-mail into the system, so this information is absent. In Java, one would typically represent the e-mail as a string or an `Email` class and represent the absence of e-mail information for a particular user by setting that reference to `null`. Similarly, in Python, we might use `None` to demonstrate the absence of a value.

This approach is dangerous because we are not encoding the possible absence of e-mail information. In any nontrivial program, deciding whether an instance attribute can be `null` requires considering every occasion in which this instance is defined. This quickly becomes impractical, so programmers either assume that a variable is not null or code too defensively.

Scala (following the lead of other functional languages) introduces the `Option[T]` type to represent an attribute that might be absent. We might then write the following:

```
class User {
  ...
  val email:Option[Email]
  ...
}
```

We have now encoded the possible absence of e-mail in the type information. It is obvious to any programmer using the `User` class that e-mail information is possibly absent. Even better, the compiler knows that the `email` field can be absent, forcing us to deal with the problem rather than recklessly ignoring it to have the application burn at runtime in a conflagration of null pointer exceptions.

All this goes back to achieving a certain level of provable correctness. Never using `null`, we know that we will never run into null pointer exceptions. Achieving the same level of correctness in languages without `Option[T]` requires writing unit tests on the client code to verify that it behaves correctly when the e-mail attribute is null.

Note that it is possible to achieve this in Java using, for instance, Google's Guava library (`https://code.google.com/p/guava-libraries/wiki/UsingAndAvoidingNullExplained`) or the `Optional` class in Java 8. It is more a matter of convention: using `null` in Java to denote the absence of a value has long been the norm.

Easier parallelism

Writing programs that take advantage of parallel architectures is challenging. It is nevertheless necessary to tackle all but the simplest data science problems.

Parallel programming is difficult because we, as programmers, tend to think sequentially. Reasoning about the order in which different events can happen in a concurrent program is very challenging.

Scala provides several abstractions that greatly facilitate the writing of parallel code. These abstractions work by imposing constraints on the way parallelism is achieved. For instance, parallel collections force the user to phrase the computation as a sequence of operations (such as **map**, **reduce**, and **filter**) on collections. Actor systems require the developer to think in terms of actors that encapsulate the application state and communicate by passing messages.

It might seem paradoxical that restricting the programmer's freedom to write parallel code as they please avoids many of the problems associated with concurrency. However, limiting the number of ways in which a program behaves facilitates thinking about its behavior. For instance, if an actor is misbehaving, we know that the problem lies either in the code for this actor or in one of the messages that the actor receives.

As an example of the power afforded by having coherent, restrictive abstractions, let's use parallel collections to solve a simple probability problem. We will calculate the probability of getting at least 60 heads out of 100 coin tosses. We can estimate this using Monte Carlo: we simulate 100 coin tosses by drawing 100 random Boolean values and check whether the number of true values is at least 60. We repeat this until results have converged to the required accuracy, or we get bored of waiting.

Let's run through this in a Scala console:

```scala
scala> val nTosses = 100
nTosses: Int = 100

scala> def trial = (0 until nTosses).count { i =>
  util.Random.nextBoolean() // count the number of heads
}
trial: Int
```

The `trial` function runs a single set of 100 throws, returning the number of heads:

```
scala> trial
Int = 51
```

To get our answer, we just need to repeat `trial` as many times as we can and aggregate the results. Repeating the same set of operations is ideally suited to parallel collections:

```
scala> val nTrials = 100000
nTrials: Int = 100000


scala> (0 until nTrials).par.count { i => trial >= 60 }
Int = 2745
```

The probability is thus approximately 2.5% to 3%. All we had to do to distribute the calculation over every CPU in our computer is use the `par` method to parallelize the range (`0 until nTrials`). This demonstrates the benefits of having a coherent abstraction: parallel collections let us trivially parallelize any computation that can be phrased in terms of higher-order functions on collections.

Clearly, not every problem is as easy to parallelize as a simple Monte Carlo problem. However, by offering a rich set of intuitive abstractions, Scala makes writing parallel applications manageable.

Interoperability with Java

Scala runs on the Java virtual machine. The Scala compiler compiles programs to Java byte code. Thus, Scala developers have access to Java libraries natively. Given the phenomenal number of applications written in Java, both open source and as part of the legacy code in organizations, the interoperability of Scala and Java helps explain the rapid uptake of Scala.

Interoperability has not just been unidirectional: some Scala libraries, such as the Play framework, are becoming increasingly popular among Java developers.

When not to use Scala

In the previous sections, we described how Scala's strong type system, preference for immutability, functional capabilities, and parallelism abstractions make it easy to write reliable programs and minimize the risk of unexpected behavior.

What reasons might you have to avoid Scala in your next project? One important reason is familiarity. Scala introduces many concepts such as implicits, type classes, and composition using traits that might not be familiar to programmers coming from the object-oriented world. Scala's type system is very expressive, but getting to know it well enough to use its full power takes time and requires adjusting to a new programming paradigm. Finally, dealing with immutable data structures can feel alien to programmers coming from Java or Python.

Nevertheless, these are all drawbacks that can be overcome with time. Scala does fall short of the other data science languages in library availability. The IPython Notebook, coupled with matplotlib, is an unparalleled resource for data exploration. There are ongoing efforts to provide similar functionality in Scala (Spark Notebooks or Apache Zeppelin, for instance), but there are no projects with the same level of maturity. The type system can also be a minor hindrance when one is exploring data or trying out different models.

Thus, in this author's biased opinion, Scala excels for more *permanent* programs. If you are writing a throwaway script or exploring data, you might be better served with Python. If you are writing something that will need to be reused and requires a certain level of provable correctness, you will find Scala extremely powerful.

Summary

Now that the obligatory introduction is over, it is time to write some Scala code. In the next chapter, you will learn about leveraging Breeze for numerical computations with Scala. For our first foray into data science, we will use logistic regression to predict the gender of a person given their height and weight.

References

By far, the best book on Scala is *Programming in Scala* by *Martin Odersky, Lex Spoon,* and *Bill Venners*. Besides being authoritative (*Martin Odersky* is the driving force behind Scala), this book is also approachable and readable.

Scala Puzzlers by *Andrew Phillips* and *Nermin Šerifović* provides a fun way to learn more advanced Scala.

Scala for Machine Learning by *Patrick R. Nicholas* provides examples of how to write machine learning algorithms with Scala.

2
Manipulating Data with Breeze

Data science is, by and large, concerned with the manipulation of structured data. A large fraction of structured datasets can be viewed as tabular data: each row represents a particular instance, and columns represent different attributes of that instance. The ubiquity of tabular representations explains the success of spreadsheet programs like Microsoft Excel, or of tools like SQL databases.

To be useful to data scientists, a language must support the manipulation of columns or tables of data. Python does this through NumPy and pandas, for instance. Unfortunately, there is no single, coherent ecosystem for numerical computing in Scala that quite measures up to the SciPy ecosystem in Python.

In this chapter, we will introduce Breeze, a library for fast linear algebra and manipulation of data arrays as well as many other features necessary for scientific computing and data science.

Code examples

The easiest way to access the code examples in this book is to clone the GitHub repository:

```
$ git clone 'https://github.com/pbugnion/s4ds'
```

The code samples for each chapter are in a single, standalone folder. You may also browse the code online on GitHub.

Installing Breeze

If you have downloaded the code examples for this book, the easiest way of using Breeze is to go into the chap02 directory and type sbt console at the command line. This will open a Scala console in which you can import Breeze.

If you want to build a standalone project, the most common way of installing Breeze (and, indeed, any Scala module) is through SBT. To fetch the dependencies required for this chapter, copy the following lines to a file called build.sbt, taking care to leave an empty line after scalaVersion:

```
scalaVersion := "2.11.7"

libraryDependencies ++= Seq(
  "org.scalanlp" %% "breeze" % "0.11.2",
  "org.scalanlp" %% "breeze-natives" % "0.11.2"
)
```

Open a Scala console in the same directory as your build.sbt file by typing sbt console in a terminal. You can check that Breeze is working correctly by importing Breeze from the Scala prompt:

```
scala> import breeze.linalg._
import breeze.linalg._
```

Getting help on Breeze

This chapter gives a reasonably detailed introduction to Breeze, but it does not aim to give a complete API reference.

To get a full list of Breeze's functionality, consult the Breeze Wiki page on GitHub at https://github.com/scalanlp/breeze/wiki. This is very complete for some modules and less complete for others. The source code (https://github.com/scalanlp/breeze/) is detailed and gives a lot of information. To understand how a particular function is meant to be used, look at the unit tests for that function.

Basic Breeze data types

Breeze is an extensive library providing fast and easy manipulation of arrays of data, routines for optimization, interpolation, linear algebra, signal processing, and numerical integration.

The basic linear algebra operations underlying Breeze rely on the `netlib-java` library, which can use system-optimized **BLAS** and **LAPACK** libraries, if present. Thus, linear algebra operations in Breeze are often extremely fast. Breeze is still undergoing rapid development and can, therefore, be somewhat unstable.

Vectors

Breeze makes manipulating one- and two-dimensional data structures easy. To start, open a Scala console through SBT and import Breeze:

```
$ sbt console
scala> import breeze.linalg._
import breeze.linalg._
```

Let's dive straight in and define a vector:

```
scala> val v = DenseVector(1.0, 2.0, 3.0)
breeze.linalg.DenseVector[Double] = DenseVector(1.0, 2.0, 3.0)
```

We have just defined a three-element vector, v. Vectors are just one-dimensional arrays of data exposing methods tailored to numerical uses. They can be indexed like other Scala collections:

```
scala> v(1)
Double = 2.0
```

They support element-wise operations with a scalar:

```
scala> v :* 2.0 // :* is 'element-wise multiplication'
breeze.linalg.DenseVector[Double] = DenseVector(2.0, 4.0, 6.0)
```

They also support element-wise operations with another vector:

```
scala> v :+ DenseVector(4.0, 5.0, 6.0) // :+ is 'element-wise addition'
breeze.linalg.DenseVector[Double] = DenseVector(5.0, 7.0, 9.0)
```

Breeze makes writing vector operations intuitive and considerably more readable than the native Scala equivalent.

Note that Breeze will refuse (at compile time) to coerce operands to the correct type:

```
scala> v :* 2 // element-wise multiplication by integer
<console>:15: error: could not find implicit value for parameter op:
...
```

It will also refuse (at runtime) to add vectors together if they have different lengths:

```
scala> v :+ DenseVector(8.0, 9.0)
java.lang.IllegalArgumentException: requirement failed: Vectors must have
same length: 3 != 2
...
```

Basic manipulation of vectors in Breeze will feel natural to anyone used to working with NumPy, MATLAB, or R.

So far, we have only looked at *element-wise* operators. These are all prefixed with a colon. All the usual suspects are present: `:+`, `:*`, `:-`, `:/`, `:%` (remainder), and `:^` (power) as well as Boolean operators. To see the full list of operators, have a look at the API documentation for `DenseVector` or `DenseMatrix` (https://github.com/scalanlp/breeze/wiki/Linear-Algebra-Cheat-Sheet).

Besides element-wise operations, Breeze vectors support the operations you might expect of mathematical vectors, such as the dot product:

```
scala> val v2 = DenseVector(4.0, 5.0, 6.0)
breeze.linalg.DenseVector[Double] = DenseVector(4.0, 5.0, 6.0)

scala> v dot v2
Double = 32.0
```

Pitfalls of element-wise operators

Besides the : + and : - operators for element-wise addition and subtraction that we have seen so far, we can also use the more traditional + and - operators:

```scala
scala> v + v2
breeze.linalg.DenseVector[Double] = DenseVector(5.0,
7.0, 9.0)
```

One must, however, be very careful with operator precedence rules when mixing : + or : * with : + operators. The : + and : * operators have very low operator precedence, so they will be evaluated last. This can lead to some counter-intuitive behavior:

```scala
scala> 2.0 :* v + v2 // !! equivalent to 2.0 :* (v + v2)
breeze.linalg.DenseVector[Double] = DenseVector(10.0,
14.0, 18.0)
```

By contrast, if we use : + instead of +, the mathematical precedence of operators is respected:

```scala
scala> 2.0 :* v :+ v2 // equivalent to (2.0 :* v) :+ v2
breeze.linalg.DenseVector[Double] = DenseVector(6.0,
9.0, 12.0)
```

In summary, one should avoid mixing the : + style operators with the + style operators as much as possible.

Dense and sparse vectors and the vector trait

All the vectors we have looked at thus far have been dense vectors. Breeze also supports sparse vectors. When dealing with arrays of numbers that are mostly zero, it may be more computationally efficient to use sparse vectors. The point at which a vector has enough zeros to warrant switching to a sparse representation depends strongly on the type of operations, so you should run your own benchmarks to determine which type to use. Nevertheless, a good heuristic is that, if your vector is about 90% zero, you may benefit from using a sparse representation.

Sparse vectors are available in Breeze as the SparseVector and HashVector classes. Both these types support many of the same operations as DenseVector but use a different internal implementation. The SparseVector instances are very memory-efficient, but adding non-zero elements is slow. HashVector is more versatile, at the cost of an increase in memory footprint and computational time for iterating over non-zero elements. Unless you need to squeeze the last bits of memory out of your application, I recommend using HashVector. We will not discuss these further in this book, but the reader should find them straightforward to use if needed. DenseVector, SparseVector, and HashVector all implement the Vector trait, giving them a common interface.

Breeze remains very experimental and, as of this writing, somewhat unstable. I have found dealing with specific implementations of the `Vector` trait, such as `DenseVector` or `SparseVector`, to be more reliable than dealing with the `Vector` trait directly. In this chapter, we will explicitly type every vector as `DenseVector`.

Matrices

Breeze allows the construction and manipulation of two-dimensional arrays in a similar manner:

```
scala> val m = DenseMatrix((1.0, 2.0, 3.0), (4.0, 5.0, 6.0))
breeze.linalg.DenseMatrix[Double] =
1.0   2.0   3.0
4.0   5.0   6.0


scala> 2.0 :* m
breeze.linalg.DenseMatrix[Double] =
2.0   4.0    6.0
8.0   10.0   12.0
```

Building vectors and matrices

We have seen how to explicitly build vectors and matrices by passing their values to the constructor (or rather, to the companion object's `apply` method): `DenseVector(1.0, 2.0, 3.0)`. Breeze offers several other powerful ways of building vectors and matrices:

```
scala> DenseVector.ones[Double](5)
breeze.linalg.DenseVector[Double] = DenseVector(1.0, 1.0, 1.0, 1.0, 1.0)


scala> DenseVector.zeros[Int](3)
breeze.linalg.DenseVector[Int] = DenseVector(0, 0, 0)
```

The `linspace` method (available in the `breeze.linalg` package object) creates a `Double` vector of equally spaced values. For instance, to create a vector of 10 values distributed uniformly between 0 and 1, perform the following:

```
scala> linspace(0.0, 1.0, 10)
breeze.linalg.DenseVector[Double] = DenseVector(0.0, 0.1111111111111111,
..., 1.0)
```

The `tabulate` method lets us construct vectors and matrices from functions:

```scala
scala> DenseVector.tabulate(4) { i => 5.0 * i }
breeze.linalg.DenseVector[Double] = DenseVector(0.0, 5.0, 10.0, 15.0)


scala> DenseMatrix.tabulate[Int](2, 3) {
   (irow, icol) => irow*2 + icol
}
breeze.linalg.DenseMatrix[Int] =
0   1   2
2   3   4
```

The first argument to `DenseVector.tabulate` is the size of the vector, and the second is a function returning the value of the vector at a particular position. This is useful for creating ranges of data, among other things.

The `rand` function lets us create random vectors and matrices:

```scala
scala> DenseVector.rand(2)
breeze.linalg.DenseVector[Double] = DenseVector(0.8072865137359484,
0.5566507203838562)


scala> DenseMatrix.rand(2, 3)
breeze.linalg.DenseMatrix[Double] =
0.5755491874682879    0.8142161471517582    0.9043780212739738
0.31530195124023974   0.2095094278911871    0.22069103504148346
```

Finally, we can construct vectors from Scala arrays:

```scala
scala> DenseVector(Array(2, 3, 4))
breeze.linalg.DenseVector[Int] = DenseVector(2, 3, 4)
```

To construct vectors from other Scala collections, you must use the *splat* operator, `:_ *`:

```scala
scala> val l = Seq(2, 3, 4)
l: Seq[Int] = List(2, 3, 4)


scala> DenseVector(l :_ *)
breeze.linalg.DenseVector[Int] = DenseVector(2, 3, 4)
```

Advanced indexing and slicing

We have already seen how to select a particular element in a vector v by its index with, for instance, v(2). Breeze also offers several powerful methods for selecting parts of a vector.

Let's start by creating a vector to play around with:

```
scala> val v = DenseVector.tabulate(5) { _.toDouble }
breeze.linalg.DenseVector[Double] = DenseVector(0.0, 1.0, 2.0, 3.0, 4.0)
```

Unlike native Scala collections, Breeze vectors support negative indexing:

```
scala> v(-1) // last element
Double = 4.0
```

Breeze lets us slice the vector using a range:

```
scala> v(1 to 3)
breeze.linalg.DenseVector[Double] = DenseVector(1.0, 2.0, 3.0)


scala v(1 until 3) // equivalent to Python v[1:3]
breeze.linalg.DenseVector[Double] = DenseVector(1.0, 2.0)


scala> v(v.length-1 to 0 by -1) // reverse view of v
breeze.linalg.DenseVector[Double] = DenseVector(4.0, 3.0, 2.0, 1.0, 0.0)
```

Indexing by a range returns a *view* of the original vector: when running val v2 = v(1 to 3), no data is copied. This means that slicing is extremely efficient. Taking a slice of a huge vector does not increase the memory footprint at all. It also means that one should be careful updating a slice, since it will also update the original vector. We will discuss mutating vectors and matrices in a subsequent section in this chapter.

Breeze also lets us select an arbitrary set of elements from a vector:

```
scala> val vSlice = v(2, 4) // Select elements at index 2 and 4
breeze.linalg.SliceVector[Int,Double] = breeze.linalg.SliceVector@9c04d22
```

This creates a `SliceVector`, which behaves like a `DenseVector` (both implement the `Vector` interface), but does not actually have memory allocated for values: it just knows how to map from its indices to values in its parent vector. One should think of `vSlice` as a specific view of `v`. We can materialize the view (give it its own data rather than acting as a lens through which `v` is viewed) by converting it to `DenseVector`:

```
scala> vSlice.toDenseVector
breeze.linalg.DenseVector[Double] = DenseVector(2.0, 4.0)
```

Note that if an element of a slice is out of bounds, an exception will only be thrown when that element is accessed:

```
scala> val vSlice = v(2, 7) // there is no v(7)
breeze.linalg.SliceVector[Int,Double] = breeze.linalg.
SliceVector@2a83f9d1


scala> vSlice(0) // valid since v(2) is still valid
Double = 2.0


scala> vSlice(1) // invalid since v(7) is out of bounds
java.lang.IndexOutOfBoundsException: 7 not in [-5,5)

    ...
```

Finally, one can index vectors using Boolean arrays. Let's start by defining an array:

```
scala> val mask = DenseVector(true, false, false, true, true)
breeze.linalg.DenseVector[Boolean] = DenseVector(true, false, false,
true, true)
```

Then, `v(mask)` results in a view containing the elements of `v` for which `mask` is `true`:

```
scala> v(mask).toDenseVector
breeze.linalg.DenseVector[Double] = DenseVector(0.0, 3.0, 4.0)
```

This can be used as a way of filtering certain elements in a vector. For instance, to select the elements of `v` which are less than `3.0`:

```
scala> val filtered = v(v :< 3.0) // :< is element-wise "less than"
breeze.linalg.SliceVector[Int,Double] = breeze.linalg.
SliceVector@2b1edef3


scala> filtered.toDenseVector
breeze.linalg.DenseVector[Double] = DenseVector(0.0, 1.0, 2.0)
```

Matrices can be indexed in much the same way as vectors. Matrix indexing functions take two arguments—the first argument selects the row(s) and the second one slices the column(s):

```scala
scala> val m = DenseMatrix((1.0, 2.0, 3.0), (5.0, 6.0, 7.0))
m: breeze.linalg.DenseMatrix[Double] =
1.0   2.0   3.0
5.0   6.0   7.0

scala> m(1, 2)
Double = 7.0

scala> m(1, -1)
Double = 7.0

scala> m(0 until 2, 0 until 2)
breeze.linalg.DenseMatrix[Double] =
1.0   2.0
5.0   6.0
```

You can also mix different slicing types for rows and columns:

```scala
scala> m(0 until 2, 0)
breeze.linalg.DenseVector[Double] = DenseVector(1.0, 5.0)
```

Note how, in this case, Breeze returns a vector. In general, slicing returns the following objects:

- A scalar when single indices are passed as the row and column arguments
- A vector when the row argument is a range and the column argument is a single index
- A vector transpose when the column argument is a range and the row argument is a single index
- A matrix otherwise

The symbol :: can be used to indicate *every element along a particular direction*. For instance, we can select the second column of m:

```scala
scala> m(::, 1)
breeze.linalg.DenseVector[Double] = DenseVector(2.0, 6.0)
```

Mutating vectors and matrices

Breeze vectors and matrices are mutable. Most of the slicing operations described above can also be used to set elements of a vector or matrix:

```scala
scala> val v = DenseVector(1.0, 2.0, 3.0)
v: breeze.linalg.DenseVector[Double] = DenseVector(1.0, 2.0, 3.0)


scala> v(1) = 22.0 // v is now DenseVector(1.0, 22.0, 3.0)
```

We are not limited to mutating single elements. In fact, all the indexing operations outlined above can be used to set the elements of vectors or matrices. When mutating slices of vectors or matrices, use the element-wise assignment operator, `:=`:

```scala
scala> v(0 until 2) := DenseVector(50.0, 51.0) // set elements at
position 0 and 1
breeze.linalg.DenseVector[Double] = DenseVector(50.0, 51.0)


scala> v
breeze.linalg.DenseVector[Double] = DenseVector(50.0, 51.0, 3.0)
```

The assignment operator, `:=`, works like other element-wise operators in Breeze. If the right-hand side is a scalar, it will automatically be broadcast to a vector of the given shape:

```scala
scala> v(0 until 2) := 0.0 // equivalent to v(0 until 2) :=
DenseVector(0.0, 0.0)
breeze.linalg.DenseVector[Double] = DenseVector(0.0, 0.0)


scala> v
breeze.linalg.DenseVector[Double] = DenseVector(0.0, 0.0, 3.0)
```

All element-wise operators have an update counterpart. For instance, the `:+=` operator acts like the element-wise addition operator `:+`, but also updates its left-hand operand:

```scala
scala> val v = DenseVector(1.0, 2.0, 3.0)
v: breeze.linalg.DenseVector[Double] = DenseVector(1.0, 2.0, 3.0)


scala> v :+= 4.0
breeze.linalg.DenseVector[Double] = DenseVector(5.0, 6.0, 7.0)


scala> v
breeze.linalg.DenseVector[Double] = DenseVector(5.0, 6.0, 7.0)
```

Notice how the update operator updates the vector in place and returns it.

We have learnt how to slice vectors and matrices in Breeze to create new views of the original data. These views are not independent of the vector they were created from—updating the view will update the underlying vector and vice-versa. This is best illustrated with an example:

```scala
scala> val v = DenseVector.tabulate(6) { _.toDouble }
breeze.linalg.DenseVector[Double] = DenseVector(0.0, 1.0, 2.0, 3.0, 4.0,
5.0)


scala> val viewEvens = v(0 until v.length by 2)
breeze.linalg.DenseVector[Double] = DenseVector(0.0, 2.0, 4.0)


scala> viewEvens := 10.0 // mutate viewEvens
breeze.linalg.DenseVector[Double] = DenseVector(10.0, 10.0, 10.0)


scala> viewEvens
breeze.linalg.DenseVector[Double] = DenseVector(10.0, 10.0, 10.0)


scala> v  // v has also been mutated!
breeze.linalg.DenseVector[Double] = DenseVector(10.0, 1.0, 10.0, 3.0,
10.0, 5.0)
```

This quickly becomes intuitive if we remember that, when we create a vector or matrix, we are creating a view of an underlying data array rather than creating the data itself:

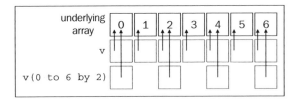

A vector slice v(0 to 6 by 2) of the v vector is just a different view of the array underlying v.
The view itself contains no data. It just contains pointers to the data in the original array. Internally,
the view is just stored as a pointer to the underlying data and a recipe for iterating over that data: in the
case of this slice, the recipe is just "start at the first element of the underlying data and go to the seventh element
of the underlying data in steps of two".

Breeze offers a `copy` function for when we want to create independent copies of data. In the previous example, we can construct a copy of `viewEvens` as:

```scala
scala> val copyEvens = v(0 until v.length by 2).copy
breeze.linalg.DenseVector[Double] = DenseVector(10.0, 10.0, 10.0)
```

We can now update `copyEvens` independently of `v`.

Matrix multiplication, transposition, and the orientation of vectors

So far, we have mostly looked at element-wise operations on vectors and matrices. Let's now look at matrix multiplication and related operations.

The matrix multiplication operator is `*`:

```scala
scala> val m1 = DenseMatrix((2.0, 3.0), (5.0, 6.0), (8.0, 9.0))
breeze.linalg.DenseMatrix[Double] =
2.0   3.0
5.0   6.0
8.0   9.0


scala> val m2 = DenseMatrix((10.0, 11.0), (12.0, 13.0))
breeze.linalg.DenseMatrix[Double]
10.0   11.0
12.0   13.0


scala> m1 * m2
56.0    61.0
122.0   133.0
188.0   205.0
```

Besides matrix-matrix multiplication, we can use the matrix multiplication operator between matrices and vectors. All vectors in Breeze are column vectors. This means that, when multiplying matrices and vectors together, a vector should be viewed as an (*n* * *1*) matrix. Let's walk through an example of matrix-vector multiplication. We want the following operation:

$$\begin{pmatrix} 2 & 3 \\ 5 & 6 \\ 8 & 9 \end{pmatrix} \begin{pmatrix} 1 \\ 2 \end{pmatrix}$$

```
scala> val v = DenseVector(1.0, 2.0)
breeze.linalg.DenseVector[Double] = DenseVector(1.0, 2.0)


scala> m1 * v
breeze.linalg.DenseVector[Double] = DenseVector(8.0, 17.0, 26.0)
```

By contrast, if we wanted:

$$\begin{pmatrix} 1 & 2 \end{pmatrix} \begin{pmatrix} 10 & 11 \\ 12 & 13 \end{pmatrix}$$

We must convert v to a row vector. We can do this using the transpose operation:

```
scala> val vt = v.t
breeze.linalg.Transpose[breeze.linalg.DenseVector[Double]] =
Transpose(DenseVector(1.0, 2.0))


scala> vt * m2
breeze.linalg.Transpose[breeze.linalg.DenseVector[Double]] =
Transpose(DenseVector(34.0, 37.0))
```

Note that the type of v.t is Transpose[DenseVector[_]]. A Transpose[DenseVector[_]] behaves in much the same way as a DenseVector as far as element-wise operations are concerned, but it does not support mutation or slicing.

Data preprocessing and feature engineering

We have now discovered the basic components of Breeze. In the next few sections, we will apply them to real examples to understand how they fit together to form a robust base for data science.

An important part of data science involves preprocessing datasets to construct useful features. Let's walk through an example of this. To follow this example and access the data, you will need to download the code examples for the book (www.github. com/pbugnion/s4ds).

You will find, in directory chap02/data/ of the code attached to this book, a CSV file with true heights and weights as well as self-reported heights and weights for 181 men and women. The original dataset was collected as part of a study on body image. Refer to the following link for more information: http://vincentarelbundock. github.io/Rdatasets/doc/car/Davis.html.

There is a helper function in the package provided with the book to load the data into Breeze arrays:

```scala
scala> val data = HWData.load
HWData [ 181 rows ]


scala> data.genders
breeze.linalg.Vector[Char] = DenseVector(M, F, F, M, ... )
```

The data object contains five vectors, each 181 element long:

- data.genders: A Char vector describing the gender of the participants
- data.heights: A Double vector of the true height of the participants
- data.weights: A Double vector of the true weight of the participants
- data.reportedHeights: A Double vector of the self-reported height of the participants
- data.reportedWeights: A Double vector of the self-reported weight of the participants

Let's start by counting the number of men and women in the study. We will define an array that contains just 'M' and do an element-wise comparison with data.genders:

```scala
scala> val maleVector = DenseVector.fill(data.genders.length)('M')
breeze.linalg.DenseVector[Char] = DenseVector(M, M, M, M, M, M,... )


scala> val isMale = (data.genders :== maleVector)
breeze.linalg.DenseVector[Boolean] = DenseVector(true, false, false, true
...)
```

The isMale vector is the same length as data.genders. It is true where the participant is male, and false otherwise. We can use this Boolean array as a mask for the other arrays in the dataset (remember that vector(mask) selects the elements of vector where mask is true). Let's get the height of the men in our dataset:

```
scala> val maleHeights = data.heights(isMale)
breeze.linalg.SliceVector[Int,Double] = breeze.linalg.
SliceVector@61717d42
```

```
scala> maleHeights.toDenseVector
breeze.linalg.DenseVector[Double] = DenseVector(182.0, 177.0, 170.0, ...
```

To count the number of men in our dataset, we can use the indicator function. This transforms a Boolean array into an array of doubles, mapping false to 0.0 and true to 1.0:

```
scala> import breeze.numerics._
import breeze.numerics._
```

```
scala> sum(I(isMale))
Double: 82.0
```

Let's calculate the mean height of men and women in the experiment. We can calculate the mean of a vector using mean(v), which we can access by importing breeze.stats._:

```
scala> import breeze.stats._
import breeze.stats._
```

```
scala> mean(data.heights)
Double = 170.75690607734808
```

To calculate the mean height of the men, we can use our isMale array to slice data.heights; data.heights(isMale) is a view of the data.heights array with all the height values for the men:

```
scala> mean(data.heights(isMale)) // mean male height
Double = 178.0121951219512
```

```
scala> mean(data.heights(!isMale)) // mean female height
Double = 164.74747474747474
```

As a somewhat more involved example, let's look at the discrepancy between real and reported weight for both men and women in this experiment. We can get an array of the percentage difference between the reported weight and the true weight:

```scala
scala> val discrepancy =
  (data.weights - data.reportedWeights) / data.weights
breeze.linalg.Vector[Double] = DenseVector(0.0, 0.1206896551724138,
-0.018867924528301886, -0.029411764705882353, ... )
```

Notice how Breeze's overloading of mathematical operators allows us to manipulate data arrays easily and elegantly.

We can now calculate the mean and standard deviation of this array for men:

```scala
scala> mean(discrepancy(isMale))
res6: Double = -0.008451852933123775
```

```scala
scala> stddev(discrepancy(isMale))
res8: Double = 0.031901519634244195
```

We can also calculate the fraction of men who overestimated their height:

```scala
scala> val overReportMask =
  (data.reportedHeights :> data.heights).toDenseVector
breeze.linalg.DenseVector[Boolean] = DenseVector(false, false, false,
false...
```

```scala
scala> sum(I(overReportMask :& isMale))
Double: 10.0
```

There are thus ten men who believe they are taller than they actually are. The element-wise AND operator `:&` returns a vector that is true for all indices for which both its arguments are true. The vector `overReportMask :& isMale` is thus true for all participants that are male and over-reported their height.

Breeze – function optimization

Having studied feature engineering, let's now look at the other end of the data science pipeline. Typically, a machine learning algorithm defines a loss function that is a function of a set of parameters. The value of the loss function represents how well the model fits the data. The parameters are then optimized to minimize (or maximize) the loss function.

In *Chapter 12, Distributed Machine Learning with MLlib*, we will look at **MLlib**, a machine learning library that contains many well-known algorithms. Often, we don't need to worry about optimizing loss functions directly since we can rely on the machine learning algorithms provided by MLlib. It is nevertheless useful to have a basic knowledge of optimization.

Breeze has an `optimize` module that contains functions for finding a local minimum:

```scala
scala> import breeze.optimize._
import breeze.optimize._
```

Let's create a toy function that we want to optimize:

$$f(x) = \sum_i x_i^2$$

We can represent this function in Scala as follows:

```scala
scala> def f(xs:DenseVector[Double]) = sum(xs :^ 2.0)
f: (xs: breeze.linalg.DenseVector[Double])Double
```

Most local optimizers also require the gradient of the function being optimized. The gradient is a vector of the same dimension as the arguments to the function. In our case, the gradient is:

$$\nabla f = 2\bar{x}$$

We can represent the gradient in Breeze with a function that takes a vector argument and returns a vector of the same length:

```scala
scala> def gradf(xs:DenseVector[Double]) = 2.0 :* xs
gradf: (xs:breeze.linalg.DenseVector[Double])breeze.linalg.
DenseVector[Double]
```

For instance, at the point $(1, 1, 1)$, we have:

```scala
scala> val xs = DenseVector.ones[Double](3)
breeze.linalg.DenseVector[Double] = DenseVector(1.0, 1.0, 1.0)

scala> f(xs)
Double = 3.0

scala> gradf(xs)
breeze.linalg.DenseVector[Double] = DenseVector(2.0, 2.0, 2.0)
```

Let's set up the optimization problem. Breeze's optimization methods require that we pass in an implementation of the `DiffFunction` trait with a single method, `calculate`. This method must return a tuple of the function and its gradient:

```
scala> val optTrait = new DiffFunction[DenseVector[Double]] {
  def calculate(xs:DenseVector[Double]) = (f(xs), gradf(xs))
}
breeze.optimize.DiffFunction[breeze.linalg.DenseVector[Double]] =
<function1>
```

We are now ready to run the optimization. The optimize module provides a `minimize` function that does just what we want. We pass it `optTrait` and a starting point for the optimization:

```
scala> val minimum = minimize(optTrait, DenseVector(1.0, 1.0, 1.0))
breeze.linalg.DenseVector[Double] = DenseVector(0.0, 0.0, 0.0)
```

The true minimum is at `(0.0, 0.0, 0.0)`. The optimizer therefore correctly finds the minimum.

The `minimize` function uses the **L-BFGS** method to run the optimization by default. It takes several additional arguments to control the optimization. We will explore these in the next sections.

Numerical derivatives

In the previous example, we specified the gradient of `f` explicitly. While this is generally good practice, calculating the gradient of a function can often be tedious. Breeze provides a gradient approximation function using finite differences. Reusing the same objective function `def f(xs:DenseVector[Double]) = sum(xs :^ 2.0)` as in the previous section:

```
scala> val approxOptTrait = new ApproximateGradientFunction(f)
breeze.optimize.ApproximateGradientFunction[Int,breeze.linalg.
DenseVector[Double]] = <function1>
```

The trait `approxOptTrait` has a `gradientAt` method that returns an approximation to the gradient at a point:

```
scala> approxOptTrait.gradientAt(DenseVector.ones(3))
breeze.linalg.DenseVector[Double] = DenseVector(2.00001000001393,
2.00001000001393, 2.00001000001393)
```

Note that this can be quite inaccurate. The `ApproximateGradientFunction` constructor takes an `epsilon` optional argument that controls the size of the step taken when calculating the finite differences. Changing the value of `epsilon` can improve the accuracy of the finite difference algorithm.

The `ApproximateGradientFunction` instance implements the `DiffFunction` trait. It can therefore be passed to `minimize` directly:

```
scala> minimize(approxOptTrait, DenseVector.ones[Double](3))
breeze.linalg.DenseVector[Double] = DenseVector(-5.000001063126813E-6,
-5.000001063126813E-6, -5.000001063126813E-6)
```

This, again, gives a result close to zero, but somewhat further away than when we specified the gradient explicitly. In general, it will be significantly more efficient and more accurate to calculate the gradient of a function analytically than to rely on Breeze's numerical gradient. It is probably best to only use the numerical gradient during data exploration or to check analytical gradients.

Regularization

The `minimize` function takes many optional arguments relevant to machine learning algorithms. In particular, we can instruct the optimizer to use a regularization parameter when performing the optimization. Regularization introduces a penalty in the loss function to prevent the parameters from growing arbitrarily. This is useful to avoid overfitting. We will discuss regularization in greater detail in *Chapter 12, Distributed Machine Learning with MLlib*.

For instance, to use `L2Regularization` with a hyperparameter of `0.5`:

```
scala> minimize(optTrait,
  DenseVector(1.0, 1.0, 1.0), L2Regularization(0.5))
breeze.linalg.DenseVector[Double] = DenseVector(0.0, 0.0, 0.0)
```

The regularization makes no difference in this case, since the parameters are zero at the minimum.

To see a list of optional arguments that can be passed to `minimize`, consult the Breeze documentation online.

An example – logistic regression

Let's now imagine we want to build a classifier that takes a person's **height** and **weight** and assigns a probability to their being **Male** or **Female**. We will reuse the height and weight data introduced earlier in this chapter. Let's start by plotting the dataset:

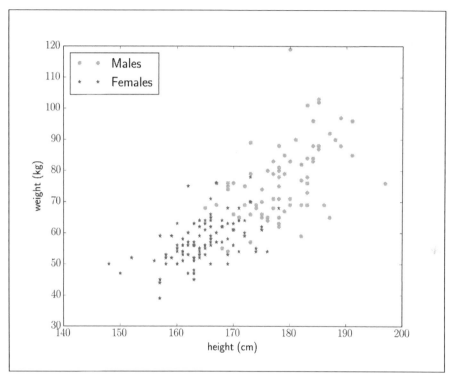

Height versus weight data for 181 men and women

There are many different algorithms for classification. A first glance at the data shows that we can, approximately, separate men from women by drawing a straight line across the plot. A linear method is therefore a reasonable initial attempt at classification. In this section, we will use logistic regression to build a classifier.

A detailed explanation of logistic regression is beyond the scope of this book. The reader unfamiliar with logistic regression is referred to *The Elements of Statistical Learning* by *Hastie, Tibshirani,* and *Friedman*. We will just give a brief summary here.

Logistic regression estimates the probability of a given *height* and *weight* belonging to a *male* with the following sigmoid function:

$$P\left(male \mid height, weight\right) = \frac{1}{1 + \exp\left(-f\left(height, weight; params\right)\right)}$$

Here, *f* is a linear function:

$$f\left(height, weight; params\right) = params\left(0\right) + height \cdot params\left(1\right) + weight \cdot params\left(2\right)$$

Here, *params* is an array of parameters that we need to determine using the training set. If we consider the height and weight as a *features = (height, weight)* matrix, we can re-write the sigmoid kernel *f* as a matrix multiplication of the *features* matrix with the *params* vector:

$$f\left(features; params\right) = params\left(0\right) + features \cdot params\left(1:\right)$$

To simplify this expression further, it is common to add a dummy feature whose value is always *1* to the *features* matrix. We can then multiply *params(0)* by this feature, allowing us to write the entire sigmoid kernel *f* as a single matrix-vector multiplication:

$$f\left(features; params\right) = params \cdot features$$

The feature matrix, *features*, is now a *(181 * 3)* matrix, where each row is *(1, height, weight)* for a particular participant.

To find the optimal values of the parameters, we can maximize the likelihood function, *L(params | features)*. The likelihood takes a given set of parameter values as input and returns the probability that these particular parameters gave rise to the training set. For a set of parameters and associated probability function *P(male | features,)*, the likelihood is:

$$L\left(params\mid features\right) = \prod_{\substack{i \\ target_i\ is\ male}} P\left(male\mid features_i\right) \times$$

$$\prod_{\substack{i \\ target_i\ not\ male}} 1 - P\left(male\mid features_i\right)$$

If we magically know, ahead of time, the gender of everyone in the population, we can assign *P(male)=1* for the men and *P(male)=0* for the women. The likelihood function would then be **1**. Conversely, any uncertainty leads to a reduction in the likelihood function. If we choose a set of parameters that consistently lead to classification errors (low *P(male)* for men or high *P(male)* for women), the likelihood function drops to *0*.

The maximum likelihood corresponds to those values of the parameters most likely to describe the observed data. Thus, to find the parameters that best describe our training set, we just need to find parameters that maximize *L(params|features)*. However, maximizing the likelihood function itself is very rarely done, since it involves multiplying many small values together, which quickly leads to floating point underflow. It is best to maximize the log of the likelihood, which has the same maximum as the likelihood. Finally, since most optimization algorithms are geared to minimize a function rather than maximize it, we will minimize $-\log\left(L\left(params\mid features\right)\right)$.

For logistic regression, this is equivalent to minimizing:

$$Cost\left(params\right) = \sum_i target_i \times \left(params \cdot features_i\right) - \log\left(\exp\left(params \cdot features_i\right) + 1\right)$$

Here, the sum runs over all participants in the training data, *features_i* is a vector $\left(1, height_i, weight_i\right)$ of the *i*-th observation in the training set, and *target_i* is *1* if the person is male, and *0* if the participant is female.

To minimize the *Cost* function, we must also know its gradient with respect to the parameters. This is:

$$\nabla_{params} Cost = \sum_i features_i \cdot \left[P\left(male\mid features_i\right) - target_i\right]$$

We will start by rescaling the height and weight by their mean and standard deviation. While this is not strictly necessary for logistic regression, it is generally good practice. It facilitates the optimization and would become necessary if we wanted to use regularization methods or build superlinear features (features that allow the boundary separating men from women to be curved rather than a straight line).

For this example, we will move away from the Scala shell and write a standalone Scala script. Here's the full code listing. Don't worry if this looks daunting. We will break it up into manageable chunks in a minute:

```scala
import breeze.linalg._
import breeze.numerics._
import breeze.optimize._
import breeze.stats._

object LogisticRegressionHWData extends App {

  val data = HWData.load

  // Rescale the features to have mean of 0.0 and s.d. of 1.0
  def rescaled(v:DenseVector[Double]) =
    (v - mean(v)) / stddev(v)

  val rescaledHeights = rescaled(data.heights)
  val rescaledWeights = rescaled(data.weights)

  // Build the feature matrix as a matrix with
  //181 rows and 3 columns.
  val rescaledHeightsAsMatrix = rescaledHeights.toDenseMatrix.t
  val rescaledWeightsAsMatrix = rescaledWeights.toDenseMatrix.t

  val featureMatrix = DenseMatrix.horzcat(
    DenseMatrix.ones[Double](rescaledHeightsAsMatrix.rows, 1),
    rescaledHeightsAsMatrix,
    rescaledWeightsAsMatrix
  )

  println(s"Feature matrix size: ${featureMatrix.rows} x " +
    s"${featureMatrix.cols}")

  // Build the target variable to be 1.0 where a participant
  // is male, and 0.0 where the participant is female.
  val target = data.genders.values.map {
```

```
    gender => if(gender == 'M') 1.0 else 0.0
  }

  // Build the loss function ready for optimization.
  // We will worry about refactoring this to be more
  // efficient later.
  def costFunction(parameters:DenseVector[Double]):Double = {
    val xBeta = featureMatrix * parameters
    val expXBeta = exp(xBeta)
    - sum((target :* xBeta) - log1p(expXBeta))
  }

  def costFunctionGradient(parameters:DenseVector[Double])
  :DenseVector[Double] = {
    val xBeta = featureMatrix * parameters
    val probs = sigmoid(xBeta)
    featureMatrix.t * (probs - target)
  }

  val f = new DiffFunction[DenseVector[Double]] {
    def calculate(parameters:DenseVector[Double]) =
      (costFunction(parameters), costFunctionGradient(parameters))
  }

  val optimalParameters = minimize(f, DenseVector(0.0, 0.0, 0.0))

  println(optimalParameters)
  // => DenseVector(-0.0751454743, 2.476293647, 2.23054540)
}
```

That was a mouthful! Let's take this one step at a time. After the obvious imports, we start with:

```
object LogisticRegressionHWData extends App {
```

By extending the built-in `App` trait, we tell Scala to treat the entire object as a `main` function. This just cuts out `def main(args:Array[String])` boilerplate. We then load the data and rescale the height and weight to have a `mean` of zero and a standard deviation of one:

```
def rescaled(v:DenseVector[Double]) =
  (v - mean(v)) / stddev(v)

val rescaledHeights = rescaled(data.heights)
val rescaledWeights = rescaled(data.weights)
```

The `rescaledHeights` and `rescaledWeights` vectors will be the features of our model. We can now build the training set matrix for this model. This is a *(181 * 3)* matrix, for which the *i*-th row is `(1, height(i), weight(i))`, corresponding to the values of the height and weight for the *i*th participant. We start by transforming both `rescaledHeights` and `rescaledWeights` from vectors to *(181 * 1)* matrices

```
val rescaledHeightsAsMatrix = rescaledHeights.toDenseMatrix.t
val rescaledWeightsAsMatrix = rescaledWeights.toDenseMatrix.t
```

We must also create a *(181 * 1)* matrix containing just *1* to act as the dummy feature. We can do this using:

```
DenseMatrix.ones[Double](rescaledHeightsAsMatrix.rows, 1)
```

We now need to combine our three *(181 * 1)* matrices together into a single feature matrix of shape *(181 * 3)*. We can use the `horzcat` method to concatenate the three matrices together:

```
val featureMatrix = DenseMatrix.horzcat(
  DenseMatrix.ones[Double](rescaledHeightsAsMatrix.rows, 1),
  rescaledHeightsAsMatrix,
  rescaledWeightsAsMatrix
)
```

The final step in the data preprocessing stage is to create the target variable. We need to convert the `data.genders` vector to a vector of ones and zeros. We assign a value of one for men and zero for women. Thus, our classifier will predict the probability that any given person is male. We will use the `.values.map` method, a method equivalent to the `.map` method on Scala collections:

```
val target = data.genders.values.map {
  gender => if(gender == 'M') 1.0 else 0.0
}
```

Note that we could also have used the indicator function which we discovered earlier:

```
val maleVector = DenseVector.fill(data.genders.size)('M')
val target = I(data.genders :== maleVector)
```

This results in the allocation of a temporary array, `maleVector`, and might therefore increase the program's memory footprint if there were many participants in the experiment.

We now have a matrix representing the training set and a vector denoting the target variable. We can write the loss function that we want to minimize. As mentioned previously, we will minimize $-\log\left(L\left(parameters\,|\,training\right)\right)$. The loss function takes as input a set of values for the linear coefficients and returns a number indicating how well those values of the linear coefficients fit the training data:

```
def costFunction(parameters:DenseVector[Double]):Double = {
  val xBeta = featureMatrix * parameters
  val expXBeta = exp(xBeta)
  - sum((target :* xBeta) - log1p(expXBeta))
}
```

Note that we use `log1p(x)` to calculate *log(1+x)*. This is robust to underflow for small values of x.

Let's explore the cost function:

```
costFunction(DenseVector(0.0, 0.0, 0.0)) // 125.45963968135031
costFunction(DenseVector(0.0, 0.1, 0.1)) // 113.33336518036882
costFunction(DenseVector(0.0, -0.1, -0.1)) // 139.17134594294433
```

We can see that the cost function is somewhat lower for slightly positive values of the height and weight parameters. This indicates that the likelihood function is larger for slightly positive values of the height and weight. This, in turn, implies (as we expect from the plot) that people who are taller and heavier than average are more likely to be male.

We also need a function that calculates the gradient of the loss function, since that will help with the optimization:

```
def costFunctionGradient(parameters:DenseVector[Double])
:DenseVector[Double] = {
  val xBeta = featureMatrix * parameters
  val probs = sigmoid(xBeta)
  featureMatrix.t * (probs - target)
}
```

Having defined the loss function and gradient, we are now in a position to set up the optimization:

```
val f = new DiffFunction[DenseVector[Double]] {
  def calculate(parameters:DenseVector[Double]) =
    (costFunction(parameters), costFunctionGradient(parameters))
}
```

All that is left now is to run the optimization. The cost function for logistic regression is convex (it has a single minimum), so the starting point for optimization is irrelevant in principle. In practice, it is common to start with a coefficient vector that is zero everywhere (equating to assigning a 0.5 probability of being male to every participant):

```
val optimalParameters = minimize(f, DenseVector(0.0, 0.0, 0.0))
```

This returns the vector of optimal parameters:

```
DenseVector(-0.0751454743, 2.476293647, 2.23054540)
```

How can we interpret the values of the optimal parameters? The coefficients for the height and weight are both positive, indicating that people who are taller and heavier are more likely to be male.

We can also get the decision boundary (the line separating (height, weight) pairs more likely to belong to a woman from (height, weight) pairs more likely to belong to a man) directly from the coefficients. The decision boundary is:

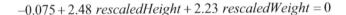

$$-0.075 + 2.48 \ rescaledHeight + 2.23 \ rescaledWeight = 0$$

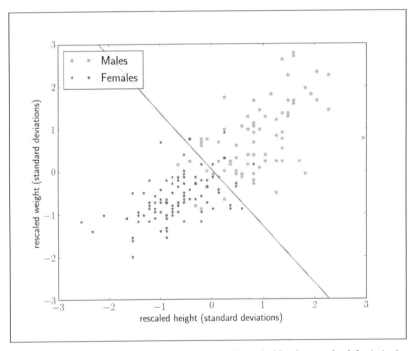

Height and weight data (shifted by the mean and rescaled by the standard deviation). The orange line is the logistic regression decision boundary. Logistic regression predicts that individuals above the boundary are male.

Towards re-usable code

In the previous section, we performed all of the computation in a single script. While this is fine for data exploration, it means that we cannot reuse the logistic regression code that we have built. In this section, we will start the construction of a machine learning library that you can reuse across different projects.

We will factor the logistic regression algorithm out into its own class. We construct a `LogisticRegression` class:

```
import breeze.linalg._
import breeze.numerics._
import breeze.optimize._

class LogisticRegression(
    val training:DenseMatrix[Double],
    val target:DenseVector[Double])
{
```

The class takes, as input, a matrix representing the training set and a vector denoting the target variable. Notice how we assign these to `vals`, meaning that they are set on class creation and will remain the same until the class is destroyed. Of course, the `DenseMatrix` and `DenseVector` objects are mutable, so the values that `training` and `target` point to might change. Since programming best practice dictates that mutable state makes reasoning about program behavior difficult, we will avoid taking advantage of this mutability.

Let's add a method that calculates the cost function and its gradient:

```
def costFunctionAndGradient(coefficients:DenseVector[Double])
:(Double, DenseVector[Double]) = {
  val xBeta = training * coefficients
  val expXBeta = exp(xBeta)
  val cost = - sum((target :* xBeta) - log1p(expXBeta))
  val probs = sigmoid(xBeta)
  val grad = training.t * (probs - target)
  (cost, grad)
}
```

We are now all set up to run the optimization to calculate the coefficients that best reproduce the training set. In traditional object-oriented languages, we might define a getOptimalCoefficients method that returns a DenseVector of the coefficients. Scala, however, is more elegant. Since we have defined the training and target attributes as vals, there is only one possible set of values of the optimal coefficients. We could, therefore, define a val optimalCoefficients = ??? class attribute that holds the optimal coefficients. The problem with this is that it forces all the computation to happen when the instance is constructed. This will be unexpected for the user and might be wasteful: if the user is only interested in accessing the cost function, for instance, the time spent minimizing it will be wasted. The solution is to use a lazy val. This value will only be evaluated when the client code requests it:

```
lazy val optimalCoefficients = ???
```

To help with the calculation of the coefficients, we will define a private helper method:

```
private def calculateOptimalCoefficients
:DenseVector[Double] = {
  val f = new DiffFunction[DenseVector[Double]] {
    def calculate(parameters:DenseVector[Double]) =
      costFunctionAndGradient(parameters)
  }

  minimize(f, DenseVector.zeros[Double](training.cols))
}

lazy val optimalCoefficients = calculateOptimalCoefficients
```

We have refactored the logistic regression into its own class, that we can reuse across different projects.

If we were planning on reusing the height-weight data, we could, similarly, refactor it into a class of its own that facilitates data loading, feature scaling, and any other functionality that we find ourselves reusing often.

Alternatives to Breeze

Breeze is the most feature-rich and approachable Scala framework for linear algebra and numeric computation. However, do not take my word for it: experiment with other libraries for tabular data. In particular, I recommend trying *Saddle*, which provides a `Frame` object similar to data frames in pandas or R. In the Java world, the *Apache Commons Maths library* provides a very rich toolkit for numerical computation. In *Chapter 10*, *Distributed Batch Processing with Spark*, *Chapter 11*, *Spark SQL and DataFrames*, and *Chapter 12*, *Distributed Machine Learning with MLlib*, we will explore *Spark* and *MLlib*, which allow the user to run distributed machine learning algorithms.

Summary

This concludes our brief overview of Breeze. We have learned how to manipulate basic Breeze data types, how to use them for linear algebra, and how to perform convex optimization. We then used our knowledge to clean a real dataset and performed logistic regression on it.

In the next chapter, we will discuss breeze-viz, a plotting library for Scala.

References

The Elements of Statistical Learning, by *Hastie*, *Tibshirani*, and *Friedman*, gives a lucid, practical description of the mathematical underpinnings of machine learning. Anyone aspiring to do more than mindlessly apply machine learning algorithms as black boxes ought to have a well-thumbed copy of this book.

Scala for Machine Learning, by *Patrick R. Nicholas*, describes practical implementations of many useful machine learning algorithms in Scala.

The Breeze documentation (`https://github.com/scalanlp/breeze/wiki/Quickstart`), API docs (`http://www.scalanlp.org/api/breeze/#package`), and source code (`https://github.com/scalanlp/breeze`) provide the most up-to-date sources of documentation on Breeze.

3
Plotting with breeze-viz

Data visualization is an integral part of data science. Visualization needs fall into two broad categories: during the development and validation of new models and, at the end of the pipeline, to distill meaning from the data and the models to provide insight to external stakeholders.

The two types of visualizations are quite different. At the data exploration and model development stage, the most important feature of a visualization library is its ease of use. It should take as few steps as possible to go from having data as arrays of numbers (or CSVs or in a database) to having data displayed on a screen. The lifetime of graphs is also quite short: once the data scientist has learned all he can from the graph or visualization, it is normally discarded. By contrast, when developing visualization widgets for external stakeholders, one is willing to tolerate increased development time for greater flexibility. The visualizations can have significant lifetime, especially if the underlying data changes over time.

The tool of choice in Scala for the first type of visualization is breeze-viz. When developing visualizations for external stakeholders, web-based visualizations (such as D3) and Tableau tend to be favored.

In this chapter, we will explore breeze-viz. In *Chapter 14*, *Visualization with D3 and the Play Framework*, we will learn how to build Scala backends for JavaScript visualizations.

Breeze-viz is (no points for guessing) Breeze's visualization library. It wraps **JFreeChart**, a very popular Java charting library. Breeze-viz is still very experimental. In particular, it is much less feature-rich than matplotlib in Python, or R or MATLAB. Nevertheless, breeze-viz allows access to the underlying JFreeChart objects so one can always fall back to editing these objects directly. The syntax for breeze-viz is inspired by MATLAB and matplotlib.

Diving into Breeze

Let's get started. We will work in the Scala console, but a program similar to this example is available in `BreezeDemo.scala` in the examples corresponding to this chapter. Create a `build.sbt` file with the following lines:

```
scalaVersion := "2.11.7"

libraryDependencies ++= Seq(
  "org.scalanlp" %% "breeze" % "0.11.2",
  "org.scalanlp" %% "breeze-viz" % "0.11.2",
  "org.scalanlp" %% "breeze-natives" % "0.11.2"
)
```

Start an sbt console:

```
$ sbt console
```

```
scala> import breeze.linalg._
import breeze.linalg._
```

```
scala> import breeze.plot._
import breeze.plot._
```

```
scala> import breeze.numerics._
import breeze.numerics._
```

Let's start by plotting a sigmoid curve, $f(x) = 1/(1 + e^{-x})$. We will first generate the data using Breeze. Recall that the `linspace` method creates a vector of doubles, uniformly distributed between two values:

```
scala> val x = linspace(-4.0, 4.0, 200)
x: DenseVector[Double] = DenseVector(-4.0, -3.959798...
```

```
scala> val fx = sigmoid(x)
fx: DenseVector[Double] = DenseVector(0.0179862099620915,...
```

We now have the data ready for plotting. The first step is to create a figure:

```
scala> val fig = Figure()
fig: breeze.plot.Figure = breeze.plot.Figure@37e36de9
```

This creates an empty Java Swing window (which may appear on your taskbar or equivalent). A figure can contain one or more plots. Let's add a plot to our figure:

```scala
scala> val plt = fig.subplot(0)
plt: breeze.plot.Plot = breeze.plot.Plot@171c2840
```

For now, let's ignore the `0` passed as argument to `.subplot`. We can add data points to our `plot`:

```scala
scala> plt += plot(x, fx)
breeze.plot.Plot = breeze.plot.Plot@63d6a0f8
```

The `plot` function takes two arguments, corresponding to the x and y values of the data series to be plotted. To view the changes, you need to refresh the figure:

```scala
scala> fig.refresh()
```

Look at the Swing window now. You should see a beautiful sigmoid, similar to the one below. Right-clicking on the window lets you interact with the plot and save the image as a PNG:

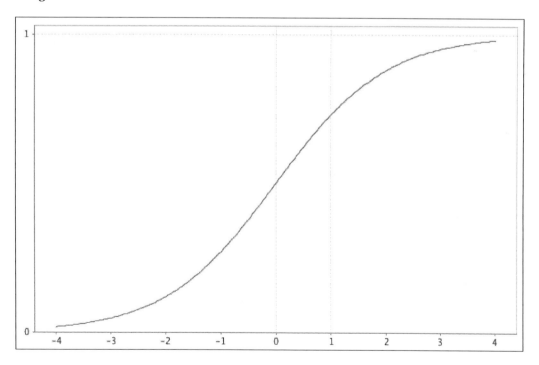

You can also save the image programmatically as follows:

```
scala> fig.saveas("sigmoid.png")
```

Breeze-viz currently only supports exporting to PNG.

Customizing plots

We now have a curve on our chart. Let's add a few more:

```
scala> val f2x = sigmoid(2.0*x)
f2x: breeze.linalg.DenseVector[Double] = DenseVector(3.353501304664E-4...

scala> val f10x = sigmoid(10.0*x)
f10x: breeze.linalg.DenseVector[Double] = DenseVector(4.2483542552
9E-18...

scala> plt += plot(x, f2x, name="S(2x)")
breeze.plot.Plot = breeze.plot.Plot@63d6a0f8

scala> plt += plot(x, f10x, name="S(10x)")
breeze.plot.Plot = breeze.plot.Plot@63d6a0f8

scala> fig.refresh()
```

Looking at the figure now, you should see all three curves in different colors. Notice that we named the data series as we added them to the plot, using the `name=""` keyword argument. To view the names, we must set the `legend` attribute:

```
scala> plt.legend = true
```

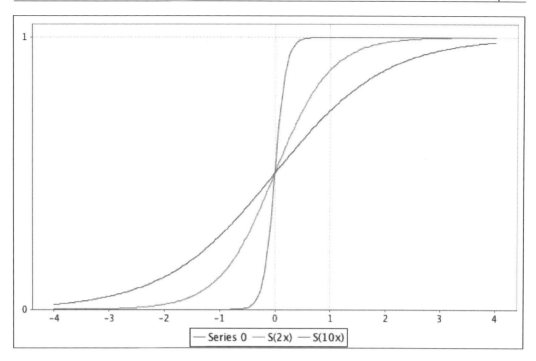

Our plot still leaves a lot to be desired. Let's start by restricting the range of the *x* axis to remove the bands of white space on either side of the plot:

```scala
scala> plt.xlim = (-4.0, 4.0)
plt.xlim: (Double, Double) = (-4.0,4.0)
```

Now, notice how, while the *x* ticks are sensibly spaced, there are only two *y* ticks: at *0* and *1*. It would be useful to have ticks every *0.1* increment. Breeze does not provide a way to set this directly. Instead, it exposes the underlying JFreeChart Axis object belonging to the current plot:

```scala
scala> plt.yaxis
org.jfree.chart.axis.NumberAxis = org.jfree.chart.axis.NumberAxis@0
```

The Axis object supports a .setTickUnit method that lets us set the tick spacing:

```scala
scala> import org.jfree.chart.axis.NumberTickUnit
import org.jfree.chart.axis.NumberTickUnit

scala> plt.yaxis.setTickUnit(new NumberTickUnit(0.1))
```

JFreeChart allows extensive customization of the Axis object. For a full list of methods available, consult the JFreeChart documentation (http://www.jfree.org/jfreechart/api/javadoc/org/jfree/chart/axis/Axis.html).

Let's also add a vertical line at *x=0* and a horizontal line at *f(x)=1*. We will need to access the underlying JFreeChart plot to add these lines. This is available (somewhat confusingly) as the .plot attribute in our Breeze Plot object:

```
scala> plt.plot
org.jfree.chart.plot.XYPlot = org.jfree.chart.plot.XYPlot@17e4db6c
```

We can use the .addDomainMarker and .addRangeMarker methods to add vertical and horizontal lines to JFreeChart XYPlot objects:

```
scala> import org.jfree.chart.plot.ValueMarker
import org.jfree.chart.plot.ValueMarker

scala> plt.plot.addDomainMarker(new ValueMarker(0.0))

scala> plt.plot.addRangeMarker(new ValueMarker(1.0))
```

Let's also add labels to the axes:

```
scala> plt.xlabel = "x"
plt.xlabel: String = x

scala> plt.ylabel = "f(x)"
plt.ylabel: String = f(x)
```

If you have run all these commands, you should have a graph that looks like this:

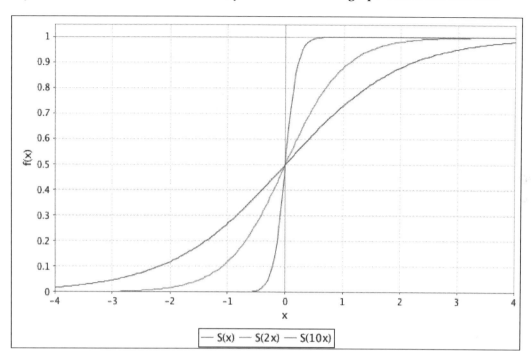

We now know how to customize the basic building blocks of a graph. The next step is to learn how to change how curves are drawn.

Customizing the line type

So far, we have just plotted lines using the default settings. Breeze lets us customize how lines are drawn, at least to some extent.

For this example, we will use the height-weight data discussed in *Chapter 2, Manipulating Data with Breeze*. We will use the Scala shell here for demonstrative purposes, but you will find a program in `BreezeDemo.scala` that follows the example shell session.

The code examples for this chapter come with a module for loading the data, `HWData.scala`, that loads the data from the CSVs:

```
scala> val data = HWData.load
data: HWData = HWData [ 181 rows ]

scala> data.heights
```

```
breeze.linalg.DenseVector[Double] = DenseVector(182.0, ...
```

```
scala> data.weights
breeze.linalg.DenseVector[Double] = DenseVector(77.0, 58.0...
```

Let's create a scatter plot of the heights against the weights:

```
scala> val fig = Figure("height vs. weight")
fig: breeze.plot.Figure = breeze.plot.Figure@743f2558
```

```
scala> val plt = fig.subplot(0)
plt: breeze.plot.Plot = breeze.plot.Plot@501ea274
```

```
scala> plt += plot(data.heights, data.weights, '+',
  colorcode="black")
breeze.plot.Plot = breeze.plot.Plot@501ea274
```

This produces a scatter-plot of the height-weight data:

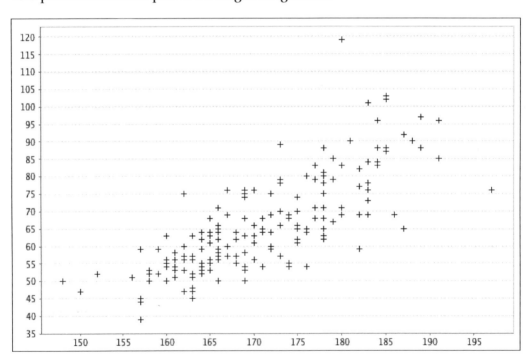

Note that we passed a third argument to the `plot` method, `'+'`. This controls the plotting style. As of this writing, there are three available styles: `'-'` (the default), `'+'`, and `'.'`. Experiment with these to see what they do. Finally, we pass a `colorcode="black"` argument to control the color of the line. This is either a color name or an RGB triple, written as a string. Thus, to plot red points, we could have passed `colorcode="[255,0,0]"`.

Looking at the height-weight plot, there is clearly a trend between height and weight. Let's try and fit a straight line through the data points. We will fit the following function:

$$weight\left(Kg\right) = a + b \times height\left(cm\right)$$

 Scientific literature suggests that it would be better to fit something more like $mass \propto height^2$. You should find it straightforward to fit a quadratic line to the data, should you wish to.

We will use Breeze's least squares function to find the values of `a` and `b`. The `leastSquares` method expects an input matrix of features and a target vector, just like the `LogisticRegression` class that we defined in the previous chapter. Recall that in *Chapter 2, Manipulating Data with Breeze*, when we prepared the training set for logistic regression classification, we introduced a dummy feature that was one for every participant to provide the degree of freedom for the *y* intercept. We will use the same approach here. Our feature matrix, therefore, contains two columns—one that is `1` everywhere and one for the height:

```scala
scala> val features = DenseMatrix.horzcat(
  DenseMatrix.ones[Double](data.npoints, 1),
  data.heights.toDenseMatrix.t
)
features: breeze.linalg.DenseMatrix[Double] =
1.0   182.0
1.0   161.0
1.0   161.0
1.0   177.0
1.0   157.0
...


scala> import breeze.stats.regression._
```

```
import breeze.stats.regression._
```

```
scala> val leastSquaresResult = leastSquares(features, data.weights)
leastSquaresResult: breeze.stats.regression.LeastSquaresRegressionResult
= <function1>
```

The `leastSquares` method returns an instance of `LeastSquareRegressionResult`, which contains a `coefficients` attribute containing the coefficients that best fit the data:

```
scala> leastSquaresResult.coefficients
breeze.linalg.DenseVector[Double] = DenseVector(-131.042322, 1.1521875)
```

The best-fit line is therefore:

$$weight(Kg) = -131.04 + 1.1522 \times height(cm)$$

Let's extract the coefficients. An elegant way of doing this is to use Scala's pattern matching capabilities:

```
scala> val Array(a, b) = leastSquaresResult.coefficients.toArray
a: Double = -131.04232269750622
b: Double = 1.1521875435418725
```

By writing `val Array(a, b) = ...`, we are telling Scala that the right-hand side of the expression is a two-element array and to bind the first element of that array to the value a and the second to the value b. See *Appendix, Pattern Matching and Extractors*, for a discussion of pattern matching.

We can now add the best-fit line to our graph. We start by generating evenly-spaced dummy height values:

```
scala> val dummyHeights = linspace(min(data.heights),
  max(data.heights), 200)
dummyHeights: breeze.linalg.DenseVector[Double] = DenseVector(148.0, ...
```

```
scala> val fittedWeights = a :+ (b :* dummyHeights)
fittedWeights: breeze.linalg.DenseVector[Double] = DenseVector(39.4814...
```

```
scala> plt += plot(dummyHeights, fittedWeights, colorcode="red")
breeze.plot.Plot = breeze.plot.Plot@501ea274
```

Let's also add the equation for the best-fit line to the graph as an annotation. We will first generate the label:

```
scala> val label = f"weight = $a%.4f + $b%.4f * height"
label: String = weight = -131.0423 + 1.1522 * height
```

To add an annotation, we must access the underlying JFreeChart plot:

```
scala> import org.jfree.chart.annotations.XYTextAnnotation
import org.jfree.chart.annotations.XYTextAnnotation


scala> plt.plot.addAnnotation(new XYTextAnnotation(label, 175.0, 105.0))
```

The XYTextAnnotation constructor takes three parameters: the annotation string and a pair of (x, y) coordinates defining the centre of the annotation on the graph. The coordinates of the annotation are expressed in the coordinate system of the data. Thus, calling new XYTextAnnotation(label, 175.0, 105.0) generates an annotation whose centroid is at the point corresponding to a height of 175 cm and weight of 105 kg:

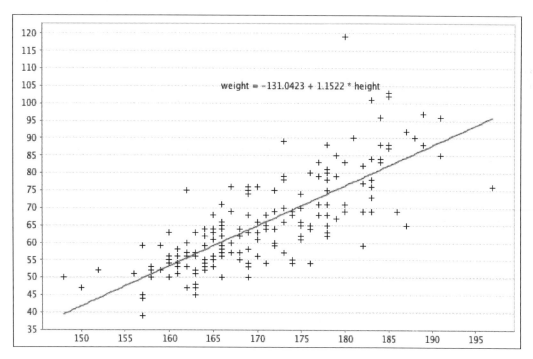

More advanced scatter plots

Breeze-viz offers a `scatter` function that adds a significant degree of customization to scatter plots. In particular, we can use the size and color of the marker points to add additional dimensions of information to the plot.

The `scatter` function takes, as its first two arguments, collections of *x* and *y* points. The third argument is a function mapping an integer `i` to a `Double` indicating the size of the *ith* point. The size of the point is measured in units of the *x* axis. If you have the sizes as a Scala collection or a Breeze vector, you can use that collection's `apply` method as the function. Let's see how this works in practice.

As with the previous examples, we will use the REPL, but you can find a sample program in `BreezeDemo.scala`:

```scala
scala> val fig = new Figure("Advanced scatter example")
fig: breeze.plot.Figure = breeze.plot.Figure@220821bc


scala> val plt = fig.subplot(0)
plt: breeze.plot.Plot = breeze.plot.Plot@668f8ae0


scala> val xs = linspace(0.0, 1.0, 100)
xs: breeze.linalg.DenseVector[Double] = DenseVector(0.0,
0.010101010101010102, 0.0202 ...


scala> val sizes = 0.025 * DenseVector.rand(100) // random sizes
sizes: breeze.linalg.DenseVector[Double] =
DenseVector(0.014879265631723166, 0.00219551...


scala> plt += scatter(xs, xs :^ 2.0, sizes.apply)
breeze.plot.Plot = breeze.plot.Plot@668f8ae0
```

Selecting custom colors works in a similar manner: we pass in a `colors` argument that maps an integer index to a `java.awt.Paint` object. Using these directly can be cumbersome, so Breeze provides some default palettes. For instance, the `GradientPaintScale` maps doubles in a given domain to a uniform color gradient. Let's map doubles in the range `0.0` to `1.0` to the colors between red and green:

```
scala> val palette = new GradientPaintScale(
  0.0, 1.0, PaintScale.RedToGreen)
palette: breeze.plot.GradientPaintScale[Double] = <function1>


scala> palette(0.5) // half-way between red and green
java.awt.Paint = java.awt.Color[r=127,g=127,b=0]


scala> palette(1.0) // green
java.awt.Paint = java.awt.Color[r=0,g=254,b=0]
```

Besides the `GradientPaintScale`, breeze-viz provides a `CategoricalPaintScale` class for categorical palettes. For an overview of the different palettes, consult the source file `PaintScale.scala` at scala: https://github.com/scalanlp/breeze/blob/master/viz/src/main/scala/breeze/plot/PaintScale.scala.

Let's use our newfound knowledge to draw a multicolor scatter plot. We will assume the same initialization as the previous example. We will assign a random color to each point:

```
scala> val palette = new GradientPaintScale(0.0, 1.0,
  PaintScale.MaroonToGold)
palette: breeze.plot.GradientPaintScale[Double] = <function1>


scala> val colors = DenseVector.rand(100).mapValues(palette)
colors: breeze.linalg.DenseVector[java.awt.Paint] = DenseVector(java.awt.
Color[r=162,g=5,b=0], ...


scala> plt += scatter(xs, xs :^ 2.0, sizes.apply, colors.apply)
breeze.plot.Plot = breeze.plot.Plot@8ff7e27
```

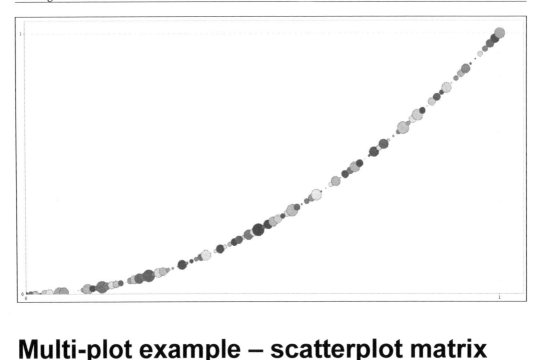

Multi-plot example – scatterplot matrix plots

In this section, we will learn how to have several plots in the same figure.

The key new method that allows multiple plots in the same figure is `fig.subplot(nrows, ncols, plotIndex)`. This method, an overloaded version of the `fig.subplot` method we have been using up to now, both sets the number of rows and columns in the figure and returns a specific subplot. It takes three arguments:

- `nrows`: The number of rows of subplots in the figure
- `ncols`: The number of columns of subplots in the figure
- `plotIndex`: The index of the plot to return

Users familiar with MATLAB or matplotlib will note that the `.subplot` method is identical to the eponymous methods in these frameworks. This might seem a little complex, so let's look at an example (you will find the code for this in `BreezeDemo.scala`):

```
import breeze.plot._

def subplotExample {
    val data = HWData.load
```

```
    val fig = new Figure("Subplot example")

    // upper subplot: plot index '0' refers to the first plot
    var plt = fig.subplot(2, 1, 0)
    plt += plot(data.heights, data.weights, '.')

    // lower subplot: plot index '1' refers to the second plot
    plt = fig.subplot(2, 1, 1)
    plt += plot(data.heights, data.reportedHeights, '.',
      colorcode="black")

    fig.refresh
  }
```

Running this example produces the following plot:

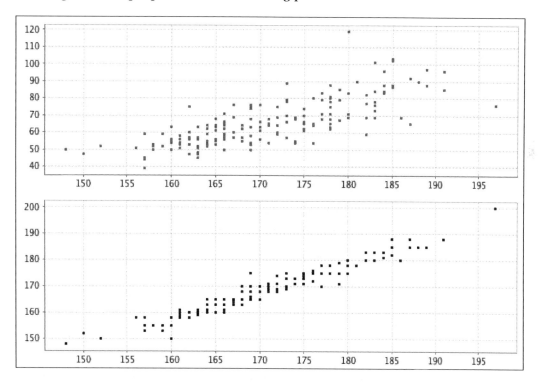

Now that we have a basic grasp of how to add several subplots to the same figure, let's do something a little more interesting. We will write a class to draw scatterplot matrices. These are useful for exploring correlations between different features.

If you are not familiar with scatterplot matrices, have a look at the figure at the end of this section for an idea of what we are constructing. The idea is to build a square matrix of scatter plots for each pair of features. Element (i, j) in the matrix is a scatter plot of feature i against feature j. Since a scatter plot of a variable against itself is of limited use, one normally draws histograms of each feature along the diagonal. Finally, since a scatter plot of feature i against feature j contains the same information as a scatter plot of feature j against feature i, one normally only plots the upper triangle or the lower triangle of the matrix.

Let's start by writing functions for the individual plots. These will take a `Plot` object referencing the correct subplot and vectors of the data to plot:

```
import breeze.plot._
import breeze.linalg._

class ScatterplotMatrix(val fig:Figure) {

  /** Draw the histograms on the diagonal */
  private def plotHistogram(plt:Plot)(
  data:DenseVector[Double], label:String) {
     plt += hist(data)
     plt.xlabel = label
  }

  /** Draw the off-diagonal scatter plots */
  private def plotScatter(plt:Plot)(
    xdata:DenseVector[Double],
    ydata:DenseVector[Double],
    xlabel:String,
    ylabel:String) {
     plt += plot(xdata, ydata, '.')
     plt.xlabel = xlabel
     plt.ylabel = ylabel
  }

  ...
```

Notice the use of `hist(data)` to draw a histogram. The argument to `hist` must be a vector of data points. The `hist` method will bin these and represent them as a histogram.

Now that we have the machinery for drawing individual plots, we just need to wire everything together. The tricky part is to know how to select the correct subplot for a given row and column position in the matrix. We can select a single plot by calling `fig.subplot(nrows, ncolumns, plotIndex)`, but translating from a (*row, column*) index pair to a single `plotIndex` is not obvious. The plots are numbered in increasing order, first from left to right, then from top to bottom:

```
0 1 2 3
4 5 6 7
...
```

Let's write a short function to select a plot at a (*row, column*) index pair:

```
private def selectPlot(ncols:Int)(irow:Int, icol:Int):Plot = {
  fig.subplot(ncols, ncols, (irow)*ncols + icol)
}
```

We are now in a position to draw the matrix plot itself:

```
/** Draw a scatterplot matrix.
  *
  * This function draws a scatterplot matrix of the correlation
  * between each pair of columns in `featureMatrix`.
  *
  * @param featureMatrix A matrix of features, with each column
  *   representing a feature.
  * @param labels Names of the features.
  */
def plotFeatures(
  featureMatrix:DenseMatrix[Double],
  labels:List[String]
) {
  val ncols = featureMatrix.cols
  require(ncols == labels.size,
    "Number of columns in feature matrix "+
    "must match length of labels"
  )
  fig.clear
  fig.subplot(ncols, ncols, 0)

  (0 until ncols) foreach { irow =>
    val p = selectPlot(ncols)(irow, irow)
    plotHistogram(p)(featureMatrix(::, irow), labels(irow))

    (0 until irow) foreach { icol =>
```

```
      val p = selectPlot(ncols)(irow, icol)
      plotScatter(p)(
        featureMatrix(::, irow),
        featureMatrix(::, icol),
        labels(irow),
        labels(icol)
      )
    }
  }
}
```

Let's write an example for our class. We will use the height-weight data again:

```
import breeze.linalg._
import breeze.numerics._
import breeze.plot._

object ScatterplotMatrixDemo extends App {

  val data = HWData.load
  val m = new ScatterplotMatrix(Figure("Scatterplot matrix demo"))

  // Make a matrix with three columns: the height, weight and
  // reported weight data.
  val featureMatrix = DenseMatrix.horzcat(
    data.heights.toDenseMatrix.t,
    data.weights.toDenseMatrix.t,
    data.reportedWeights.toDenseMatrix.t
  )
  m.plotFeatures(featureMatrix,
    List("height", "weight", "reportedWeights"))

}
```

Running this through SBT produces the following plot:

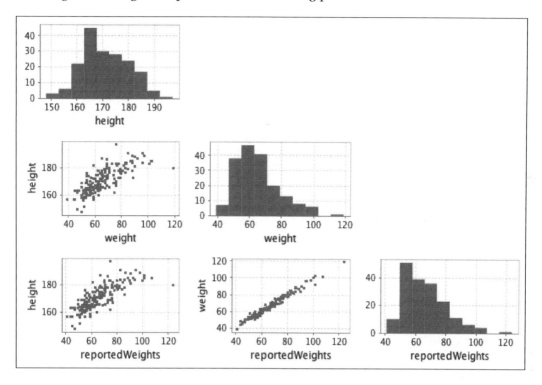

Managing without documentation

Breeze-viz is unfortunately rather poorly documented. This can make the learning curve somewhat steep. Fortunately, it is still quite a small project: at the time of writing, there are just ten source files (`https://github.com/scalanlp/breeze/tree/master/viz/src/main/scala/breeze/plot`). A good way to understand exactly what breeze-viz does is to read the source code. For instance, to see what methods are available on a `Plot` object, read the source file `Plot.scala`. If you need functionality beyond that provided by Breeze, consult the documentation for JFreeChart to discover if you can implement what you need by accessing the underlying JFreeChart objects.

Breeze-viz reference

Writing a reference in a programming book is a dangerous exercise: you quickly become out of date. Nevertheless, given the paucity of documentation for breeze-viz, this section becomes more relevant – it is easier to compete against something that does not exist. Take this section with a pinch of salt, and if a command in this section does not work, head over to the source code:

Command	Description
`plt += plot(xs, ys)`	This plots a series of (xs, ys) values. The xs and ys values must be collection-like objects (Breeze vectors, Scala arrays, or lists, for instance).

`plt += scatter(xs, ys, size)`
 	
`plt += scatter(xs, ys, size, color)`
	This plots a series of (xs, ys) values as a scatter plot. The `size` argument is an `(Int) => Double` function mapping the index of a point to its size (in the same units as the *x* axis). The `color` argument is an `(Int) => java.awt.Paint` function mapping from integers to colors. Read the *more advanced scatter plots* section for further details.

`plt += hist(xs)`
 	
`plt += hist(xs, bins=10)`
	This bins xs and plots a histogram. The `bins` argument controls the number of bins.

`plt += image(mat)`	This plots an image or matrix. The `mat` argument should be `Matrix[Double]`. Read the `package.scala` source file in `breeze.plot` for details (`https://github.com/scalanlp/breeze/blob/master/viz/src/main/scala/breeze/plot/package.scala`).

It is also useful to summarize the options available on a `plot` object:

Attribute	Description
`plt.xlabel = "x-label"` `plt.ylabel = "y-label"`	This sets the axis label
`plt.xlim = (0.0, 1.0)` `plt.ylim = (0.0, 1.0)`	This sets the axis maximum and minimum value
`plt.logScaleX = true` `plt.logScaleY = true`	This switches the axis to a log scale
`plt.title = "title"`	This sets the plot title

Data visualization beyond breeze-viz

Other tools for data visualization in Scala are emerging: Spark notebooks (`https://github.com/andypetrella/spark-notebook#description`) based on the IPython notebook and Apache Zeppelin (`https://zeppelin.incubator.apache.org`). Both of these rely on Apache Spark, which we will explore later in this book.

Summary

In this chapter, we learned how to draw simple charts with breeze-viz. In the last chapter of this book, we will learn how to build interactive visualizations using JavaScript libraries.

Next, we will learn about basic Scala concurrency constructs—specifically, parallel collections.

4
Parallel Collections and Futures

Data science often involves processing medium or large amounts of data. Since the previously exponential growth in the speed of individual CPUs has slowed down and the amount of data continues to increase, leveraging computers effectively must entail parallel computation.

In this chapter, we will look at ways of parallelizing computation and data processing over a single computer. Virtually all new computers have more than one processing unit, and distributing a calculation over these cores can be an effective way of hastening medium-sized calculations.

Parallelizing calculations over a single chip is suitable for calculations involving gigabytes or a few terabytes of data. For larger data flows, we must resort to distributing the computation over several computers in parallel. We will discuss Apache Spark, a framework for parallel data processing in *Chapter 10, Distributed Batch Processing with Spark*.

In this book, we will look at three common ways of leveraging parallel architectures in a single machine: parallel collections, futures, and actors. We will consider the first two in this chapter, and leave the study of actors to *Chapter 9, Concurrency with Akka*.

Parallel collections

Parallel collections offer an extremely easy way to parallelize independent tasks. The reader, being familiar with Scala, will know that many tasks can be phrased as operations on collections, such as *map, reduce, filter*, or *groupBy*. Parallel collections are an implementation of Scala collections that parallelize these operations to run over several threads.

Let's start with an example. We want to calculate the frequency of occurrence of each letter in a sentence:

```
scala> val sentence = "The quick brown fox jumped over the lazy dog"
sentence: String = The quick brown fox jumped ...
```

Let's start by converting our sentence from a string to a vector of characters:

```
scala> val characters = sentence.toVector
Vector[Char] = Vector(T, h, e,  , q, u, i, c, k, ...)
```

We can now convert `characters` to a *parallel* vector, a `ParVector`. To do this, we use the `par` method:

```
scala> val charactersPar = characters.par
ParVector[Char] = ParVector(T, h, e,  , q, u, i, c, k,  , ...)
```

`ParVector` collections support the same operations as regular vectors, but their methods are executed in parallel over several threads.

Let's start by filtering out the spaces in `charactersPar`:

```
scala> val lettersPar = charactersPar.filter { _ != ' ' }
ParVector[Char] = ParVector(T, h, e, q, u, i, c, k, ...)
```

Notice how Scala hides the execution details. The `filter` operation was performed using multiple threads, and you barely even noticed! The interface and behavior of a parallel vector is identical to its serial counterpart, save for a few details that we will explore in the next section.

Let's now use the `toLower` function to make the letters lowercase:

```
scala> val lowerLettersPar = lettersPar.map { _.toLower }
ParVector[Char] = ParVector(t, h, e, q, u, i, c, k, ...)
```

As before, the `map` method was applied in parallel. To find the frequency of occurrence of each letter, we use the `groupBy` method to group characters into vectors containing all the occurrences of that character:

```
scala> val intermediateMap = lowerLettersPar.groupBy(identity)
ParMap[Char,ParVector[Char]] = ParMap(e -> ParVector(e, e, e, e), ...)
```

Note how the `groupBy` method has created a `ParMap` instance, the parallel equivalent of an immutable map. To get the number of occurrences of each letter, we do a `mapValues` call on `intermediateMap`, replacing each vector by its length:

```scala
scala> val occurenceNumber = intermediateMap.mapValues { _.length }
ParMap[Char,Int] = ParMap(e -> 4, x -> 1, n -> 1, j -> 1, ...)
```

Congratulations! We've written a multi-threaded algorithm for finding the frequency of occurrence of each letter in a few lines of code. You should find it straightforward to adapt this to find the frequency of occurrence of each word in a document, a common preprocessing problem for analyzing text data.

Parallel collections make it very easy to parallelize some operation pipelines: all we had to do was call `.par` on the `characters` vector. All subsequent operations were parallelized. This makes switching from a serial to a parallel implementation very easy.

Limitations of parallel collections

Part of the power and the appeal of parallel collections is that they present the same interface as their serial counterparts: they have a `map` method, a `foreach` method, a `filter` method, and so on. By and large, these methods work in the same way on parallel collections as they do in serial. There are, however, some notable caveats. The most important one has to do with side effects. If an operation on a parallel collection has a side effect, this may result in a race condition: a situation in which the final result depends on the order in which the threads perform their operations.

Side effects in collections arise most commonly when we update a variable defined outside of the collection. To give a trivial example of unexpected behavior, let's define a `count` variable and increment it a thousand times using a parallel range:

```scala
scala> var count = 0
count: Int = 0


scala> (0 until 1000).par.foreach { i => count += 1 }


scala> count
count: Int = 874 // not 1000!
```

What happened here? The function passed to foreach has a side effect: it increments count, a variable outside of the scope of the function. This is a problem because the += operator is a sequence of two operations:

- Retrieve the value of count and add one to it
- Assign the result back to count

To understand why this causes unexpected behavior, let's imagine that the foreach loop has been parallelized over two threads. **Thread A** might read the **count** variable when it is **832** and add one to it to give **833**. Before it has time to reassign **833** to **count**, **Thread B** reads **count**, still at **832**, and adds one to give **833**. **Thread A** then assigns **833** to **count**. **Thread B** then assigns **833** to **count**. We've run through two updates but only incremented the count by one. The problem arises because += can be separated into two instructions: it is not *atomic*. This leaves room for threads to interleave their operations:

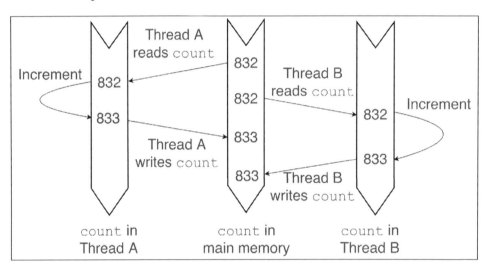

The anatomy of a race condition: both thread A and thread B are trying to update count concurrently, resulting in one of the updates being overwritten. The final value of count is 833 instead of 834.

To give a somewhat more realistic example of problems caused by non-atomicity, let's look at a different method for counting the frequency of occurrence of each letter in our sentence. We define a mutable Char -> Int hash map outside of the loop. Each time we encounter a letter, we increment the corresponding integer in the map:

```scala
scala> import scala.collection.mutable
import scala.collection.mutable


scala> val occurenceNumber = mutable.Map.empty[Char, Int]
```

```
occurenceNumber: mutable.Map[Char,Int] = Map()

scala> lowerLettersPar.foreach { c =>
  occurenceNumber(c) = occurenceNumber.getOrElse(c, 0) + 1
}

scala> occurenceNumber('e') // Should be 4
Int = 2
```

The discrepancy occurs because of the non-atomicity of the operations in the `foreach` loop.

In general, it is good practice to avoid side effects in higher-order functions on collections. They make the code harder to understand and preclude switching from serial to parallel collections. It is also good practice to avoid exposing mutable state: immutable objects can be shared freely between threads and cannot be affected by side effects.

Another limitation of parallel collections occurs in reduction (or folding) operations. The function used to combine items together must be *associative*. For instance:

```
scala> (0 until 1000).par.reduce {_ - _ } // should be -499500
Int = 63620
```

The *minus* operator, $-$, is not associative. The order in which consecutive operations are applied matters: `(a - b) - c` is not the same as `a - (b - c)`. The function used to reduce a parallel collection must be associative because the order in which the reduction occurs is not tied to the order of the collection.

Error handling

In single-threaded programs, exception handling is relatively straightforward: if an exception occurs, the function can either handle it or escalate it. This is not nearly as obvious when parallelism is introduced: a single thread might fail, but the others might return successfully.

Parallel collection methods will throw an exception if they fail on any element, just like their serial counterparts:

```
scala> Vector(2, 0, 5).par.map { 10 / _ }
java.lang.ArithmeticException: / by zero

...
```

There are cases when this isn't the behavior that we want. For instance, we might be using a parallel collection to retrieve a large number of web pages in parallel. We might not mind if a few of the pages cannot be fetched.

Scala's `Try` type was designed for sandboxing code that might throw exceptions. It is similar to `Option` in that it is a one-element container:

```
scala> import scala.util._
import scala.util._

scala> Try { 2 + 2 }
Try[Int] = Success(4)
```

Unlike the `Option` type, which indicates whether an expression has a useful value, the `Try` type indicates whether an expression can be executed without throwing an exception. It takes on the following two values:

- `Try { 2 + 2 } == Success(4)` if the expression in the `Try` statement is evaluated successfully
- `Try { 2 / 0 } == Failure(java.lang.ArithmeticException: / by zero)` if the expression in the `Try` block results in an exception

This will make more sense with an example. To see the `Try` type in action, we will try to fetch web pages in a fault tolerant manner. We will use the built-in `Source.fromURL` method which fetches a web page and opens an iterator of the page's content. If it fails to fetch the web page, it throws an error:

```
scala> import scala.io.Source
import scala.io.Source

scala> val html = Source.fromURL("http://www.google.com")
scala.io.BufferedSource = non-empty iterator

scala> val html = Source.fromURL("garbage")
java.net.MalformedURLException: no protocol: garbage
...
```

Instead of letting the expression propagate out and crash the rest of our code, we can wrap the call to `Source.fromURL` in `Try`:

```
scala> Try { Source.fromURL("http://www.google.com") }
```

```
Try[BufferedSource] = Success(non-empty iterator)
```

```scala
scala> Try { Source.fromURL("garbage") }
```
```
Try[BufferedSource] = Failure(java.net.MalformedURLException: no
protocol: garbage)
```

To see the power of our `Try` statement, let's now retrieve a list of URLs in parallel in a fault tolerant manner:

```scala
scala> val URLs = Vector("http://www.google.com",
  "http://www.bbc.co.uk",
  "not-a-url"
)
```
```
URLs: Vector[String] = Vector(http://www.google.com, http://www.bbc.
co.uk, not-a-url)
```

```scala
scala> val pages = URLs.par.map { url =>
  url -> Try { Source.fromURL(url) }
}
```
```
pages: ParVector[(String, Try[BufferedSource])] = ParVector((http://
www.google.com,Success(non-empty iterator)), (http://www.bbc.
co.uk,Success(non-empty iterator)), (not-a-url,Failure(java.net.
MalformedURLException: no protocol: not-a-url)))
```

We can then use a `collect` statement to act on the pages we could fetch successfully. For instance, to get the number of characters on each page:

```scala
scala> pages.collect { case(url, Success(it)) => url -> it.size }
```
```
ParVector[(String, Int)] = ParVector((http://www.google.com,18976),
(http://www.bbc.co.uk,132893))
```

By making good use of Scala's built-in `Try` classes and parallel collections, we have built a fault tolerant, multithreaded URL retriever in a few lines of code. (Compare this to the myriad of Java/C++ books that prefix code examples with 'error handling is left out for clarity'.)

The Try type versus try/catch statements

Programmers with imperative or object-oriented backgrounds will be more familiar with try/catch blocks for handling exceptions. We could have accomplished similar functionality here by wrapping the code for fetching URLs in a try block, returning null if the call raises an exception.

However, besides being more verbose, returning null is less satisfactory: we lose all information about the exception and null is less expressive than `Failure(exception)`. Furthermore, returning a `Try[T]` type forces the caller to consider the possibility that the function might fail, by encoding this possibility in the type of the return value. In contrast, just returning `T` and coding failure with a null value allows the caller to ignore failure, raising the possibility of a confusing `NullPointerException` being thrown at a completely different point in the program.

In short, `Try[T]` is just another higher-order type, like `Option[T]` or `List[T]`. Treating the possibility of failure in the same way as the rest of the code adds coherence to the program and encourages programmers to tackle the possibility of exceptions explicitly.

Setting the parallelism level

So far, we have considered parallel collections as black boxes: add `par` to a normal collection and all the operations are performed in parallel. Often, we will want more control over how the tasks are executed.

Internally, parallel collections work by distributing an operation over multiple threads. Since the threads share memory, parallel collections do not need to copy any data. Changing the number of threads available to the parallel collection will change the number of CPUs that are used to perform the tasks.

Parallel collections have a `tasksupport` attribute that controls task execution:

```scala
scala> val parRange = (0 to 100).par
parRange: ParRange = ParRange(0, 1, 2, 3, 4, 5,...


scala> parRange.tasksupport
TaskSupport = scala.collection.parallel.ExecutionContextTaskSupport@311a0
b3e


scala> parRange.tasksupport.parallelismLevel
Int = 8 // Number of threads to be used
```

The task support object of a collection is an *execution context*, an abstraction capable of executing Scala expressions in a separate thread. By default, the execution context in Scala 2.11 is a *work-stealing thread pool*. When a parallel collection submits tasks, the context allocates these tasks to its threads. If a thread finds that it has finished its queued tasks, it will try and steal outstanding tasks from the other threads. The default execution context maintains a thread pool with number of threads equal to the number of CPUs.

The number of threads over which the parallel collection distributes the work can be changed by changing the task support. For instance, to parallelize the operations performed by a range over four threads:

```
scala> import scala.collection.parallel._
import scala.collection.parallel._


scala> parRange.tasksupport = new ForkJoinTaskSupport(
  new scala.concurrent.forkjoin.ForkJoinPool(4)
)
parRange.tasksupport: scala.collection.parallel.TaskSupport = scala.
collection.parallel.ForkJoinTaskSupport@6e1134e1


scala> parRange.tasksupport.parallelismLevel
Int: 4
```

An example – cross-validation with parallel collections

Let's apply what you have learned so far to solve data science problems. There are many parts of a machine learning pipeline that can be parallelized trivially. One such part is cross-validation.

We will give a brief description of cross-validation here, but you can refer to *The Elements of Statistical Learning*, by *Hastie*, *Tibshirani*, and *Friedman* for a more in-depth discussion.

Typically, a supervised machine learning problem involves training an algorithm over a training set. For instance, when we built a model to calculate the probability of a person being male based on their height and weight, the training set was the (height, weight) data for each participant, together with the male/female label for each row. Once the algorithm is trained on the training set, we can use it to classify new data. This process only really makes sense if the training set is representative of the new data that we are likely to encounter.

The training set has a finite number of entries. It will thus, inevitably, have idiosyncrasies that are not representative of the population at large, merely due to its finite nature. These idiosyncrasies will result in prediction errors when predicting whether a new person is male or female, over and above the prediction error of the algorithm on the training set itself. Cross-validation is a tool for estimating the error caused by the idiosyncrasies of the training set that do not reflect the population at large.

Cross-validation works by dividing the training set in two parts: a smaller, new training set and a cross-validation set. The algorithm is trained on the reduced training set. We then see how well the algorithm models the cross-validation set. Since we know the right answer for the cross-validation set, we can measure how well our algorithm is performing when shown new information. We repeat this procedure many times with different cross-validation sets.

There are several different types of cross-validation, which differ in how we choose the cross-validation set. In this chapter, we will look at repeated random subsampling: we select k rows at random from the training data to form the cross-validation set. We do this many times, calculating the cross-validation error for each subsample. Since each iteration is independent of the previous ones, we can parallelize this process trivially. It is therefore a good candidate for parallel collections. We will look at an alternative form of cross-validation, *k-fold cross-validation*, in *Chapter 12, Distributed Machine Learning with MLlib*.

We will build a class that performs cross-validation in parallel. I encourage you to write the code as you go, but you will find the source code corresponding to these examples on GitHub (`https://github.com/pbugnion/s4ds`). We will use parallel collections to handle the parallelism and Breeze data types in the inner loop. The `build.sbt` file is identical to the one we used in *Chapter 2, Manipulating Data with Breeze*:

```
scalaVersion := "2.11.7"


libraryDependencies ++= Seq(
  "org.scalanlp" %% "breeze" % "0.11.2",
  "org.scalanlp" %% "breeze-natives" % "0.11.2"
)
```

We will build a `RandomSubsample` class. The class exposes a type alias, `CVFunction`, for a function that takes two lists of indices—the first corresponding to the reduced training set and the second to the validation set—and returns a `Double` corresponding to the cross-validation error:

```
type CVFunction = (Seq[Int], Seq[Int]) => Double
```

The `RandomSubsample` class will expose a single method, `mapSamples`, which takes a `CVFunction`, repeatedly passes it different partitions of indices, and returns a vector of the errors. This is what the class looks like:

```scala
// RandomSubsample.scala

import breeze.linalg._
import breeze.numerics._

/** Random subsample cross-validation
 *
 * @param nElems Total number of elements in the training set.
 * @param nCrossValidation Number of elements to leave out of
 * training set.
 */
class RandomSubsample(val nElems:Int, val nCrossValidation:Int) {

  type CVFunction = (Seq[Int], Seq[Int]) => Double

  require(nElems > nCrossValidation,
    "nCrossValidation, the number of elements " +
    "withheld, must be < nElems")

  private val indexList = DenseVector.range(0, nElems)

  /** Perform multiple random sub-sample CV runs on f
   *
   * @param nShuffles Number of random sub-sample runs.
   * @param f user-defined function mapping from a list of
   *    indices in the training set and a list of indices in the
   *    test-set to a double indicating the out-of sample score
   *    for this split.
   * @returns DenseVector of the CV error for each random split.
   */
  def mapSamples(nShuffles:Int)(f:CVFunction)
  :DenseVector[Double] = {
    val cvResults = (0 to nShuffles).par.map { i =>

      // Randomly split indices between test and training
      val shuffledIndices = breeze.linalg.shuffle(indexList)
      val Seq(testIndices, trainingIndices) =
        split(shuffledIndices, Seq(nCrossValidation))

      // Apply f for this split
```

```
      f(trainingIndices.toScalaVector,
        testIndices.toScalaVector)
    }
    DenseVector(cvResults.toArray)
  }
}
```

Let's look at what happens in more detail, starting with the arguments passed to the constructor:

```
class RandomSubsample(val nElems:Int, val nCrossValidation:Int)
```

We pass the total number of elements in the training set and the number of elements to leave out for cross-validation in the class constructor. Thus, passing 100 to nElems and 20 to nCrossValidation implies that our training set will have 80 random elements of the total data and that the test set will have 20 elements.

We then construct a list of all integers between 0 and nElems:

```
private val indexList = DenseVector.range(0, nElems)
```

For each iteration of the cross-validation, we will shuffle this list and take the first nCrossValidation elements to be the indices of rows in our test set and the remaining to be the indices of rows in our training set.

Our class exposes a single method, mapSamples, that takes two curried arguments: nShuffles, the number of times to perform random subsampling, and f, a CVFunction:

```
def mapSamples(nShuffles:Int)(f:CVFunction):DenseVector[Double]
```

With all this set up, the code for doing cross-validation is deceptively simple. We generate a parallel range from 0 to nShuffles and, for each item in the range, generate a new train-test split and calculate the cross-validation error:

```
val cvResults = (0 to nShuffles).par.map { i =>
  val shuffledIndices = breeze.linalg.shuffle(indexList)
  val Seq(testIndices, trainingIndices) =
    split(shuffledIndices, Seq(nCrossValidation))
  f(trainingIndices.toScalaVector, testIndices.toScalaVector)
}
```

The only tricky part of this function is splitting the shuffled index list into a list of indices for the training set and a list of indices for the test set. We use Breeze's split method. This takes a vector as its first argument and a list of split-points as its second, and returns a list of fragments of the original vector. We then use pattern matching to extract the individual parts.

Finally, `mapSamples` converts `cvResults` to a Breeze vector:

```
DenseVector(cvResults.toArray)
```

Let's see this in action. We can test our class by running cross-validation on the logistic regression example developed in *Chapter 2, Manipulating Data with Breeze*. In that chapter, we developed a `LogisticRegression` class that takes a training set (in the form of a `DenseMatrix`) and target (in the form of a `DenseVector`) at construction time. The class then calculates the parameters that best represent the training set. We will first add two methods to the `LogisticRegression` class to use the trained model to classify previously unseen examples:

- The `predictProbabilitiesMany` method uses the trained model to calculate the probability of having the target variable set to one. In the context of our example, this is the probability of being male, given a height and weight.

- The `classifyMany` method assigns classification labels (one or zero) to members of a test set. We will assign a one if `predictProbabilitiesMany` returns a value greater than `0.5`.

With these two functions, our `LogisticRegression` class becomes:

```scala
// Logistic Regression.scala

class LogisticRegression(
  val training:DenseMatrix[Double],
  val target:DenseVector[Double]
) {
  ...
  /** Probability of classification for each row
    * in test set.
    */
  def predictProbabilitiesMany(test:DenseMatrix[Double])
  :DenseVector[Double] = {
    val xBeta = test * optimalCoefficients
    sigmoid(xBeta)
  }

  /** Predict the value of the target variable
    * for each row in test set.
    */
  def classifyMany(test:DenseMatrix[Double])
  :DenseVector[Double] = {
    val probabilities = predictProbabilitiesMany(test)
    I((probabilities :> 0.5).toDenseVector)
  }
  ...
}
```

We can now put together an example program for our RandomSubsample class. We will use the same height-weight data as in *Chapter 2, Manipulating Data with Breeze*. The data preprocessing will be similar. The code examples for this chapter provide a helper module, HWData, to load the height-weight data into Breeze vectors. The data itself is in the data/ directory of the code examples for this chapter (available on GitHub at https://github.com/pbugnion/s4ds/tree/master/chap04).

For each new subsample, we create a new LogisticRegression instance, train it on the subset of the training set to get the best coefficients for this train-test split, and use classifyMany to generate predictions on the cross-validation set in this split. We then calculate the classification error and report the average classification error over every train-test split:

```scala
// RandomSubsampleDemo.scala

import breeze.linalg._
import breeze.linalg.functions.manhattanDistance
import breeze.numerics._
import breeze.stats._

object RandomSubsampleDemo extends App {

  /* Load and pre-process data */
  val data = HWData.load

  val rescaledHeights:DenseVector[Double] =
    (data.heights - mean(data.heights)) / stddev(data.heights)

  val rescaledWeights:DenseVector[Double] =
    (data.weights - mean(data.weights)) / stddev(data.weights)

  val featureMatrix:DenseMatrix[Double] =
    DenseMatrix.horzcat(
      DenseMatrix.ones[Double](data.npoints, 1),
      rescaledHeights.toDenseMatrix.t,
      rescaledWeights.toDenseMatrix.t
    )

  val target:DenseVector[Double] = data.genders.values.map {
    gender => if(gender == 'M') 1.0 else 0.0
  }

  /* Cross-validation */
  val testSize = 20
```

```scala
val cvCalculator = new RandomSubsample(data.npoints, testSize)

// Start parallel CV loop
val cvErrors = cvCalculator.mapSamples(1000) {
  (trainingIndices, testIndices) =>

  val regressor = new LogisticRegression(
    data.featureMatrix(trainingIndices, ::).toDenseMatrix,
    data.target(trainingIndices).toDenseVector
  )
  // Predictions on test-set
  val genderPredictions = regressor.classifyMany(
    data.featureMatrix(testIndices, ::).toDenseMatrix
  )
  // Calculate number of mis-classified examples
  val dist = manhattanDistance(
    genderPredictions, data.target(testIndices)
  )
  // Calculate mis-classification rate
  dist / testSize.toDouble
}

println(s"Mean classification error: ${mean(cvErrors)}")
}
```

Running this program on the height-weight data gives a classification error of 10%.

We now have a fully working, parallelized cross-validation class. Scala's parallel range made it simple to repeatedly compute the same function in different threads.

Futures

Parallel collections offer a simple, yet powerful, framework for parallel operations. However, they are limited in one respect: the total amount of work must be known in advance, and each thread must perform the same function (possibly on different inputs).

Imagine that we want to write a program that fetches a web page (or queries a web API) every few seconds and extracts data for further processing from this web page. A typical example might involve querying a web API to maintain an up-to-date value of a particular stock price. Fetching data from an external web page takes a few hundred milliseconds, typically. If we perform this operation on the main thread, it will needlessly waste CPU cycles waiting for the web server to reply.

The solution is to wrap the code for fetching the web page in a *future*. A future is a one-element container containing the future result of a computation. When you create a future, the computation in it gets off-loaded to a different thread in order to avoid blocking the main thread. When the computation finishes, the result is written to the future and thus made accessible to the main thread.

As an example, we will write a program that queries the "Markit on demand" API to fetch the price of a given stock. For instance, the URL for the current price of a Google share is `http://dev.markitondemand.com/MODApis/Api/v2/Quote?symbol=GOOG`. Go ahead and paste this in the address box of your web browser. You will see an XML string appear with, among other things, the current stock price. Let's fetch this programmatically without resorting to a future first:

```
scala> import scala.io._

import scala.io_


scala> val url = "http://dev.markitondemand.com/MODApis/Api/v2/
Quote?symbol=GOOG"

url: String = http://dev.markitondemand.com/MODApis/Api/v2/
Quote?symbol=GOOG


scala> val response = Source.fromURL(url).mkString

response: String = <StockQuote><Status>SUCCESS</Status>

...
```

Notice how it takes a little bit of time to query the API. Let's now do the same, but using a future (don't worry about the imports for now, we will discuss what they mean in more detail further on):

```
scala> import scala.concurrent._

import scala.concurrent._


scala> import scala.util._

import scala.util._


scala> import scala.concurrent.ExecutionContext.Implicits.global

import scala.concurrent.ExecutionContext.Implicits.global


scala> val response = Future { Source.fromURL(url).mkString }

response: Future[String] = Promise$DefaultPromise@3301801b
```

If you run this, you will notice that control returns to the shell instantly before the API has had a chance to respond. To make this evident, let's simulate a slow connection by adding a call to `Thread.sleep`:

```scala
scala> val response = Future {
  Thread.sleep(10000) // sleep for 10s
  Source.fromURL(url).mkString
}
response: Future[String] = Promise$DefaultPromise@231f98ef
```

When you run this, you do not have to wait for ten seconds for the next prompt to appear: you regain control of the shell straightaway. The bit of code in the future is executed asynchronously: its execution is independent of the main program flow.

How do we retrieve the result of the computation? We note that `response` has type `Future[String]`. We can check whether the computation wrapped in the future has finished by querying the future's `isCompleted` attribute:

```scala
scala> response.isCompleted
Boolean = true
```

The future exposes a `value` attribute that contains the computation result:

```scala
scala> response.value
Option[Try[String]] = Some(Success(<StockQuote><Status>SUCCESS</Status>
...
```

The `value` attribute of a future has type `Option[Try[T]]`. We have already seen how to use the `Try` type to handle exceptions gracefully in the context of parallel collections. It is used in the same way here. A future's `value` attribute is `None` until the future is complete, then it is set to `Some(Success(value))` if the future ran successfully, or `Some(Failure(error))` if an exception was thrown.

Repeatedly calling `f.value` until the future completes works well in the shell, but it does not generalize to more complex programs. Instead, we want to tell the computer to do something once the future is complete: we want to bind a *callback* function to the future. We can do this by setting the future's `onComplete` attribute. Let's tell the future to print the API response when it completes:

```scala
scala> response.onComplete {
  case Success(s) => println(s)
```

```
    case Failure(e) => println(s"Error fetching page: $e")
}
```

```
scala>
// Wait for response to complete, then prints:
<StockQuote><Status>SUCCESS</Status><Name>Alphabet Inc</
Name><Symbol>GOOGL</Symbol><LastPrice>695.22</LastPrice><Chan...
```

The function passed to `onComplete` runs when the future is finished. It takes a single argument of type `Try[T]` containing the result of the future.

Failure is normal: how to build resilient applications

By wrapping the output of the code that it runs in a `Try` type, futures force the client code to consider the possibility that the code might fail. The client can isolate the effect of failure to avoid crashing the whole application. They might, for instance, log the exception. In the case of a web API query, they might add the offending URL to be queried again at a later date. In the case of a database failure, they might roll back the transaction.

By treating failure as a first-class citizen rather than through exceptional control flow bolted on at the end, we can build applications that are much more resilient.

Future composition – using a future's result

In the previous section, you learned about the `onComplete` method to bind a callback to a future. This is useful to cause a side effect to happen when the future is complete. It does not, however, let us transform the future's return value easily.

To carry on with our stocks example, let's imagine that we want to convert the query response from a string to an XML object. Let's start by including the `scala-xml` library as a dependency in `build.sbt`:

```
libraryDependencies += "org.scala-lang" % "scala-xml" % "2.11.0-M4"
```

Let's restart the console and reimport the dependencies on `scala.concurrent._`, `scala.concurrent.ExecutionContext.Implicits.global`, and `scala.io._`. We also want to import the XML library:

```
scala> import scala.xml.XML
import scala.xml.XML
```

We will use the same URL as in the previous section:

```
http://dev.markitondemand.com/MODApis/Api/v2/Quote?symbol=GOOG
```

It is sometimes useful to think of a future as a collection that either contains one element if a calculation has been successful, or zero elements if it has failed. For instance, if the web API has been queried successfully, our future contains a string representation of the response. Like other container types in Scala, futures support a map method that applies a function to the element contained in the future, returning a new future, and does nothing if the calculation in the future failed. But what does this mean in the context of a computation that might not be finished yet? The map method gets applied as soon as the future is complete, like the onComplete method.

We can use the future's map method to apply a transformation to the result of the future asynchronously. Let's poll the "Markit on demand" API again. This time, instead of printing the result, we will parse it as XML.

```
scala> val strResponse = Future {
  Thread.sleep(20000) // Sleep for 20s
  val res = Source.fromURL(url).mkString
  println("finished fetching url")
  res
}
strResponse: Future[String] = Promise$DefaultPromise@1dda9bc8


scala> val xmlResponse = strResponse.map { s =>
  println("applying string to xml transformation")
  XML.loadString(s)
}
xmlResponse: Future[xml.Elem] = Promise$DefaultPromise@25d1262a


// wait while the remainder of the 20s elapses
finished fetching url
applying string to xml transformation


scala> xmlResponse.value
Option[Try[xml.Elem]] = Some(Success(<StockQuote><Status>SUCCESS</
Status>...
```

By registering subsequent maps on futures, we are providing a road map to the executor running the future for what to do.

If any of the steps fail, the failed `Try` instance containing the exception gets propagated instead:

```scala
scala> val strResponse = Future {
  Source.fromURL("empty").mkString
}


scala> val xmlResponse = strResponse.map {
  s => XML.loadString(s)
}


scala> xmlResponse.value
Option[Try[xml.Elem]] = Some(Failure(MalformedURLException: no protocol:
empty))
```

This behavior makes sense if you think of a failed future as an empty container. When applying a map to an empty list, it returns the same empty list. Similarly, when applying a map to an empty (failed) future, the empty future is returned.

Blocking until completion

The code for fetching stock prices works fine in the shell. However, if you paste it in a standalone program, you will notice that nothing gets printed and the program finishes straightaway. Let's look at a trivial example of this:

```scala
// BlockDemo.scala
import scala.concurrent._
import scala.concurrent.ExecutionContext.Implicits.global
import scala.concurrent.duration._

object BlockDemo extends App {
  val f = Future { Thread.sleep(10000) }
  f.onComplete { _ => println("future completed") }
  // "future completed" is not printed
}
```

The program stops running as soon as the main thread has completed its tasks, which, in this example, just involves creating the futures. In particular, the line `"future completed"` is never printed. If we want the main thread to wait for a future to execute, we must explicitly tell it to block execution until the future has finished running. This is done using the `Await.ready` or `Await.result` methods. Both these methods block the execution of the main thread until the future completes. We could make the above program work as intended by adding this line:

```
Await.ready(f, 1 minute)
```

The `Await` methods take the future as their first argument and a `Duration` object as the second. If the future takes longer to complete than the specified duration, a `TimeoutException` is thrown. Pass `Duration.Inf` to set an infinite timeout.

The difference between `Await.ready` and `Await.result` is that the latter returns the value inside the future. In particular, if the future resulted in an exception, that exception will get thrown. In contrast, `Await.ready` returns the future itself.

In general, one should try to avoid blocking as much as possible: the whole point of futures is to run code in background threads in order to keep the main thread of execution responsive. However, a common, legitimate use case for blocking is at the end of a program. If we are running a large-scale integration process, we might dispatch several futures to query web APIs, read from text files, or insert data into a database. Embedding the code in futures is more scalable than performing these operations sequentially. However, as the majority of the intensive work is running in background threads, we are left with many outstanding futures when the main thread completes. It makes sense, at this stage, to block until all the futures have completed.

Controlling parallel execution with execution contexts

Now that we know how to define futures, let's look at controlling how they run. In particular, you might want to control the number of threads to use when running a large number of futures.

When a future is defined, it is passed an *execution context*, either directly or implicitly. An execution context is an object that exposes an `execute` method that takes a block of code and runs it, possibly asynchronously. By changing the execution context, we can change the "backend" that runs the futures. We have already seen how to use execution contexts to control the execution of parallel collections.

So far, we have just been using the default execution context by importing `scala.concurrent.ExecutionContext.Implicits.global`. This is a fork / join thread pool with as many threads as there are underlying CPUs.

Let's now define a new execution context that uses sixteen threads:

```scala
scala> import java.util.concurrent.Executors
import java.util.concurrent.Executors

scala> val ec = ExecutionContext.fromExecutorService(
  Executors.newFixedThreadPool(16)
)
ec: ExecutionContextExecutorService = ExecutionContextImpl$$anon$1@1351
ce60
```

Having defined the execution context, we can pass it explicitly to futures as they are defined:

```scala
scala> val f = Future { Thread.sleep(1000) } (ec)
f: Future[Unit] = Promise$DefaultPromise@458b456
```

Alternatively, we can define the execution context implicitly:

```scala
scala> implicit val context = ec
context: ExecutionContextExecutorService = ExecutionContextImpl$$anon$1@1
351ce60
```

It is then passed as an implicit parameter to all new futures as they are constructed:

```scala
scala> val f = Future { Thread.sleep(1000) }
f: Future[Unit] = Promise$DefaultPromise@3c4b7755
```

You can shut the execution context down to destroy the thread pool:

```scala
scala> ec.shutdown()
```

When an execution context receives a shutdown command, it will finish executing its current tasks but will refuse any new tasks.

Futures example – stock price fetcher

Let's bring some of the concepts that we covered in this section together to build a command-line application that prompts the user for the name of a stock and fetches the value of that stock. The catch is that, to keep the UI responsive, we will fetch the stock using a future:

```scala
// StockPriceDemo.scala

import scala.concurrent._
```

```scala
import scala.concurrent.ExecutionContext.Implicits.global
import scala.io._
import scala.xml.XML
import scala.util._

object StockPriceDemo extends App {

  /* Construct URL for a stock symbol */
  def urlFor(stockSymbol:String) =
    ("http://dev.markitondemand.com/MODApis/Api/v2/Quote?" +
    s"symbol=${stockSymbol}")

  /* Build a future that fetches the stock price */
  def fetchStockPrice(stockSymbol:String):Future[BigDecimal] = {
    val url = urlFor(stockSymbol)
    val strResponse = Future { Source.fromURL(url).mkString }
    val xmlResponse = strResponse.map { s => XML.loadString(s) }
    val price = xmlResponse.map {
      r => BigDecimal((r \ "LastPrice").text)
    }
    price
  }

  /* Command line interface */
  println("Enter symbol at prompt.")
  while (true) {
    val symbol = readLine("> ") // Wait for user input
    // When user puts in symbol, fetch data in background
    // thread and print to screen when complete
    fetchStockPrice(symbol).onComplete { res =>
      println()
      res match {
        case Success(price) => println(s"$symbol: USD $price")
        case Failure(e) => println(s"Error fetching  $symbol: $e")
      }
      print("> ") // Simulate the appearance of a new prompt
    }
  }

}
```

Try running the program and entering the code for some stocks:

```
[info] Running StockPriceDemo
Enter symbol at prompt:
> GOOG
> MSFT
>
GOOG: USD 695.22
>
MSFT: USD 47.48
> AAPL
>
AAPL: USD 111.01
```

Let's summarize how the code works. when you enter a stock, the main thread constructs a future that fetches the stock information from the API, converts it to XML, and extracts the price. We use `(r \ "LastPrice").text` to extract the text inside the `LastPrice` tag from the XML node `r`. We then convert the value to a big decimal. When the transformations are complete, the result is printed to screen by binding a callback through `onComplete`. Exception handling is handled naturally through our use of `.map` methods to handle transformations.

By wrapping the code for fetching a stock price in a future, we free up the main thread to just respond to the user. This means that the user interface does not get blocked if we have, for instance, a slow internet connection.

This example is somewhat artificial, but you could easily wrap much more complicated logic: stock prices could be written to a database and we could add additional commands to plot the stock price over time, for instance.

We have only scratched the surface of what futures can offer in this section. We will revisit futures in more detail when we look at polling web APIs in *Chapter 7, Web APIs* and *Chapter 9, Concurrency with Akka*.

Futures are a key part of the data scientist's toolkit for building scalable systems. Moving expensive computation (either in terms of CPU time or wall time) to background threads improves scalability greatly. For this reason, futures are an important part of many Scala libraries such as **Akka** and the **Play** framework.

Summary

By providing high-level concurrency abstractions, Scala makes writing parallel code intuitive and straightforward. Parallel collections and futures form an invaluable part of a data scientist's toolbox, allowing them to parallelize their code with minimal effort. However, while these high-level abstractions obviate the need to deal directly with threads, an understanding of the internals of Scala's concurrency model is necessary to avoid race conditions.

In the next chapter, we will put concurrency on hold and study how to interact with SQL databases. However, this is only temporary: futures will play an important role in many of the remaining chapters in this book.

References

Aleksandar Prokopec, Learning Concurrent Programming in Scala. This is a detailed introduction to the basics of concurrent programming in Scala. In particular, it explores parallel collections and futures in much greater detail than this chapter.

Daniel Westheide's blog gives an excellent introduction to many Scala concepts, in particular:

- **Futures**: http://danielwestheide.com/blog/2013/01/09/the-neophytes-guide-to-scala-part-8-welcome-to-the-future.html
- **The Try type**: http://danielwestheide.com/blog/2012/12/26/the-neophytes-guide-to-scala-part-6-error-handling-with-try.html

For a discussion of cross-validation, see *The Elements of Statistical Learning* by *Hastie, Tibshirani*, and *Friedman*.

5
Scala and SQL through JDBC

One of data science's raison d'être is the difficulty of manipulating large datasets. Much of the data of interest to a company or research group cannot fit conveniently in a single computer's RAM. Storing the data in a way that is easy to query is therefore a complex problem.

Relational databases have been successful at solving the data storage problem. Originally proposed in 1970 (`http://www.seas.upenn.edu/~zives/03f/cis550/codd.pdf`), the overwhelming majority of databases in active use today are still relational. In that time, the price of RAM per megabyte has decreased by a factor of a hundred million. Similarly, hard drive capacity has increased from tens or hundreds of megabytes to terabytes. It is remarkable that, despite this exponential growth in data storage capacity, the relational model has remained dominant.

Virtually all relational databases are described and queried with variants of **SQL** (**Structured Query Language**). With the advent of distributed computing, the position of SQL databases as the de facto data storage standard is being challenged by other types of databases, commonly grouped under the umbrella term NoSQL. Many NoSQL databases are more partition-tolerant than SQL databases: they can be split into several parts residing on different computers. While this author expects that NoSQL databases will become increasingly popular, SQL databases are likely to remain prevalent as a data persistence mechanism; hence, a significant portion of this book is devoted to interacting with SQL from Scala.

While SQL is standardized, most implementations do not follow the full standard. Additionally, most implementations provide extensions to the standard. This means that, while many of the concepts in this book will apply to all SQL backends, the exact syntax will need to be adjusted. We will consider only the MySQL implementation here.

In this chapter, you will learn how to interact with SQL databases from Scala using JDBC, a bare bones Java API. In the next chapter, we will consider Slick, an **Object Relational Mapper (ORM)** that gives a more Scala-esque feel to interacting with SQL.

This chapter is roughly composed of two sections: we will first discuss the basic functionality for connecting and interacting with SQL databases, and then discuss useful functional patterns that can be used to create an elegant, loosely coupled, and coherent data access layer.

This chapter assumes that you have a basic working knowledge of SQL. If you do not, you would be better off first reading one of the reference books mentioned at the end of the chapter.

Interacting with JDBC

JDBC is an API for connecting to SQL databases in Java. It remains the simplest way of connecting to SQL databases from Scala. Furthermore, the majority of higher-level abstractions for interacting with databases still use JDBC as a backend.

JDBC is not a library in itself. Rather, it exposes a set of interfaces to interact with databases. Relational database vendors then provide specific implementations of these interfaces.

Let's start by creating a `build.sbt` file. We will declare a dependency on the MySQL JDBC connector:

```
scalaVersion := "2.11.7"

libraryDependencies += "mysql" % "mysql-connector-java" % "5.1.36"
```

First steps with JDBC

Let's start by connecting to JDBC from the command line. To follow with the examples, you will need access to a running MySQL server. If you added the MySQL connector to the list of dependencies, open a Scala console by typing the following command:

```
$ sbt console
```

Let's import JDBC:

```
scala> import java.sql._
import java.sql._
```

We then need to tell JDBC to use a specific connector. This is normally done using reflection, loading the driver at runtime:

```
scala> Class.forName("com.mysql.jdbc.Driver")
Class[_] = class com.mysql.jdbc.Driver
```

This loads the appropriate driver into the namespace at runtime. If this seems somewhat magical to you, it's probably not worth worrying about exactly how this works. This is the only example of reflection that we will consider in this book, and it is not particularly idiomatic Scala.

Connecting to a database server

Having specified the SQL connector, we can now connect to a database. Let's assume that we have a database called `test` on host `127.0.0.1`, listening on port `3306`. We create a connection as follows:

```
scala> val connection = DriverManager.getConnection(
  "jdbc:mysql://127.0.0.1:3306/test",
  "root", // username when connecting
  "" // password
)
java.sql.Connection = com.mysql.jdbc.JDBC4Connection@12e78a69
```

The first argument to `getConnection` is a URL-like string with `jdbc:mysql://host[:port]/database`. The second and third arguments are the username and password. Pass in an empty string if you can connect without a password.

Creating tables

Now that we have a database connection, let's interact with the server. For these examples, you will find it useful to have a MySQL shell open (or a MySQL GUI such as **MySQLWorkbench**) as well as the Scala console. You can open a MySQL shell by typing the following command in a terminal:

```
$ mysql
```

As an example, we will create a small table to keep track of famous physicists. In a `mysql` shell, we would run the following command:

```
mysql> USE test;
mysql> CREATE TABLE physicists (
    id INT(11) AUTO_INCREMENT PRIMARY KEY,
    name VARCHAR(32) NOT NULL
);
```

To achieve the same with Scala, we send a JDBC statement to the connection:

```
scala> val statementString = """
CREATE TABLE physicists (
    id INT(11) AUTO_INCREMENT PRIMARY KEY,
    name VARCHAR(32) NOT NULL
)
"""

scala> val statement = connection.prepareStatement(statementString)
PreparedStatement = JDBC4PreparedStatement@c983201: CREATE TABLE ...

scala> statement.executeUpdate()
results: Int = 0
```

Let's ignore the return value of `executeUpdate` for now.

Inserting data

Now that we have created a table, let's insert some data into it. We can do this with a SQL `INSERT` statement:

```
scala> val statement = connection.prepareStatement("""
    INSERT INTO physicists (name) VALUES ('Isaac Newton')
""")

scala> statement.executeUpdate()
Int = 1
```

In this case, executeUpdate returns 1. When inserting rows, it returns the number of rows that were inserted. Similarly, if we had used a SQL UPDATE statement, this would return the number of rows that were updated. For statements that do not manipulate rows directly (such as the CREATE TABLE statement in the previous section), executeUpdate just returns 0.

Let's just jump into a mysql shell to verify the insertion performed correctly:

```
mysql> select * from physicists ;
+----+--------------+
| id | name         |
+----+--------------+
|  1 | Isaac Newton |
+----+--------------+
1 row in set (0.00 sec)
```

Let's quickly summarize what we have seen so far: to execute SQL statements that do not return results, use the following:

```
val statement = connection.prepareStatement("SQL statement string")
statement.executeUpdate()
```

In the context of data science, we frequently need to insert or update many rows at a time. For instance, we might have a list of physicists:

```
scala> val physicistNames = List("Marie Curie", "Albert Einstein", "Paul Dirac")
```

We want to insert all of these into the database. While we could create a statement for each physicist and send it to the database, this is quite inefficient. A better solution is to create a *batch* of statements and send them to the database together. We start by creating a statement template:

```
scala> val statement = connection.prepareStatement("""
    INSERT INTO physicists (name) VALUES (?)
""")
PreparedStatement = JDBC4PreparedStatement@621a8225: INSERT INTO physicists (name) VALUES (** NOT SPECIFIED **)
```

This is identical to the previous prepareStatement calls, except that we replaced the physicist's name with a ? placeholder. We can set the placeholder value with the statement.setString method:

```
scala> statement.setString(1, "Richard Feynman")
```

This replaces the first placeholder in the statement with the string `Richard Feynman`:

```
scala> statement
com.mysql.jdbc.JDBC4PreparedStatement@5fdd16c3:
INSERT INTO physicists (name) VALUES ('Richard Feynman')
```

Note that JDBC, somewhat counter-intuitively, counts the placeholder positions from 1 rather than 0.

We have now created the first statement in the batch of updates. Run the following command:

```
scala> statement.addBatch()
```

By running the preceding command, we initiate a batch insert: the statement is added to a temporary buffer that will be executed when we run the `executeBatch` method. Let's add all the physicists in our list:

```
scala> physicistNames.foreach { name =>
  statement.setString(1, name)
  statement.addBatch()
}
```

We can now execute all the statements in the batch:

```
scala> statement.executeBatch
Array[Int] = Array(1, 1, 1, 1)
```

The return value of `executeBatch` is an array of the number of rows altered or inserted by each item in the batch.

Note that we used `statement.setString` to fill in the template with a particular name. The `PreparedStatement` object has `setXXX` methods for all basic types. To get a complete list, read the `PreparedStatement` API documentation (http://docs. oracle.com/javase/7/docs/api/java/sql/PreparedStatement.html).

Reading data

Now that we know how to insert data into a database, let's look at the converse: reading data. We use SQL `SELECT` statements to query the database. Let's do this in the MySQL shell first:

```
mysql> SELECT * FROM physicists;
+----+-----------------+
| id | name            |
```

```
+----+----------------+
|  1 | Isaac Newton   |
|  2 | Richard Feynman |
|  3 | Marie Curie    |
|  4 | Albert Einstein |
|  5 | Paul Dirac     |
+----+----------------+
5 rows in set (0.01 sec)
```

To extract this information in Scala, we define a `PreparedStatement`:

```
scala> val statement = connection.prepareStatement("""
    SELECT name FROM physicists
""")
PreparedStatement = JDBC4PreparedStatement@3c577c9d:
SELECT name FROM physicists
```

We execute this statement by running the following command:

```
scala> val results = statement.executeQuery()
results: java.sql.ResultSet = com.mysql.jdbc.JDBC4ResultSet@74a2e158
```

This returns a JDBC `ResultSet` instance. The `ResultSet` is an abstraction representing a set of rows from the database. Note that we used `statement.executeQuery` rather than `statement.executeUpdate`. In general, one should execute statements that return data (in the form of `ResultSet`) with `executeQuery`. Statements that modify the database without returning data (insert, create, alter, or update statements, among others) are executed with `executeUpdate`.

The `ResultSet` object behaves somewhat like an iterator. It exposes a `next` method that advances itself to the next record, returning `true` if there are records left in `ResultSet`:

```
scala> results.next // Advance to the first record
Boolean = true
```

When the `ResultSet` instance points to a record, we can extract fields in this record by passing in the field name:

```
scala> results.getString("name")
String = Isaac Newton
```

We can also extract fields using positional arguments. The fields are indexed from one:

```
scala> results.getString(1) // first positional argument
String = Isaac Newton
```

When we are done with a particular record, we call the `next` method to advance the `ResultSet` to the next record:

```
scala> results.next // advances the ResultSet by one record
Boolean = true


scala> results.getString("name")
String = Richard Feynman
```

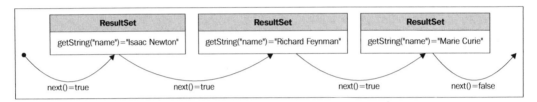

A ResultSet object supports the getXXX(fieldName) methods to access the fields of a record and a `next` method to advance to the next record in the result set.

One can iterate over a result set using a `while` loop:

```
scala> while(results.next) { println(results.getString("name")) }
Marie Curie
Albert Einstein
Paul Dirac
```

A word of warning applies to reading fields that are nullable. While one might expect JDBC to return null when faced with a null SQL field, the return type depends on the get XXX command used. For instance, get Int and getLong will return 0 for any field that is null. Similarly, getDouble and getFloat return 0.0. This can lead to some subtle bugs in code. In general, one should be careful with getters that return Java value types (int, long) rather than objects. To find out if a value is null in the database, query it first with get Int (or getLong or getDouble, as appropriate), then use the wasNull method that returns a Boolean if the last read value was null:

```scala
scala> rs.getInt("field")

0

scala> rs.wasNull // was the last item read null?

true
```

This (surprising) behavior makes reading from ResultSet instances error-prone. One of the goals of the second part of this chapter is to give you the tools to build an abstraction layer on top of the ResultSet interface to avoid having to call methods such as get Int directly.

Reading values directly from ResultSet objects feels quite unnatural in Scala. We will look, further on in this chapter, at constructing a layer through which you can access the result set using type classes.

We now know how to read and write to a database. Having finished with the database for now, we close the result sets, prepared statements, and connections:

```scala
scala> results.close
```

```scala
scala> statement.close
```

```scala
scala> connection.close
```

While closing statements and connections is not important in the Scala shell (they will get closed when you exit), it is important when you run programs; otherwise, the objects will persist, leading to "out of memory exceptions". In the next sections, we will look at establishing connections and statements with the **loan pattern**, a design pattern that closes a resource automatically when we finish using it.

JDBC summary

We now have an overview of JDBC. The rest of this chapter will concentrate on writing abstractions that sit above JDBC, making database accesses feel more natural. Before we do this, let's summarize what we have seen so far.

We have used three JDBC classes:

- The `Connection` class represents a connection to a specific SQL database. Instantiate a connection as follows:

```
import java.sql._
Class.forName("com.mysql.jdbc.Driver")
val connection = DriverManager.getConnection(
  "jdbc:mysql://127.0.0.1:3306/test",
  "root", // username when connecting
  "" // password
)
```

  Our main use of `Connection` instances has been to generate `PreparedStatement` objects:

```
connection.prepareStatement("SELECT * FROM physicists")
```

- A `PreparedStatement` instance represents a SQL statement about to be sent to the database. It also represents the template for a SQL statement with placeholders for values yet to be filled in. The class exposes the following methods:

`statement.executeUpdate`	This sends the statement to the database. Use this for SQL statements that modify the database and do not return any data, such as INSERT, UPDATE, DELETE, and CREATE statements.
`val results = statement.executeQuery`	This sends the statement to the database. Use this for SQL statements that return data (predominantly, the SELECT statements). This returns a ResultSet instance.
`statement.addBatch` `statement.executeBatch`	The addBatch method adds the current statement to a batch of statements, and executeBatch sends the batch of statements to the database.

statement.setString(1, "Scala") statement.setInt(1, 42) statement.setBoolean(1, true)	Fill in the placeholder values in the PreparedStatement. The first argument is the position in the statement (counting from 1). The second argument is the value. One common use case for these is in a batch update or insert: we might have a Scala list of objects that we want to insert into the database. We fill in the placeholders for each object in the list using the .setXXX methods, then add this statement to the batch using .addBatch. We can then send the entire batch to the database using .executeBatch.
statement.setNull(1, java.sql.Types.BOOLEAN)	This sets a particular item in the statement to NULL. The second argument specifies the NULL type. If we are setting a cell in a Boolean column, for instance, this should be Types.BOOLEAN. A full list of types is given in the API documentation for the java.sql.Types package (http://docs.oracle.com/javase/7/docs/api/java/sql/Types.html).

- A ResultSet instance represents a set of rows returned by a SELECT or SHOW statement. ResultSet exposes methods to access fields in the current row:

rs.getString(i) rs.getInt(i)	These methods get the value of the ith field in the current row; i is measured from 1.
rs.getString("name") rs.getInt("age")	These methods get the value of a specific field, which is indexed by the column name.
rs.wasNull	This returns whether the last column read was NULL. This is particularly important when reading Java value types, such as getInt, getBoolean, or getDouble, as these return a default value when reading a NULL value.

The ResultSet instance exposes the .next method to move to the next row; .next returns true until the ResultSet has advanced to just beyond the last row.

Functional wrappers for JDBC

We now have a basic overview of the tools afforded by JDBC. All the objects that we have interacted with so far feel somewhat clunky and out of place in Scala. They do not encourage a functional style of programming.

Of course, elegance is not necessarily a goal in itself (or, at least, you will probably struggle to convince your CEO that he should delay the launch of a product because the code lacks elegance). However, it is usually a symptom: either the code is not extensible or too tightly coupled, or it is easy to introduce bugs. The latter is particularly the case for JDBC. Forgot to check `wasNull`? That will come back to bite you. Forgot to close your connections? You'll get an "out of memory exception" (hopefully not in production).

In the next sections, we will look at patterns that we can use to wrap JDBC types in order to mitigate many of these risks. The patterns that we introduce here are used very commonly in Scala libraries and applications. Thus, besides writing robust classes to interact with JDBC, learning about these patterns will, I hope, give you greater understanding of Scala programming.

Safer JDBC connections with the loan pattern

We have already seen how to connect to a JDBC database and send statements to the database for execution. This technique, however, is somewhat error prone: you have to remember to close statements; otherwise, you will quickly run out of memory. In more traditional imperative style, we write the following try-finally block around every connection:

```scala
// WARNING: poor Scala code
val connection = DriverManager.getConnection(url, user, password)
try {
  // do something with connection
}
finally {
  connection.close()
}
```

Scala, with first-class functions, provides us with an alternative: the *loan pattern*. We write a function that is responsible for opening the connection, loaning it to the client code to do something interesting with it, and then closing it when the client code is done. Thus, the client code is not responsible for closing the connection any more.

Let's create a new `SqlUtils` object with a `usingConnection` method that leverages the loan pattern:

```scala
// SqlUtils.scala

import java.sql._

object SqlUtils {

  /** Create an auto-closing connection using
    * the loan pattern */
  def usingConnection[T](
    db:String,
    host:String="127.0.0.1",
    user:String="root",
    password:String="",
    port:Int=3306
  )(f:Connection => T):T = {

    // Create the connection
    val Url = s"jdbc:mysql://$host:$port/$db"
    Class.forName("com.mysql.jdbc.Driver")
    val connection = DriverManager.getConnection(
      Url, user, password)

    // give the connection to the client, through the callable
    // `f` passed in as argument
    try {
      f(connection)
    }
    finally {
      // When client is done, close the connection
      connection.close()
    }
  }
}
```

Let's see this function in action:

```scala
scala> SqlUtils.usingConnection("test") {
  connection => println(connection)
}
com.mysql.jdbc.JDBC4Connection@46fd3d66
```

Thus, the client doesn't have to remember to close the connection, and the resultant code (for the client) feels much more like Scala.

How does our `usingConnection` function work? The function definition is
`def usingConnection( ... )(f : Connection => T ):T`. It takes, as its
second set of arguments, a function that acts on a `Connection` object. The body of
`usingConnection` creates the connection, then passes it to `f`, and finally closes the
connection. This syntax is somewhat similar to code blocks in Ruby or the `with`
statement in Python.

> Be careful when mixing the loan pattern with lazy operations. This
> applies particularly to returning iterators, streams, and futures from
> `f`. As soon as the thread of execution leaves `f`, the connection will be
> closed. Any data structure that is not materialized at this point will
> not be able to carry on accessing the connection.

The loan pattern is, of course, not exclusive to database connections. It is useful
whenever you have the following pattern, in pseudocode:

```
open resource (eg. database connection, file ...)
use resource somehow // loan resource to client for this part.
close resource
```

Enriching JDBC statements with the "pimp my library" pattern

In the previous section, we saw how to create self-closing connections with the
loan pattern. This allows us to open connections to the database without having
to remember to close them. However, we still have to remember to close any
`ResultSet` and `PreparedStatement` that we open:

```
// WARNING: Poor Scala code
SqlUtils.usingConnection("test") { connection =>
  val statement = connection.prepareStatement(
    "SELECT * FROM physicists")
  val results = statement.executeQuery
  // do something useful with the results
  results.close
  statement.close
}
```

Having to open and close the statement is somewhat ugly and error prone. This is another natural use case for the loan pattern. Ideally, we would like to write the following:

```
usingConnection("test") { connection =>
  connection.withQuery("SELECT * FROM physicists") {
    resultSet => // process results
  }
}
```

How can we define a `.withQuery` method on the `Connection` class? We do not control the `Connection` class definition as it is part of the JDBC API. We would like to be able to somehow reopen the `Connection` class definition to add the `withQuery` method.

Scala does not let us reopen classes to add new methods (a practice known as monkey-patching). We can still, however, enrich existing libraries with implicit conversions using the **pimp my library** pattern (`http://www.artima.com/weblogs/viewpost.jsp?thread=179766`). We first define a `RichConnection` class that contains the `withQuery` method. This `RichConnection` class is created from an existing `Connection` instance.

```scala
// RichConnection.scala

import java.sql.{Connection, ResultSet}

class RichConnection(val underlying:Connection) {

  /** Execute a SQL query and process the ResultSet */
  def withQuery[T](query:String)(f:ResultSet => T):T = {
    val statement = underlying.prepareStatement(query)
    val results = statement.executeQuery
    try {
      f(results) // loan the ResultSet to the client
    }
    finally {
      // Ensure all the resources get freed.
      results.close
      statement.close
    }
  }
}
```

We could use this class by just wrapping every `Connection` instance in a `RichConnection` instance:

```scala
// Warning: poor Scala code
SqlUtils.usingConnection("test") { connection =>
  val richConnection = new RichConnection(connection)
  richConnection.withQuery("SELECT * FROM physicists") {
    resultSet => // process resultSet
  }
}
```

This adds unnecessary boilerplate: we have to remember to convert every connection instance to `RichConnection` to use `withQuery`. Fortunately, Scala provides an easier way with implicit conversions: we tell Scala how to convert from `Connection` to `RichConnection` and vice versa, and tell it to perform this conversion automatically (implicitly), if necessary:

```scala
// Implicits.scala
import java.sql.Connection

// Implicit conversion methods are often put in
// an object called Implicits.
object Implicits {
  implicit def pimpConnection(conn:Connection) =
    new RichConnection(conn)
  implicit def depimpConnection(conn:RichConnection) =
    conn.underlying
}
```

Now, whenever `pimpConnection` and `depimpConnection` are in the current scope, Scala will automatically use them to convert from `Connection` instances to `RichConnection` and back as needed.

We can now write the following (I have added type information for emphasis):

```scala
// Bring the conversion functions into the current scope
import Implicits._

SqlUtils.usingConnection("test") { (connection:Connection) =>
  connection.withQuery("SELECT * FROM physicists") {
    // Wow! It's like we have just added
    // .withQuery to the JDBC Connection class!
    resultSet => // process results
  }
}
```

This might look like magic, so let's step back and look at what happens when we call `withQuery` on a `Connection` instance. The Scala compiler will first look to see if the class definition of `Connection` defines a `withQuery` method. When it finds that it does not, it will look for implicit methods that convert a `Connection` instance to a class that defines `withQuery`. It will find that the `pimpConnection` method allows conversion from `Connection` to `RichConnection`, which defines `withQuery`. The Scala compiler automatically uses `pimpConnection` to transform the `Connection` instance to `RichConnection`.

Note that we used the names `pimpConnection` and `depimpConnection` for the conversion functions, but they could have been anything. We never call these methods explicitly.

Let's summarize how to use the *pimp my library* pattern to add methods to an existing class:

1. Write a class that wraps the class you want to enrich: `class RichConnection(val underlying:Connection)`. Add all the methods that you wish the original class had.

2. Write a method to convert from your original class to your enriched class as part of an object called (conventionally) `Implicits`. Make sure that you tell Scala to use this conversion automatically with the `implicit` keyword: `implicit def pimpConnection(conn:Connection):RichConnection`. You can also tell Scala to automatically convert back from the enriched class to the original class by adding the reverse conversion method.

3. Allow implicit conversions by importing the implicit conversion methods: `import Implicits._`.

Wrapping result sets in a stream

The JDBC `ResultSet` object plays very badly with Scala collections. The only real way of doing anything useful with it is to loop through it directly with a `while` loop. For instance, to get a list of the names of physicists in our database, we could write the following code:

```
// WARNING: poor Scala code
import Implicits._ // import implicit conversions

SqlUtils.usingConnection("test") { connection =>
  connection.withQuery("SELECT * FROM physicists") { resultSet =>
    var names = List.empty[String]
    while(resultSet.next) {
```

```
        val name = resultSet.getString("name")
        names = name :: names
      }
    names
  }
}
//=> List[String] = List(Paul Dirac, Albert Einstein, Marie Curie,
Richard Feynman, Isaac Newton)
```

The `ResultSet` interface feels unnatural because it behaves very differently from Scala collections. In particular, it does not support the higher-order functions that we take for granted in Scala: no `map`, `filter`, `fold`, or `for` comprehensions. Thankfully, writing a *stream* that wraps `ResultSet` is quite straightforward. A Scala stream is a lazily evaluated list: it evaluates the next element in the collection when it is needed and forgets previous elements when they are no longer used.

We can define a `stream` method that wraps `ResultSet` as follows:

```
// SqlUtils.scala
object SqlUtils {
  ...
  def stream(results:ResultSet):Stream[ResultSet] =
    if (results.next) { results #:: stream(results) }
    else { Stream.empty[ResultSet] }
}
```

This might look quite confusing, so let's take it slowly. We define a `stream` method that wraps `ResultSet`, returning a `Stream[ResultSet]`. When the client calls `stream` on an empty result set, this just returns an empty stream. When the client calls `stream` on a non-empty `ResultSet`, the `ResultSet` instance is advanced by one row, and the client gets back `results #:: stream(results)`. The `#::` operator on a stream is similar to the cons operator, `::`, on a list: it prepends `results` to an existing `Stream`. The critical difference is that, unlike a list, `stream(results)` does not get evaluated until necessary. This, therefore, avoids duplicating the entire `ResultSet` in memory.

Let's use our brand new `stream` function to get the name of all the physicists in our database:

```
import Implicits._

SqlUtils.usingConnection("test") { connection =>
  connection.withQuery("SELECT * FROM physicists") { results =>
    val resultsStream = SqlUtils.stream(results)
```

```
      resultsStream.map { _.getString("name") }.toVector
    }
  }
  //=> Vector(Richard Feynman, Albert Einstein, Marie Curie, Paul Dirac)
```

Streaming the results, rather than using the result set directly, lets us interact with the data much more naturally as we are now dealing with just a Scala collection.

When you use `stream` in a `withQuery` block (or, generally, in a block that automatically closes the result set), you must always materialize the stream within the function, hence the call to `toVector`. Otherwise, the stream will wait until its elements are needed to materialize them, and by then, the `ResultSet` instance will be closed.

Looser coupling with type classes

So far, we have been reading and writing simple types to the database. Let's imagine that we want to add a `gender` column to our database. We will store the gender as an enumeration in our physicists database. Our table is now as follows:

```
mysql> CREATE TABLE physicists (
        id INT(11) AUTO_INCREMENT PRIMARY KEY,
        name VARCHAR(32) NOT NULL,
        gender ENUM("Female", "Male") NOT NULL
);
```

How can we represent genders in Scala? A good way of doing this is with an enumeration:

```
// Gender.scala

object Gender extends Enumeration {
  val Male = Value
  val Female = Value
}
```

However, we now have a problem when deserializing objects from the database: JDBC has no built-in mechanism to convert from a SQL ENUM type to a Scala `Gender` type. We could achieve this by just converting manually every time we need to read gender information:

```
resultsStream.map {
  rs => Gender.withName(rs.getString("gender"))
}.toVector
```

However, we would need to write this everywhere that we want to read the gender field. This goes against the DRY (don't repeat yourself) principle, leading to code that is difficult to maintain. If we decide to change the way gender is stored in the database, we would need to find every instance in the code where we read the gender field and change it.

A somewhat better solution would be to add a getGender method to the ResultSet class using the pimp my library idiom that we used extensively in this chapter. This solution is still not optimal. We are adding unnecessary specificity to ResultSet: it is now coupled to the structure of our databases.

We could create a subclass of ResultSet using inheritance, such as PhysicistResultSet, that can read the fields in a specific table. However, this approach is not composable: if we had another table that kept track of pets, with name, species, and gender fields, we would have to either reimplement the code for reading gender in a new PetResultSet or factor out a GenderedResultSet superclass. As the number of tables grows, the inheritance hierarchy would become unmanageable. A better approach would let us compose the functionality that we need. In particular, we want to decouple the process of extracting Scala objects from a result set from the code for iterating over a result set.

Type classes

Scala provides an elegant solution using *type classes*. Type classes are a very powerful arrow in the Scala architect's quiver. However, they can present a bit of a learning curve, especially as there is no direct equivalent in object-oriented programming.

Instead of presenting an abstract explanation, I will dive into an example: I will describe how we can leverage type classes to convert fields in a ResultSet to Scala types. The aim is to define a read[T](field) method on ResultSet that knows exactly how to deserialize to objects of type T. This method will replace and extend the getXXX methods in ResultSet:

```
// results is a ResultSet instance
val name = results.read[String]("name")
val gender = results.read[Gender.Value]("gender")
```

We start by defining an abstract `SqlReader[T]` trait that exposes a `read` method to read a specific field from a `ResultSet` and return an instance of type `T`:

```
// SqlReader.scala

import java.sql._

trait SqlReader[T] {
  def read(results:ResultSet, field:String):T
}
```

We now need to provide a concrete implementation of `SqlReader[T]` for every `T` type that we want to read. Let's provide concrete implementations for the `Gender` and `String` fields. We will place the implementation in a `SqlReader` companion object:

```
// SqlReader.scala

object SqlReader {
  implicit object StringReader extends SqlReader[String] {
    def read(results:ResultSet, field:String):String =
      results.getString(field)
  }

  implicit object GenderReader extends SqlReader[Gender.Value] {
    def read(results:ResultSet, field:String):Gender.Value =
      Gender.withName(StringReader.read(results, field))
  }
}
```

We could now use our `ReadableXXX` objects to read from a result set:

```
import SqlReader._
val name = StringReader.read(results, "name")
val gender = GenderReader.read(results, "gender")
```

This is already somewhat better than using the following:

```
Gender.withName(results.getString("gender"))
```

This is because the code to map from a `ResultSet` field to `Gender.Value` is centralized in a single place: `ReadableGender`. However, it would be great if we could tell Scala to use `ReadableGender` whenever it needs to read `Gender.Value`, and use `ReadableString` whenever it needs to read a String value. This is exactly what type classes do.

Coding against type classes

We defined a `Readable[T]` interface that abstracts how to read an object of type `T` from a field in a `ResultSet`. How do we tell Scala that it needs to use this `Readable` object to convert from the `ResultSet` fields to the appropriate Scala type?

The key is the `implicit` keyword that we used to prefix the `GenderReader` and `StringReader` object definitions. It lets us write:

```
implicitly[SqlReader[Gender.Value]].read(results, "gender")
implicitly[SqlReader[String]].read(results, "name")
```

By writing `implicitly[SqlReader[T]]`, we are telling the Scala compiler to find a class (or an object) that extends `SqlReader[T]` that is marked for implicit use. Try this out by pasting the following in the command line, for instance:

```
scala> :paste

import Implicits._ // Connection to RichConnection conversion
SqlUtils.usingConnection("test") {
  _.withQuery("select * from physicists") {
    rs => {
      rs.next() // advance to first record
      implicitly[SqlReader[Gender.Value]].read(rs, "gender")
    }
  }
}
```

Of course, using `implicitly[SqlReader[T]]` everywhere is not particularly elegant. Let's use the pimp my library idiom to add a `read[T]` method to `ResultSet`. We first define a `RichResultSet` class that we can use to "pimp" the `ResultSet` class:

```
// RichResultSet.scala

import java.sql.ResultSet

class RichResultSet(val underlying:ResultSet) {
  def read[T : SqlReader](field:String):T = {
    implicitly[SqlReader[T]].read(underlying, field)
  }
}
```

The only unfamiliar part of this should be the `read[T : SqlReader]` generic definition. We are stating here that `read` will accept any `T` type, provided an instance of `SqlReader[T]` exists. This is called a *context bound*.

We must also add implicit methods to the `Implicits` object to convert from `ResultSet` to `RichResultSet`. You should be familiar with this now, so I will not bore you with the details. You can now call `results.read[T](fieldName)` for any `T` for which you have a `SqlReader[T]` implicit object defined:

```
import Implicits._

SqlUtils.usingConnection("test") { connection =>
  connection.withQuery("SELECT * FROM physicists") {
    results =>
      val resultStream = SqlUtils.stream(results)
      resultStream.map { row =>
        val name = row.read[String]("name")
        val gender = row.read[Gender.Value]("gender")
        (name, gender)
      }.toVector
  }
}
//=> Vector[(String, Gender.Value)] = Vector((Albert Einstein,Male),
(Marie Curie,Female))
```

Let's summarize the steps needed for type classes to work. We will do this in the context of deserializing from SQL, but you will be able to adapt these steps to solve other problems:

- Define an abstract generic trait that provides the interface for the type class, for example, `SqlReader[T]`. Any functionality that is independent of `T` can be added to this base trait.

- Create the companion object for the base trait and add implicit objects extending the trait for each `T`, for example,

  `implicit object StringReader extends SqlReader[T]`.

- Type classes are always used in generic methods. A method that relies on the existence of a type class for an argument must contain a context bound in the generic definition, for example, `def read[T : SqlReader](field:String):T`. To access the type class in this method, use the `implicitly` keyword: `implicitly[SqlReader[T]]`.

When to use type classes

Type classes are useful when you need a particular behavior for many different types, but exactly how this behavior is implemented varies between these types. For instance, we need to be able to read several different types from ResultSet, but exactly how each type is read differs between types: for strings, we must read from ResultSet using getString, whereas for integers, we must use getInt followed by wasNull.

A good rule of thumb is when you start thinking "Oh, I could just write a generic method to do this. Ah, but wait, I will have to write the Int implementation as a specific edge case as it behaves differently. Oh, and the Gender implementation. I wonder if there's a better way?", then type classes might be useful.

Benefits of type classes

Data scientists frequently have to deal with new input streams, changing requirements, and new data types. Having an object-relational mapping layer that is easy to extend or alter is therefore critical to responding to changes efficiently. Minimizing coupling between code entities and separation of concerns are the only ways to ensure that the code can be changed in response to new data.

With type classes, we maintain orthogonality between accessing records in the database (through the ResultSet class) and how individual fields are transformed to Scala objects: both can vary independently. The only coupling between these two concerns is through the SqlReader[T] interface.

This means that both concerns can evolve independently: to read a new data type, we just need to implement a SqlReader[T] object. Conversely, we can add functionality to ResultSet without needing to reimplement how fields are converted. For instance, we could add a getColumn method that returns a Vector[T] of all the values of a field in a ResultSet instance:

```
def getColumn[T : SqlReader](field:String):Vector[T] = {
  val resultStream = SqlUtils.stream(results)
  resultStream.map { _.read[T](field) }.toVector
}
```

Note how we could do this without increasing the coupling to the way in which individual fields are read.

Creating a data access layer

Let's bring together everything that we have seen and build a *data-mapper* class for fetching `Physicist` objects from the database. These classes (also called *data access objects*) are useful to decouple the internal representation of an object from its representation in the database.

We start by defining the `Physicist` class:

```
// Physicist.scala
case class Physicist(
  val name:String,
  val gender:Gender.Value
)
```

The data access object will expose a single method, `readAll`, that returns a `Vector[Physicist]` of all the physicists in our database:

```
// PhysicistDao.scala

import java.sql.{ ResultSet, Connection }
import Implicits._ // implicit conversions

object PhysicistDao {

  /* Helper method for reading a single row */
  private def readFromResultSet(results:ResultSet):Physicist = {
    Physicist(
      results.read[String]("name"),
      results.read[Gender.Value]("gender")
    )
  }

  /* Read the entire 'physicists' table. */
  def readAll(connection:Connection):Vector[Physicist] = {
    connection.withQuery("SELECT * FROM physicists") {
      results =>
        val resultStream = SqlUtils.stream(results)
        resultStream.map(readFromResultSet).toVector
    }
  }
}
```

The data access layer can be used by client code as in the following example:

```scala
object PhysicistDaoDemo extends App {

  val physicists = SqlUtils.usingConnection("test") {
    connection => PhysicistDao.readAll(connection)
  }

  // physicists is a Vector[Physicist] instance.
  physicists.foreach { println }
  //=> Physicist(Albert Einstein,Male)
  //=> Physicist(Marie Curie,Female)
}
```

Summary

In this chapter, we learned how to interact with SQL databases using JDBC. We wrote a library to wrap native JDBC objects, aiming to give them a more functional interface.

In the next chapter, you will learn about Slick, a Scala library that provides functional wrappers to interact with relational databases.

References

The API documentation for JDBC is very complete: `http://docs.oracle.com/javase/7/docs/api/java/sql/package-summary.html`

The API documentation for the `ResultSet` interface (`http://docs.oracle.com/javase/7/docs/api/java/sql/ResultSet.html`), for the `PreparedStatement` class (`http://docs.oracle.com/javase/7/docs/api/java/sql/PreparedStatement.html`) and the `Connection` class (`http://docs.oracle.com/javase/7/docs/api/java/sql/Connection.html`) is particularly relevant.

The data mapper pattern is described extensively in Martin Fowler's *Patterns of Enterprise Application Architecture*. A brief description is also available on his website (`http://martinfowler.com/eaaCatalog/dataMapper.html`).

For an introduction to SQL, I suggest *Learning SQL* by *Alan Beaulieu* (*O'Reilly*).

For another discussion of type classes, read `http://danielwestheide.com/blog/2013/02/06/the-neophytes-guide-to-scala-part-12-type-classes.html`.

This post describes how some common object-oriented design patterns can be reimplemented more elegantly in Scala using type classes:

`https://staticallytyped.wordpress.com/2013/03/24/gang-of-four-patterns-with-type-classes-and-implicits-in-scala-part-2/`

This post by *Martin Odersky* details the *Pimp my Library* pattern:

`http://www.artima.com/weblogs/viewpost.jsp?thread=179766`

6
Slick – A Functional Interface for SQL

In *Chapter 5*, *Scala and SQL through JDBC*, we investigated how to access SQL databases with JDBC. As interacting with JDBC feels somewhat unnatural, we extended JDBC using custom wrappers. The wrappers were developed to provide a functional interface to hide the imperative nature of JDBC.

With the difficulty of interacting directly with JDBC from Scala and the ubiquity of SQL databases, you would expect there to be existing Scala libraries that wrap JDBC. *Slick* is such a library.

Slick styles itself as a *functional-relational mapping* library, a play on the more traditional *object-relational mapping* name used to denote libraries that build objects from relational databases. It presents a functional interface to SQL databases, allowing the client to interact with them in a manner similar to native Scala collections.

FEC data

In this chapter, we will use a somewhat more involved example dataset. The **Federal Electoral Commission of the United States** (**FEC**) records all donations to presidential candidates greater than $200. These records are publicly available. We will look at the donations for the campaign leading up to the 2012 general elections that resulted in Barack Obama's re-election. The data includes donations to the two presidential candidates, Obama and Romney, and also to the other contenders in the Republican primaries (there were no Democrat primaries).

In this chapter, we will take the transaction data provided by the FEC, store it in a table, and learn how to query and analyze it.

The first step is to acquire the data. If you have downloaded the code samples from the Packt website, you should already have two CSVs in the data directory of the code samples for this chapter. If not, you can download the files using the following links:

- data.scala4datascience.com/fec/ohio.csv.gz (or ohio.csv.zip)
- data.scala4datascience.com/fec/us.csv.gz (or us.csv.zip)

Decompress the two files and place them in a directory called data/ in the same location as the source code examples for this chapter. The data files correspond to the following:

- The ohio.csv file is a CSV of all the donations made by donors in Ohio.
- The us.csv file is a CSV of all the donations made by donors across the country. This is quite a large file, with six million rows.

The two CSV files contain identical columns. Use the Ohio dataset for more responsive behavior, or the nationwide data file if you want to wrestle with a larger dataset. The dataset is adapted from a list of contributions downloaded from http://www.fec.gov/disclosurep/PDownload.do.

Let's start by creating a Scala case class to represent a transaction. In the context of this chapter, a transaction is a single donation from an individual to a candidate:

```
// Transaction.scala
import java.sql.Date

case class Transaction(
  id:Option[Int], // unique identifier
  candidate:String, // candidate receiving the donation
  contributor:String, // name of the contributor
  contributorState:String, // contributor state
  contributorOccupation:Option[String], // contributor job
  amount:Long, // amount in cents
  date:Date // date of the donation
)
```

The code repository for this chapter includes helper functions in an FECData singleton object to load the data from CSVs:

```
scala> val ohioData = FECData.loadOhio
s4ds.FECData = s4ds.FECData@718454de
```

Calling `FECData.loadOhio` or `FECData.loadAll` will create an `FECData` object with a single attribute, `transactions`, which is an iterator over all the donations coming from Ohio or the entire United States:

```
scala> val ohioTransactions = ohioData.transactions
Iterator[Transaction] = non-empty iterator


scala> ohioTransactions.take(5).foreach(println)
Transaction(None,Paul, Ron,BROWN, TODD W MR.,OH,Some(ENGINE
ER),5000,2011-01-03)

Transaction(None,Paul, Ron,DIEHL, MARGO SONJA,OH,Some(RETIR
ED),2500,2011-01-03)

Transaction(None,Paul, Ron,KIRCHMEYER, BENJAMIN,OH,Some(COMPUTER
PROGRAMMER),20120,2011-01-03)

Transaction(None,Obama, Barack,KEYES, STEPHEN,OH,Some(HR EXECUTIVE /
ATTORNEY),10000,2011-01-03)

Transaction(None,Obama, Barack,MURPHY, MIKE W,OH,Some(MANAG
ER),5000,2011-01-03)
```

Now that we have some data to play with, let's try and put it in the database so that we can run some useful queries on it.

Importing Slick

To add Slick to the list of dependencies, you will need to add `"com.typesafe.slick"` `%% "slick" % "2.1.0"` to the list of dependencies in your `build.sbt` file. You will also need to make sure that Slick has access to a JDBC driver. In this chapter, we will connect to a MySQL database, and must, therefore, add the MySQL connector `"mysql" % "mysql-connector-java" % "5.1.37"` to the list of dependencies.

Slick is imported by importing a specific database driver. As we are using MySQL, we must import the following:

```
scala> import slick.driver.MySQLDriver.simple._
import slick.driver.MySQLDriver.simple._
```

To connect to a different flavor of SQL database, import the relevant driver. The easiest way of seeing what drivers are available is to consult the API documentation for the `slick.driver` package, which is available at http://slick.typesafe.com/doc/2.1.0/api/#scala.slick.driver.package. All the common SQL flavors are supported (including **H2**, **PostgreSQL**, **MS SQL Server**, and **SQLite**).

Defining the schema

Let's create a table to represent our transactions. We will use the following schema:

```
CREATE TABLE transactions(
    id INT(11) AUTO_INCREMENT PRIMARY KEY,
    candidate VARCHAR(254) NOT NULL,
    contributor VARCHAR(254) NOT NULL,
    contributor_state VARCHAR(2) NOT NULL,
    contributor_occupation VARCHAR(254),
    amount BIGINT(20) NOT NULL,
    date DATE
);
```

Note that the donation amount is in *cents*. This allows us to use an integer field (rather than a fixed point decimal, or worse, a float).

> You should never use a floating point format to represent money or, in fact, any discrete quantity because floats cannot represent most fractions exactly:
>
> **scala> 0.1 + 0.2**
>
> **Double = 0.30000000000000004**
>
> This seemingly nonsensical result occurs because there is no way to store 0.3 exactly in doubles.
>
> This post gives an extensive discussion of the limitations of the floating point format:
>
> http://docs.oracle.com/cd/E19957-01/806-3568/ncg_goldberg.html

To use Slick with tables in our database, we first need to tell Slick about the database schema. We do this by creating a class that extends the `Table` abstract class. The way in which a schema is defined is quite straightforward, so let's dive straight into the code. We will store our schema in a `Tables` singleton. We define a `Transactions` class that provides the mapping to go from collections of `Transaction` instances to SQL tables structured like the `transactions` table:

```
// Tables.scala

import java.sql.Date
import slick.driver.MySQLDriver.simple._

/** Singleton object for table definitions */
```

```scala
object Tables {

  // Transactions table definition
  class Transactions(tag:Tag)
  extends Table[Transaction](tag, "transactions") {
    def id = column[Int]("id", O.PrimaryKey, O.AutoInc)
    def candidate = column[String]("candidate")
    def contributor = column[String]("contributor")
    def contributorState = column[String](
      "contributor_state", O.DBType("VARCHAR(2)"))
    def contributorOccupation = column[Option[String]](
      "contributor_occupation")
    def amount = column[Long]("amount")
    def date = column[Date]("date")

    def * = (id.?, candidate, contributor,
      contributorState, contributorOccupation, amount, date) <> (
      Transaction.tupled, Transaction.unapply)
  }

  val transactions = TableQuery[Transactions]

}
```

Let's go through this line by line. We first define a `Transactions` class, which must take a Slick `Tag` object as its first argument. The `Tag` object is used by Slick internally to construct SQL statements. The `Transactions` class extends a `Table` object, passing it the tag and name of the table in the database. We could, optionally, have added a database name by extending `Table[Transaction](tag, Some("fec"), "transactions")` rather than just `Table[Transaction](tag, "transactions")`. The `Table` type is parametrized by `Transaction`. This means that running SELECT statements on the database returns `Transaction` objects. Similarly, we will insert data into the database by passing a transaction or list of transactions to the relevant Slick methods.

Let's look at the `Transactions` class definition in more detail. The body of the class starts by listing the database columns. For instance, the `id` column is defined as follows:

```scala
def id = column[Int]("id", O.PrimaryKey, O.AutoInc)
```

We tell Slick that it should read the column called `id` and transform it to a Scala integer. Additionally, we tell Slick that this column is the primary key and that it is auto-incrementing. The Slick documentation contains a list of available options for `column`.

The `candidate` and `contributor` columns are straightforward: we tell Slick to read these as `String` from the database. The `contributor_state` column is a little more interesting. Besides specifying that it should be read from the database as a `String`, we also tell Slick that it should be stored in the database with type `VARCHAR(2)`.

The `contributor_occupation` column in our table can contain `NULL` values. When defining the schema, we pass the `Option[String]` type to the column method:

```
def contributorOccupation =
  column[Option[String]]("contributor_occupation")
```

When reading from the database, a `NULL` field will get converted to `None` for columns specified as `Option[T]`. Conversely, if the field has a value, it will be returned as `Some(value)`.

The last line of the class body is the most interesting part: it specifies how to transform the raw data read from the database into a `Transaction` object and how to convert a `Transaction` object to raw fields ready for insertion:

```
def * = (id.?, candidate, contributor,
contributorState, contributorOccupation, amount, date) <> (
Transaction.tupled, Transaction.unapply)
```

The first part is just a tuple of fields to be read from the database: `(id.?, candidate, contributor, contributorState, contributorOccupation, amount, date)`, with a small amount of metadata. The second part is a pair of functions that describe how to transform this tuple into a `Transaction` object and back. In this case, as `Transaction` is a case class, we can take advantage of the `Transaction.tupled` and `Transaction.unapply` methods automatically provided for case classes.

Notice how we followed the `id` entry with `.?`. In our `Transaction` class, the donation `id` has the `Option[Int]` type, but the column in the database has the `INT` type with the additional `O.AutoInc` option. The `.?` suffix tells Slick to use the default value provided by the database (in this case, the database's auto-increment) if `id` is `None`.

Finally, we define the value:

```
val transactions = TableQuery[Transactions]
```

This is the handle that we use to actually interact with the database. For instance, as we will see later, to get a list of donations to Barack Obama, we run the following query (don't worry about the details of the query for now):

```
Tables.transactions.filter {_.candidate === "Obama, Barack"}.list
```

Let's summarize the parts of our `Transactions` mapper class:

- The `Transactions` class must extend the `Table` abstract class parametrized by the type that we want to return: `Table[Transaction]`.

- We define the columns to read from the database explicitly using `column`, for example, `def contributorState = column[String]("contributor_state", O.DBType("VARCHAR(2)"))`. The `[String]` type parameter defines the Scala type that this column gets read as. The first argument is the SQL column name. Consult the Slick documentation for a full list of additional arguments (`http://slick.typesafe.com/doc/2.1.0/schemas.html`).

- We describe how to convert from a tuple of the column values to a Scala object and vice versa using `def * = (id.?, candidate, ...) <> (Transaction.tupled, Transaction.unapply)`.

Connecting to the database

So far, you have learned how to define `Table` classes that encode the transformation from rows in a SQL table to Scala case classes. To move beyond table definitions and start interacting with a database server, we must connect to a database. As in the previous chapter, we will assume that there is a MySQL server running on localhost on port `3306`.

We will use the console to demonstrate the functionality in this chapter, but you can find an equivalent sample program in `SlickDemo.scala`. Let's open a Scala console and connect to the database running on port `3306`:

```
scala> import slick.driver.MySQLDriver.simple._
import slick.driver.MySQLDriver.simple._


scala> val db = Database.forURL(
  "jdbc:mysql://127.0.0.1:3306/test",
  driver="com.mysql.jdbc.Driver"
)
db: slick.driver.MySQLDriver.backend.DatabaseDef = slick.jdbc.JdbcBackend
$DatabaseDef@3632d1dd
```

If you have read the previous chapter, you will recognize the first argument as a JDBC-style URL. The URL starts by defining a protocol, in this case, `jdbc:mysql`, followed by the IP address and port of the database server, followed by the database name (`test`, here).

The second argument to `forURL` is the class name of the JDBC driver. This driver is imported at runtime using reflection. Note that the driver specified here must match the Slick driver imported statically.

Having defined the database, we can now use it to create a connection:

```scala
scala> db.withSession { implicit session =>
  // do something useful with the database
  println(session)
}
scala.slick.jdbc.JdbcBackend$BaseSession@af5a276
```

Slick functions that require access to the database take a `Session` argument implicitly: if a `Session` instance marked as implicit is available in scope, they will use it. Thus, preceding `session` with the `implicit` keyword saves us having to pass `session` explicitly every time we run an operation on the database.

If you have read the previous chapter, you will recognize that Slick deals with the need to close connections with the *loan pattern*: a database connection is created in the form of a `session` object and passed temporarily to the client. When the client code returns, the session is closed, ensuring that all opened connections are closed. The client code is therefore spared the responsibility of closing the connection.

The loan pattern is very useful in production code, but it can be somewhat cumbersome in the shell. Slick lets us create a session explicitly as follows:

```scala
scala> implicit val session = db.createSession
session: slick.driver.MySQLDriver.backend.Session = scala.slick.jdbc.Jdbc
Backend$BaseSession@2b775b49


scala> session.close
```

Creating tables

Let's use our new connection to create the transaction table in the database. We can access methods to create and drop tables using the `ddl` attribute on our `TableQuery[Transactions]` instance:

```scala
scala> db.withSession { implicit session =>
  Tables.transactions.ddl.create
}
```

If you jump into a `mysql` shell, you will see that a `transactions` table has been created:

```
mysql> describe transactions ;

+-------------------------+--------------+------+-----+
| Field                   | Type         | Null | Key |
+-------------------------+--------------+------+-----+
| id                      | int(11)      | NO   | PRI |
| candidate               | varchar(254) | NO   |     |
| contributor             | varchar(254) | NO   |     |
| contributor_state       | varchar(2)   | NO   |     |
| contributor_occupation  | varchar(254) | YES  |     |
| amount                  | bigint(20)   | NO   |     |
| date                    | date         | NO   |     |
+-------------------------+--------------+------+-----+

7 rows in set (0.01 sec)
```

The `ddl` attribute also includes a `drop` method to drop the table. Incidentally, `ddl` stands for "data-definition language" and is commonly used to refer to the parts of SQL relevant to schema and constraint definitions.

Inserting data

Slick `TableQuery` instances let us interact with SQL tables with an interface similar to Scala collections.

Let's create a transaction first. We will pretend that a donation occurred on the 22nd of June, 2010. Unfortunately, the code to create dates in Scala and pass these to JDBC is particularly clunky. We first create a `java.util.Date` instance, which we must then convert to a `java.sql.Date` to use in our newly created transaction:

```scala
scala> import java.text.SimpleDateFormat
import java.text.SimpleDateFormat

scala> val date = new SimpleDateFormat("dd-MM-yyyy").parse("22-06-2010")
date: java.util.Date = Tue Jun 22 00:00:00 BST 2010

scala> val sqlDate = new java.sql.Date(date.getTime())
sqlDate: java.sql.Date = 2010-06-22

scala> val transaction = Transaction(
```

```
  None, "Obama, Barack", "Doe, John", "TX", None, 200, sqlDate
)
transaction: Transaction = Transaction(None,Obama, Barack,Doe,
John,TX,None,200,2010-06-22)
```

Much of the interface provided by the `TableQuery` instance mirrors that of a mutable list. To insert a single row in the transaction table, we can use the `+=` operator:

```
scala> db.withSession {
  implicit session => Tables.transactions += transaction
}
Int = 1
```

Under the hood, this will create a JDBC prepared statement and run this statement's `executeUpdate` method.

If you are committing many rows at a time, you should use Slick's bulk insert operator: `++=`. This takes a `List[Transaction]` as input and inserts all the transactions in a single batch by taking advantage of JDBC's `addBatch` and `executeBatch` functionality.

Let's insert all the FEC transactions so that we have some data to play with when running queries in the next section. We can load an iterator of transactions for Ohio by calling the following:

```
scala> val transactions = FECData.loadOhio.transactions
transactions: Iterator[Transaction] = non-empty iterator
```

We can also load the transactions for the whole of United States:

```
scala> val transactions = FECData.loadAll.transactions
transactions: Iterator[Transaction] = non-empty iterator
```

To avoid materializing all the transactions in a single fell swoop—thus potentially exceeding our computer's available memory—we will take batches of transactions from the iterator and insert them:

```
scala> val batchSize = 100000
batchSize: Int = 100000


scala> val transactionBatches = transactions.grouped(batchSize)
transactionBatches: transactions.GroupedIterator[Transaction] = non-empty
iterator
```

An iterator's `grouped` method splits the iterator into batches. It is useful to split a long collection or iterator into manageable batches that can be processed one after the other. This is important when integrating or processing large datasets.

All that we have to do now is iterate over our batches, inserting them into the database as we go:

```scala
scala> db.withSession { implicit session =>
  transactionBatches.foreach {
    batch => Tables.transactions ++= batch.toList
  }
}
```

While this works, it is sometimes useful to see progress reports when doing long-running integration processes. As we have split the integration into batches, we know (to the nearest batch) how far into the integration we are. Let's print the progress information at the beginning of every batch:

```scala
scala> db.withSession { implicit session =>
  transactionBatches.zipWithIndex.foreach {
    case (batch, batchNumber) =>
      println(s"Processing row ${batchNumber*batchSize}")
      Tables.transactions ++= batch.toList
  }
}
Processing row 0
Processing row 100000
...
```

We use the `.zipWithIndex` method to transform our iterator over batches into an iterator of (*batch, current index*) pairs. In a full-scale application, the progress information would probably be written to a log file rather than to the screen.

Slick's well-designed interface makes inserting data very intuitive, integrating well with native Scala types.

Querying data

In the previous section, we used Slick to insert donation data into our database. Let's explore this data now.

When defining the `Transactions` class, we defined a `TableQuery` object, `transactions`, that acts as the handle for accessing the transaction table. It exposes an interface similar to Scala iterators. For instance, to see the first five elements in our database, we can call `take(5)`:

```scala
scala> db.withSession { implicit session =>
  Tables.transactions.take(5).list
}
List[Tables.Transactions#TableElementType] =
List(Transaction(Some(1),Obama, Barack,Doe, ...
```

Internally, Slick implements the `.take` method using a SQL `LIMIT`. We can, in fact, get the SQL statement using the `.selectStatement` method on the query:

```scala
scala> db.withSession { implicit session =>
  println(Tables.transactions.take(5).selectStatement)
}
select x2.`id`, x2.`candidate`, x2.`contributor`, x2.`contributor_
state`, x2.`contributor_occupation`, x2.`amount`, x2.`date` from
(select x3.`date` as `date`, x3.`contributor` as `contributor`,
x3.`amount` as `amount`, x3.`id` as `id`, x3.`candidate` as `candidate`,
x3.`contributor_state` as `contributor_state`, x3.`contributor_
occupation` as `contributor_occupation` from `transactions` x3 limit 5)
x2
```

Our Slick query is made up of the following two parts:

- `.take(n)`: This part is called the *invoker*. Invokers build up the SQL statement but do not actually fire it to the database. You can chain many invokers together to build complex SQL statements.

- `.list`: This part sends the statement prepared by the invoker to the database and converts the result to Scala object. This takes a `session` argument, possibly implicitly.

Invokers

Invokers are the components of a Slick query that build up the SQL select statement. Slick exposes a variety of invokers that allow the construction of complex queries. Let's look at some of these invokers here:

- The `map` invoker is useful to select individual columns or apply operations to columns:

```
scala> db.withSession { implicit session =>
  Tables.transactions.map {
    _.candidate
  }.take(5).list
}
List[String] = List(Obama, Barack, Paul, Ron, Paul, Ron, Paul,
Ron, Obama, Barack)
```

- The `filter` invoker is the equivalent of the WHERE statements in SQL. Note that Slick fields must be compared using `===`:

```
scala> db.withSession { implicit session =>
  Tables.transactions.filter {
    _.candidate === "Obama, Barack"
  }.take(5).list
}
List[Tables.Transactions#TableElementType] =
List(Transaction(Some(1),Obama, Barack,Doe,
John,TX,None,200,2010-06-22), ...
```

  Similarly, to filter out donations to Barack Obama, use the `=!=` operator:

```
scala> db.withSession { implicit session =>
  Tables.transactions.filter {
    _.candidate =!= "Obama, Barack"
  }.take(5).list
}
List[Tables.Transactions#TableElementType] =
List(Transaction(Some(2),Paul, Ron,BROWN, TODD W MR.,OH,...
```

- The `sortBy` invoker is the equivalent of the ORDER BY statement in SQL:

```
scala> db.withSession { implicit session =>
  Tables.transactions.sortBy {
    _.date.desc
```

```
    }.take(5).list

  }
  List[Tables.Transactions#TableElementType] = List(Transactio
  n(Some(65536),Obama, Barack,COPELAND,  THOMAS,OH,Some(COLLEGE
  TEACHING),10000,2012-01-02)
```

- The `leftJoin`, `rightJoin`, `innerJoin`, and `outerJoin` invokers are used for joining tables. As we do not cover interactions between multiple tables in this tutorial, we cannot demonstrate joins. See the Slick documentation (`http://slick.typesafe.com/doc/2.1.0/queries.html#joining-and-zipping`) for examples of these.

- Aggregation invokers such as `length`, `min`, `max`, `sum`, and `avg` can be used for computing summary statistics. These must be executed using `.run`, rather than `.list`, as they return single numbers. For instance, to get the total donations to Barack Obama:

```scala
scala> db.withSession { implicit session =>

  Tables.transactions.filter {

    _.candidate === "Obama, Barack"

  }.map { _.amount }.sum.run

}

Option[Int] = Some(849636799) // (in cents)
```

Operations on columns

In the previous section, you learned about the different invokers and how they mapped to SQL statements. We brushed over the methods supported by columns themselves, however: we can compare for equality using `===`, but what other operations are supported by Slick columns?

Most of the SQL functions are supported. For instance, to get the total donations to candidates whose name starts with `"O"`, we could run the following:

```scala
scala> db.withSession { implicit session =>

  Tables.transactions.filter {

    _.candidate.startsWith("O")

  }.take(5).list

}

List[Tables.Transactions#TableElementType] = List(Transaction(So
me(1594098)...
```

Similarly, to count donations that happened between January 1, 2011 and February 1, 2011, we can use the `.between` method on the `date` column:

```scala
scala> val dateParser = new SimpleDateFormat("dd-MM-yyyy")
dateParser: java.text.SimpleDateFormat = SimpleDateFormat

scala> val startDate = new java.sql.Date(dateParser.parse("01-01-2011").
getTime())
startDate: java.sql.Date = 2011-01-01

scala> val endDate = new java.sql.Date(dateParser.parse("01-02-2011").
getTime())
endDate: java.sql.Date = 2011-02-01

scala> db.withSession { implicit session =>
  Tables.transactions.filter {
    _.date.between(startDate, endDate)
  }.length.run
}
Int = 9772
```

The equivalent of the SQL IN (...) operator that selects values in a specific set is `inSet`. For instance, to select all transactions to Barack Obama and Mitt Romney, we can use the following:

```scala
scala> val candidateList = List("Obama, Barack", "Romney, Mitt")
candidateList: List[String] = List(Obama, Barack, Romney, Mitt)

scala> val donationCents = db.withSession { implicit session =>
  Tables.transactions.filter {
    _.candidate.inSet(candidateList)
  }.map { _.amount }.sum.run
}
donationCents: Option[Long] = Some(2874484657)

scala> val donationDollars = donationCents.map { _ / 100 }
donationDollars: Option[Long] = Some(28744846)
```

So, between them, Mitt Romney and Barack Obama received over 28 million dollars in registered donations.

We can also negate a Boolean column with the ! operator. For instance, to calculate the total amount of donations received by all candidates apart from Barack Obama and Mitt Romney:

```
scala> db.withSession { implicit session =>
  Tables.transactions.filter {
    ! _.candidate.inSet(candidateList)
  }.map { _.amount }.sum.run
}.map { _ / 100 }
Option[Long] = Some(1930747)
```

Column operations are added by implicit conversion on the base Column instances. For a full list of methods available on String columns, consult the API documentation for the StringColumnExtensionMethods class (http://slick.typesafe.com/doc/2.1.0/api/#scala.slick.lifted.StringColumnExtensionMethods). For the methods available on Boolean columns, consult the API documentation for the BooleanColumnExtensionMethods class (http://slick.typesafe.com/doc/2.1.0/api/#scala.slick.lifted.BooleanColumnExtensionMethods). For the methods available on numeric columns, consult the API documentation for NumericColumnExtensionMethods (http://slick.typesafe.com/doc/2.1.0/api/#scala.slick.lifted.NumericColumnExtensionMethods).

Aggregations with "Group by"

Slick also provides a groupBy method that behaves like the groupBy method of native Scala collections. Let's get a list of candidates with all the donations for each candidate:

```
scala> val grouped = Tables.transactions.groupBy { _.candidate }
grouped: scala.slick.lifted.Query[(scala.slick.lifted.Column[...


scala> val aggregated = grouped.map {
  case (candidate, group) =>
    (candidate -> group.map { _.amount }.sum)
}
aggregated: scala.slick.lifted.Query[(scala.slick.lifted.Column[...


scala> val groupedDonations = db.withSession {
  implicit session => aggregated.list
}
```

```
groupedDonations: List[(String, Option[Long])] = List((Bachmann,
Michele,Some(7439272)),...
```

Let's break this down. The first statement, `transactions.groupBy { _.candidate }`, specifies the key by which to group. You can think of this as building an intermediate list of `(String, List[Transaction])` tuples mapping the group key to a list of all the table rows that satisfy this key. This behavior is identical to calling `groupBy` on a Scala collection.

The call to `groupBy` must be followed by a `map` that aggregates the groups. The function passed to `map` must take the tuple `(String, List[Transaction])` pair created by the `groupBy` call as its sole argument. The `map` call is responsible for aggregating the `List[Transaction]` object. We choose to first pick out the `amount` field of each transaction, and then to run a sum over these. Finally, we call `.list` on the whole pipeline to actually run the query. This just returns a Scala list. Let's convert the total donations from cents to dollars:

```scala
scala> val groupedDonationDollars = groupedDonations.map {
  case (candidate, donationCentsOption) =>
    candidate -> (donationCentsOption.getOrElse(0L) / 100)
}
groupedDonationDollars: List[(String, Long)] = List((Bachmann,
Michele,74392),...
```

```scala
scala> groupedDonationDollars.sortBy {
  _._2
}.reverse.foreach { println }
(Romney, Mitt,20248496)
(Obama, Barack,8496347)
(Paul, Ron,565060)
(Santorum, Rick,334926)
(Perry, Rick,301780)
(Gingrich, Newt,277079)
(Cain, Herman,210768)
(Johnson, Gary Earl,83610)
(Bachmann, Michele,74392)
(Pawlenty, Timothy,42500)
(Huntsman, Jon,23571)
(Roemer, Charles E. 'Buddy' III,8579)
(Stein, Jill,5270)
(McCotter, Thaddeus G,3210)
```

Accessing database metadata

Commonly, especially during development, you might start the script by dropping the table if it exists, then recreating it. We can find if a table is defined by accessing the database metadata through the MTable object. To get a list of tables with name matching a certain pattern, we can run MTable.getTables(pattern):

```
scala> import slick.jdbc.meta.MTable
import slick.jdbc.meta.MTable


scala> db.withSession { implicit session =>
  MTable.getTables("transactions").list
}
List[scala.slick.jdbc.meta.MTable] = List(MTable(MQName(fec.transactions)
,TABLE,,None,None,None) ...)
```

Thus, to drop the transactions table if it exists, we can run the following:

```
scala> db.withSession { implicit session =>
  if(MTable.getTables("transactions").list.nonEmpty) {
    Tables.transactions.ddl.drop
  }
}
```

The MTable instance contains a lot of metadata about the table. Go ahead and recreate the transactions table if you dropped it in the previous example. Then, to find information about the table's primary keys:

```
scala> db.withSession { implicit session =>
  val tableMeta = MTable.getTables("transactions").first
  tableMeta.getPrimaryKeys.list
}
List[MPrimaryKey] = List(MPrimaryKey(MQName(test.transactions),id,1,Some(
PRIMARY)))
```

For a full list of methods available on MTable instances, consult the Slick documentation (http://slick.typesafe.com/doc/2.1.0/api/index.html#scala.slick.jdbc.meta.MTable).

Slick versus JDBC

This chapter and the previous one introduced two different ways of interacting with SQL. In the previous chapter, we described how to use JDBC and build extensions on top of JDBC to make it more usable. In this chapter, we introduced Slick, a library that provides a functional interface on top of JDBC.

Which method should you choose? If you are starting a new project, you should consider using Slick. Even if you spend a considerable amount of time writing wrappers that sit on top of JDBC, it is unlikely that you will achieve the fluidity that Slick offers.

If you are working on an existing project that makes extensive use of JDBC, I hope that the previous chapter demonstrates that, with a little time and effort, you can write JDBC wrappers that reduce the impedance between the imperative style of JDBC and Scala's functional approach.

Summary

In the previous two chapters, we looked extensively at how to query relational databases from Scala. In this chapter, you learned how to use Slick, a "functional-relational" mapper that allows interacting with SQL databases as one would with Scala collections.

In the next chapter, you will learn how to ingest data by querying web APIs.

References

To learn more about Slick, you can refer to the Slick documentation (`http://slick.typesafe.com/doc/2.1.0/`) and its API documentation (`http://slick.typesafe.com/doc/2.1.0/api/#package`).

7
Web APIs

Data scientists and data engineers get data from a variety of different sources. Often, data might come as CSV files or database dumps. Sometimes, we have to obtain the data through a web API.

An individual or organization sets up a web API to distribute data to programs over the Internet (or an internal network). Unlike websites, where the data is intended to be consumed by a web browser and shown to the user, the data provided by a web API is agnostic to the type of program querying it. Web servers serving HTML and web servers backing an API are queried in essentially the same way: through HTTP requests.

We have already seen an example of a web API in *Chapter 4*, *Parallel Collections and Futures*, where we queried the "Markit on demand" API for current stock prices. In this chapter, we will explore how to interact with web APIs in more detail; specifically, how to convert the data returned by the API to Scala objects and how to add additional information to the request through HTTP headers (for authentication, for instance).

The "Markit on demand" API returned the data formatted as an XML object, but increasingly, new web APIs return data formatted as JSON. We will therefore focus on JSON in this chapter, but the concepts will port easily to XML.

JSON is a language for formatting structured data. Many readers will have come across JSON in the past, but if not, there is a brief introduction to the syntax and concepts later on in this chapter. You will find it quite straightforward.

In this chapter, we will poll the GitHub API. GitHub has, over the last few years, become the de facto tool for collaborating on open source software. It provides a powerful, feature-rich API that gives programmatic access to nearly all the data available through the website.

Let's get a taste of what we can do. Type `api.github.com/users/odersky` in your web browser address bar. This will return the data offered by the API on a particular user (Martin Odersky, in this case):

```
{
  "login": "odersky",
  "id": 795990,
  ...
  "public_repos": 8,
  "public_gists": 3,
  "followers": 707,
  "following": 0,
  "created_at": "2011-05-18T14:51:21Z",
  "updated_at": "2015-09-15T15:14:33Z"
}
```

The data is returned as a JSON object. This chapter is devoted to learning how to access and parse this data programmatically. In *Chapter 13, Web APIs with Play*, you will learn how to build your own web API.

 The GitHub API is extensive and very well-documented. We will explore some of the features of the API in this chapter. To see the full extent of the API, visit the documentation (`https://developer.github.com/v3/`).

A whirlwind tour of JSON

JSON is a format for transferring structured data. It is flexible, easy for computers to generate and parse, and relatively readable for humans. It has become very common as a means of persisting program data structures and transferring data between programs.

JSON has four basic types: **Numbers**, **Strings**, **Booleans**, and **null**, and two compound types: **Arrays** and **Objects**. Objects are unordered collections of key-value pairs, where the key is always a string and the value can be any simple or compound type. We have already seen a JSON object: the data returned by the API call `api.github.com/users/odersky`.

Arrays are ordered lists of simple or compound types. For instance, type `api.github.com/users/odersky/repos` in your browser to get an array of objects, each representing a GitHub repository:

```
[
  {
    "id": 17335228,
    "name": "dotty",
    "full_name": "odersky/dotty",
    ...
  },
  {
    "id": 15053153,
    "name": "frontend",
    "full_name": "odersky/frontend",
    ...
  },
  ...
]
```

We can construct complex structures by nesting objects within other objects or arrays. Nevertheless, most web APIs return JSON structures with no more than one or two levels of nesting. If you are not familiar with JSON, I encourage you to explore the GitHub API through your web browser.

Querying web APIs

The easiest way of querying a web API from Scala is to use `Source.fromURL`. We have already used this in *Chapter 4, Parallel Collections and Futures*, when we queried the "Markit on demand" API. `Source.fromURL` presents an interface similar to `Source.fromFile`:

```
scala> import scala.io._
import scala.io._

scala> val response = Source.fromURL(
  "https://api.github.com/users/odersky"
).mkString
response: String = {"login":"odersky","id":795990, ...
```

`Source.fromURL` returns an iterator over the characters of the response. We materialize the iterator into a string using its `.mkString` method. We now have the response as a Scala string. The next step is to parse the string with a JSON parser.

JSON in Scala – an exercise in pattern matching

There are several libraries for manipulating JSON in Scala. We prefer json4s, but if you are a die-hard fan of another JSON library, you should be able to readily adapt the examples in this chapter. Let's create a `build.sbt` file with a dependency on `json4s`:

```
// build.sbt
scalaVersion := "2.11.7"

libraryDependencies += "org.json4s" %% "json4s-native" % "3.2.11"
```

We can then import `json4s` into an SBT console session with:

```
scala> import org.json4s._
import org.json4s._


scala> import org.json4s.native.JsonMethods._
import org.json4s.native.JsonMethods._
```

Let's use `json4s` to parse the response to our GitHub API query:

```
scala> val jsonResponse = parse(response)
jsonResponse: org.json4s.JValue = JObject(List((login,JString(odersky)),(
id,JInt(795990))),...
```

The `parse` method takes a string (that contains well-formatted JSON) and converts it to a `JValue`, a supertype for all `json4s` objects. The runtime type of the response to this particular query is `JObject`, which is a `json4s` type representing a JSON object.

`JObject` is a wrapper around a `List[JField]`, and `JField` represents an individual key-value pair in the object. We can use *extractors* to access this list:

```
scala> val JObject(fields) = jsonResponse
fields: List[JField] = List((login,Jstring(odersky)),...
```

What's happened here? By writing `val JObject(fields) = ...`, we are telling Scala:

- The right-hand side has runtime type of `JObject`
- Go into the `JObject` instance and bind the list of fields to the constant `fields`

Readers familiar with Python might recognize the similarity with tuple unpacking, though Scala extractors are much more powerful and versatile. Extractors are used extensively to extract Scala types from `json4s` types.

Pattern matching using case classes

How exactly does the Scala compiler know what to do with an extractor such as:

```
val JObject(fields) = ...
```

`JObject` is a case class with the following constructor:

```
case class JObject(obj:List[JField])
```

Case classes all come with an extractor that reverses the constructor exactly. Thus, writing `val JObject(fields)` will bind `fields` to the `obj` attribute of the `JObject`. For further details on how extractors work, read *Appendix, Pattern Matching and Extractors*.

We have now extracted `fields`, a (plain old Scala) list of fields from the `JObject`. A `JField` is a key-value pair, with the key being a string and value being a subtype of `JValue`. Again, we can use extractors to extract the values in the field:

```
scala> val firstField = fields.head
firstField: JField = (login,JString(odersky))


scala> val JField(key, JString(value)) = firstField
key: String = login
value: String = odersky
```

We matched the right-hand side against the pattern `JField(_, JString(_))`, binding the first element to `key` and the second to `value`. What happens if the right-hand side does not match the pattern?

```
scala> val JField(key, JInt(value)) = firstField
scala.MatchError: (login,JString(odersky)) (of class scala.Tuple2)
...
```

The code throws a `MatchError` at runtime. These examples demonstrate the power of nested pattern matching: in a single line, we managed to verify the type of `firstField`, that its value has type `JString`, and we have bound the key and value to the `key` and `value` variables, respectively. As another example, if we *know* that the first field is the login field, we can both verify this and extract the value:

```scala
scala> val JField("login", JString(loginName)) = firstField
loginName: String = odersky
```

Notice how this style of programming is *declarative* rather than imperative: we declare that we want a `JField("login", JString(_))` variable on the right-hand side. We then let the language figure out how to check the variable types. Pattern matching is a recurring theme in functional languages.

We can also use pattern matching in a for loop when looping over fields. When used in a for loop, a pattern match defines a *partial function*: only elements that match the pattern pass through the loop. This lets us filter the collection for elements that match a pattern and also apply a transformation to these elements. For instance, we can extract every string field in our `fields` list:

```scala
scala> for {
  JField(key, JString(value)) <- fields
} yield (key -> value)
List[(String, String)] = List((login,odersky), (avatar_url,https://
avatars.githubusercontent.com/...
```

We can use this to search for specific fields. For instance, to extract the `"followers"` field:

```scala
scala> val followersList = for {
  JField("followers", JInt(followers)) <- fields
} yield followers
followersList: List[Int] = List(707)


scala> val followers = followersList.headOption
blogURL: Option[Int] = Some(707)
```

We first extracted all fields that matched the pattern `JField("follower", JInt(_))`, returning the integer inside the `JInt`. As the source collection, `fields`, is a list, this returns a list of integers. We then extract the first value from this list using `headOption`, which returns the head of the list if the list has at least one element, or `None` if the list is empty.

We are not limited to extracting a single field at a time. For instance, to extract the `"id"` and `"login"` fields together:

```scala
scala> {
  for {
    JField("login", JString(loginName)) <- fields
    JField("id", JInt(id)) <- fields
  } yield (id -> loginName)
}.headOption
Option[(BigInt, String)] = Some((795990,odersky))
```

Scala's pattern matching and extractors provide you with an extremely powerful way of traversing the json4s tree, extracting the fields that we need.

JSON4S types

We have already discovered parts of json4s's type hierarchy: strings are wrapped in JString objects, integers (or big integers) are wrapped in JInt, and so on. In this section, we will take a step back and formalize the type structure and what Scala types they extract to. These are the json4s runtime types:

- `val JString(s) // => extracts to a String`
- `val JDouble(d) // => extracts to a Double`
- `val JDecimal(d) // => extracts to a BigDecimal`
- `val JInt(i) // => extracts to a BigInt`
- `val JBool(b) // => extracts to a Boolean`
- `val JObject(l) // => extracts to a List[JField]`
- `val JArray(l) // => extracts to a List[JValue]`
- `JNull // => represents a JSON null`

All these types are subclasses of JValue. The compile-time result of `parse` is JValue, which you normally need to cast to a concrete type using an extractor.

The last type in the hierarchy is JField, which represents a key-value pair. JField is just a type alias for the `(String, JValue)` tuple. It is thus not a subtype of JValue. We can extract the key and value using the following extractor:

```scala
val JField(key, JInt(value)) = ...
```

Extracting fields using XPath

In the previous sections, you learned how to traverse JSON objects using extractors. In this section, we will look at a different way of traversing JSON objects and extracting specific fields: the *XPath DSL* (domain-specific language). XPath is a query language for traversing tree-like structures. It was originally designed for addressing specific nodes in an XML document, but it works just as well with JSON. We have already seen an example of XPath syntax when we extracted the stock price from the XML document returned by the "Markit on demand" API in *Chapter 4, Parallel Collections and Futures*. We extracted the node with tag `"LastPrice"` using `r \ "LastPrice"`. The `\` operator was defined by the `scala.xml` package.

The `json4s` package exposes a similar DSL to extract fields from `JObject` instances. For instance, we can extract the `"login"` field from the JSON object `jsonResponse`:

```scala
scala> jsonResponse \ "login"
org.json4s.JValue = JString(odersky)
```

This returns a `JValue` that we can transform into a Scala string using an extractor:

```scala
scala> val JString(loginName) = jsonResponse \ "login"
loginName: String = odersky
```

Notice the similarity between the XPath DSL and traversing a filesystem: we can think of `JObject` instances as directories. Field names correspond to file names and the field value to the content of the file. This is more evident for nested structures. The `users` endpoint of the GitHub API does not have nested documents, so let's try another endpoint. We will query the API for the repository corresponding to this book: `"https://api.github.com/repos/pbugnion/s4ds"`. The response has the following structure:

```
{
  "id": 42269470,
  "name": "s4ds",
  ...
  "owner": { "login": "pbugnion", "id": 1392879 ... }
  ...
}
```

Let's fetch this document and use the XPath syntax to extract the repository owner's login name:

```scala
scala> val jsonResponse = parse(Source.fromURL(
  "https://api.github.com/repos/pbugnion/s4ds"
).mkString)
jsonResponse: JValue = JObject(List((id,JInt(42269470)),
(name,JString(s4ds))...
```

```scala
scala> val JString(ownerLogin) = jsonResponse \ "owner" \ "login"
ownerLogin: String = pbugnion
```

Again, this is much like traversing a filesystem: `jsonResponse \ "owner"` returns a `JObject` corresponding to the `"owner"` object. This `JObject` can, in turn, be queried for the `"login"` field, returning the value `JString(pbugnion)` associated with this key.

What if the API response is an array? The filesystem analogy breaks down somewhat. Let's query the API endpoint listing Martin Odersky's repositories: `https://api.github.com/users/odersky/repos`. The response is an array of JSON objects, each of which represents a repository:

```
[
  {
    "id": 17335228,
    "name": "dotty",
    "size": 14699,
    ...
  },
  {
    "id": 15053153,
    "name": "frontend",
    "size": 392,
    ...
  },
  {
    "id": 2890092,
    "name": "scala",
    "size": 76133,
    ...
  },
  ...
]
```

Let's fetch this and parse it as JSON:

```scala
scala> val jsonResponse = parse(Source.fromURL(
  "https://api.github.com/users/odersky/repos"
).mkString)
jsonResponse: JValue = JArray(List(JObject(List((id,JInt(17335228)),
(name,Jstring(dotty)), ...
```

This returns a `JArray`. The XPath DSL works in the same way on a `JArray` as on a `JObject`, but now, instead of returning a single `JValue`, it returns an array of fields matching the path in every object in the array. Let's get the size of all Martin Odersky's repositories:

```scala
scala> jsonResponse \ "size"
JValue = JArray(List(JInt(14699), JInt(392), ...
```

We now have a `JArray` of the values corresponding to the `"size"` field in every repository. We can iterate over this array with a `for` comprehension and use extractors to convert elements to Scala objects:

```scala
scala> for {
  JInt(size) <- (jsonResponse \ "size")
} yield size
List[BigInt] = List(14699, 392, 76133, 32010, 98166, 1358, 144, 273)
```

Thus, combining extractors with the XPath DSL gives us powerful, complementary tools to extract information from JSON objects.

There is much more to the XPath syntax than we have space to cover here, including the ability to extract fields nested at any level of depth below the current root or fields that match a predicate or a certain type. We find that well-designed APIs obviate the need for many of these more powerful functions, but do consult the documentation (`json4s.org`) to get an overview of what you can do.

In the next section, we will look at extracting JSON directly into case classes.

Extraction using case classes

In the previous sections, we extracted specific fields from the JSON response using Scala extractors. We can do one better and extract full case classes.

When moving beyond the REPL, programming best practice dictates that we move from json4s types to Scala objects as soon as possible rather than passing json4s types around the program. Converting from json4s types to Scala types (or case classes representing domain objects) is good practice because:

- It decouples the program from the structure of the data that we receive from the API, something we have little control over.

- It improves type safety: a JObject is, as far as the compiler is concerned, always a JObject, whatever fields it contains. By contrast, the compiler will never mistake a User for a Repository.

Json4s lets us extract case classes directly from JObject instances, making writing the layer converting JObject instances to custom types easy.

Let's define a case class representing a GitHub user:

```scala
scala> case class User(id:Long, login:String)
defined class User
```

To extract a case class from a JObject, we must first define an implicit Formats value that defines how simple types should be serialized and deserialized. We will use the default DefaultFormats provided with json4s:

```scala
scala> implicit val formats = DefaultFormats
formats: DefaultFormats.type = DefaultFormats$@750e685a
```

We can now extract instances of User. Let's do this for Martin Odersky:

```scala
scala> val url = "https://api.github.com/users/odersky"
url: String = https://api.github.com/users/odersky


scala> val jsonResponse = parse(Source.fromURL(url).mkString)
jsonResponse: JValue = JObject(List((login,JString(odersky)), ...


scala> jsonResponse.extract[User]
User = User(795990,odersky)
```

This works as long as the object is well-formatted. The extract method looks for fields in the JObject that match the attributes of User. In this case, extract will note that the JObject contains the "login": "odersky" field and that JString("odersky") can be converted to a Scala string, so it binds "odersky" to the login attribute in User.

What if the attribute names differ from the field names in the JSON object? We must first transform the object to have the correct fields. For instance, let's rename the `login` attribute to `userName` in our `User` class:

```scala
scala> case class User(id:Long, userName:String)
defined class User
```

If we try to use `extract[User]` on `jsonResponse`, we will get a mapping error because the deserializer is missing a `login` field in the response. We can fix this using the `transformField` method on `jsonResponse` to rename the `login` field:

```scala
scala> jsonResponse.transformField {
  case("login", n) => "userName" -> n
}.extract[User]
User = User(795990,odersky)
```

What about optional fields? Let's assume that the JSON object returned by the GitHub API does not always contain the login field. We could symbolize this in our object model by giving the `login` parameter the type `Option[String]` rather than `String`:

```scala
scala> case class User(id:Long, login:Option[String])
defined class User
```

This works just as you would expect. When the response contains a non-null `login` field, calling `extract[User]` will deserialize it to `Some(value)`, and when it's missing or `JNull`, it will produce `None`:

```scala
scala> jsonResponse.extract[User]
User = User(795990,Some(odersky))


scala> jsonResponse.removeField {
  case(k, _) => k == "login" // remove the "login" field
}.extract[User]
User = User(795990,None)
```

Let's wrap this up in a small program. The program will take a single command-line argument, the user's login name, extract a `User` instance, and print it to screen:

```scala
// GitHubUser.scala

import scala.io._
import org.json4s._
```

```scala
import org.json4s.native.JsonMethods._

object GitHubUser {

  implicit val formats = DefaultFormats

  case class User(id:Long, userName:String)

  /** Query the GitHub API corresponding to `url`
    * and convert the response to a User.
    */
  def fetchUserFromUrl(url:String):User = {
    val response = Source.fromURL(url).mkString
    val jsonResponse = parse(response)
    extractUser(jsonResponse)
  }

  /** Helper method for transforming the response to a User */
  def extractUser(obj:JValue):User = {
    val transformedObject = obj.transformField {
      case ("login", name) => ("userName", name)
    }
    transformedObject.extract[User]
  }

  def main(args:Array[String]) {
    // Extract username from argument list
    val name = args.headOption.getOrElse {
      throw new IllegalArgumentException(
        "Missing command line argument for user.")
    }

    val user = fetchUserFromUrl(
      s"https://api.github.com/users/$name")

    println(s"** Extracted for $name:")
    println()
    println(user)

  }

}
```

We can run this from an SBT console as follows:

```
$ sbt
> runMain GitHubUser pbugnion
** Extracted for pbugnion:
User(1392879,pbugnion)
```

Concurrency and exception handling with futures

While the program that we wrote in the previous section works, it is very brittle. It will crash if we enter a non-existent user name or the GitHub API changes or returns a badly-formatted response. We need to make it fault-tolerant.

What if we also wanted to fetch multiple users? The program, as written, is entirely single-threaded. The fetchUserFromUrl method fires a call to the API and blocks until the API sends data back. A better solution would be to fetch multiple users in parallel.

As you learned in *Chapter 4, Parallel Collections and Futures*, there are two straightforward ways to implement both fault tolerance and parallel execution: we can either put all the user names in a parallel collection and wrap the code for fetching and extracting the user in a Try block or we can wrap each query in a future.

When querying web APIs, it is sometimes the case that a request can take abnormally long. To prevent this from blocking the other threads, it is preferable to rely on futures rather than parallel collections for concurrency, as we saw in the *Parallel collection or Future?* section at the end of *Chapter 4, Parallel Collections and Futures*.

Let's rewrite the code from the previous section to handle fetching multiple users concurrently in a fault-tolerant manner. We will change the fetchUserFromUrl method to query the API asynchronously. This is not terribly different from *Chapter 4, Parallel Collections and Futures*, in which we queried the "Markit on demand" API:

```scala
// GitHubUserConcurrent.scala

import scala.io._
import scala.concurrent._
import scala.concurrent.duration._
import ExecutionContext.Implicits.global
import scala.util._

import org.json4s._
```

```scala
import org.json4s.native.JsonMethods._

object GitHubUserConcurrent {

  implicit val formats = DefaultFormats

  case class User(id:Long, userName:String)

  // Fetch and extract the `User` corresponding to `url`
  def fetchUserFromUrl(url:String):Future[User] = {
    val response = Future { Source.fromURL(url).mkString }
    val parsedResponse = response.map { r => parse(r) }
    parsedResponse.map { extractUser }
  }

  // Helper method for extracting a user from a JObject
  def extractUser(jsonResponse:JValue):User = {
    val o = jsonResponse.transformField {
      case ("login", name) => ("userName", name)
    }
    o.extract[User]
  }

  def main(args:Array[String]) {
    val names = args.toList

    // Loop over each username and send a request to the API
    // for that user
    val name2User = for {
      name <- names
      url = s"https://api.github.com/users/$name"
      user = fetchUserFromUrl(url)
    } yield name -> user

    // callback function
    name2User.foreach { case(name, user) =>
      user.onComplete {
        case Success(u) => println(s" ** Extracted for $name: $u")
        case Failure(e) => println(s" ** Error fetching $name:
          $e")
      }
    }

    // Block until all the calls have finished.
```

```
      Await.ready(Future.sequence(name2User.map { _._2 }), 1 minute)
   }
}
```

Let's run the code through `sbt`:

```
$ sbt

> runMain GitHubUserConcurrent odersky derekwyatt not-a-user-675

 ** Error fetching user not-a-user-675: java.io.FileNotFoundException:
https://api.github.com/users/not-a-user-675

 ** Extracted for odersky: User(795990,odersky)

 ** Extracted for derekwyatt: User(62324,derekwyatt)
```

The code itself should be straightforward. All the concepts used here have been explored in this chapter or in *Chapter 4, Parallel Collections and Futures,* apart from the last line:

```
      Await.ready(Future.sequence(name2User.map { _._2 }), 1 minute)
```

This statement tells the program to wait until all futures in our list have been completed. `Await.ready(..., 1 minute)` takes a future as its first argument and blocks execution until this future returns. The second argument is a time-out on this future. The only catch is that we need to pass a single future to `Await` rather than a list of futures. We can use `Future.sequence` to merge a collection of futures into a single future. This future will be completed when all the futures in the sequence have completed.

Authentication – adding HTTP headers

So far, we have been using the GitHub API without authentication. This limits us to sixty requests per hour. Now that we can query the API in parallel, we could exceed this limit in seconds.

Fortunately, GitHub is much more generous if you authenticate when you query the API. The limit increases to 5,000 requests per hour. You must have a GitHub user account to authenticate, so go ahead and create one now if you need to. After creating an account, navigate to `https://github.com/settings/tokens` and click on the **Generate new token** button. Accept the default settings and enter a token description and a long hexadecimal number should appear on the screen. Copy the token for now.

HTTP – a whirlwind overview

Before using our newly generated token, let's take a few minutes to review how HTTP works.

HTTP is a protocol for transferring information between different computers. It is the protocol that we have been using throughout the chapter, though Scala hid the details from us in the call to `Source.fromURL`. It is also the protocol that you use when you point your web browser to a website, for instance.

In HTTP, a computer will typically make a *request* to a remote server, and the server will send back a *response*. Requests contain a *verb*, which defines the type of request, and a URL identifying a *resource*. For instance, when we typed `api.github.com/users/pbugnion` in our browsers, this was translated into a GET (the verb) request for the `users/pbugnion` resource. All the calls that we have made so far have been GET requests. You might use a different type of request, for instance, a POST request, to modify (rather than just view) some content on GitHub.

Besides the verb and resource, there are two more parts to an HTTP request:

- The *headers* include metadata about the request, such as the expected format and character set of the response or the authentication credentials. Headers are just a list of key-value pairs. We will pass the OAuth token that we have just generated to the API using the `Authorization` header. This Wikipedia article lists commonly used header fields: `en.wikipedia.org/wiki/List_of_HTTP_header_fields`.

- The request body is not used in GET requests but becomes important for requests that modify the resource they query. For instance, if I wanted to create a new repository on GitHub programmatically, I would send a POST request to `/pbugnion/repos`. The POST body would then be a JSON object describing the new repository. We will not use the request body in this chapter.

Adding headers to HTTP requests in Scala

We will pass the OAuth token as a header with our HTTP request. Unfortunately, the `Source.fromURL` method is not particularly suited to adding headers when creating a GET request. We will, instead, use a library, `scalaj-http`.

Let's add `scalaj-http` to the dependencies in our `build.sbt`:

```
libraryDependencies += "org.scalaj" %% "scalaj-http" % "1.1.6"
```

We can now import `scalaj-http`:

```
scala> import scalaj.http._
import scalaj.http._
```

We start by creating an `HttpRequest` object:

```
scala> val request = Http("https://api.github.com/users/pbugnion")
request:scalaj.http.HttpRequest = HttpRequest(api.github.com/users/
pbugnion,GET,...
```

We can now add the authorization header to the request (add your own token string here):

```
scala> val authorizedRequest = request.header("Authorization", "token
e836389ce ...")
authorizedRequest:scalaj.http.HttpRequest = HttpRequest(api.github.com/
users/pbugnion,GET,...
```

> The `.header` method returns a new `HttpRequest` instance.
> It does not modify the request in place. Thus, just calling
> `request.header(...)` does not actually add the header to
> request itself, which can be a source of confusion.

Let's fire the request. We do this through the request's `asString` method, which queries the API, fetches the response, and parses it as a Scala `String`:

```
scala> val response = authorizedRequest.asString
response:scalaj.http.HttpResponse[String] = HttpResponse({"login":"pbugni
on",...
```

The response is made up of three components:

- The status code, which should be `200` for a successful request:
  ```
  scala> response.code
  Int = 200
  ```

- The response body, which is the part that we are interested in:
  ```
  scala> response.body
  String = {"login":"pbugnion","id":1392879,...
  ```

- The response headers (metadata about the response):
  ```
  scala> response.headers
  Map[String,String] = Map(Access-Control-Allow-Credentials -> true,
  ...
  ```

To verify that the authorization was successful, query the X-RateLimit-Limit header:

```
scala> response.headers("X-RateLimit-Limit")
String = 5000
```

This value is the maximum number of requests per hour that you can make to the GitHub API from a single IP address.

Now that we have some understanding of how to add authentication to GET requests, let's modify our script for fetching users to use the OAuth token for authentication. We first need to import scalaj-http:

```
import scalaj.http._
```

Injecting the value of the token into the code can be somewhat tricky. You might be tempted to hardcode it, but this prohibits you from sharing the code. A better solution is to use an *environment variable*. Environment variables are a set of variables present in your terminal session that are accessible to all processes running in that session. To get a list of the current environment variables, type the following on Linux or Mac OS:

```
$ env
HOME=/Users/pascal
SHELL=/bin/zsh
...
```

On Windows, the equivalent command is SET. Let's add the GitHub token to the environment. Use the following command on Mac OS or Linux:

```
$ export GHTOKEN="e83638..." # enter your token here
```

On Windows, use the following command:

```
$ SET GHTOKEN="e83638..."
```

If you were to reuse this environment variable across many projects, entering export GHTOKEN=... in the shell for every session gets old quite quickly. A more permanent solution is to add export GHTOKEN="e83638..." to your shell configuration file (your .bashrc file if you are using Bash). This is safe provided your .bashrc is readable by the user only. Any new shell session will have access to the GHTOKEN environment variable.

We can access environment variables from a Scala program using `sys.env`, which returns a `Map[String, String]` of the variables. Let's add a `lazy val token` to our class, containing the `token` value:

```
lazy val token:Option[String] = sys.env.get("GHTOKEN") orElse {
  println("No token found: continuing without authentication")
  None
}
```

Now that we have the token, the only part of the code that must change, to add authentication, is the `fetchUserFromUrl` method:

```
def fetchUserFromUrl(url:String):Future[User] = {
  val baseRequest = Http(url)
  val request = token match {
    case Some(t) => baseRequest.header(
      "Authorization", s"token $t")
    case None => baseRequest
  }
  val response = Future {
    request.asString.body
  }
  val parsedResponse = response.map { r => parse(r) }
  parsedResponse.map(extractUser)
}
```

Additionally, we can, to gain clearer error messages, check that the response's status code is 200. As this is straightforward, it is left as an exercise.

Summary

In this chapter, you learned how to query the GitHub API, converting the response to Scala objects. Of course, merely printing results to screen is not terribly interesting. In the next chapter, we will look at the next step of the data ingestion process: storing data in a database. We will query the GitHub API and store the results in a MongoDB database.

In *Chapter 13, Web APIs with Play*, we will look at building our own simple web API.

References

The GitHub API, with its extensive documentation, is a good place to explore how a rich API is constructed. It has a **Getting Started** section that is worth reading:

`https://developer.github.com/guides/getting-started/`

Of course, this is not specific to Scala: it uses cURL to query the API.

Read the documentation (`http://json4s.org`) and source code (`https://github.com/json4s/json4s`) for `json4s` for a complete reference. There are many parts of this package that we have not explored, in particular, how to build JSON from Scala.

8
Scala and MongoDB

In *Chapter 5*, *Scala and SQL through JDBC*, and *Chapter 6*, *Slick – A Functional Interface for SQL*, you learned how to insert, transform, and read data in SQL databases. These databases remain (and are likely to remain) very popular in data science, but NoSQL databases are emerging as strong contenders.

The needs for data storage are growing rapidly. Companies are producing and storing more data points in the hope of acquiring better business intelligence. They are also building increasingly large teams of data scientists, who all need to access the data store. Maintaining constant access time as the data load increases requires taking advantage of parallel architectures: we need to distribute the database across several computers so that, as the load on the server increases, we can just add more machines to improve throughput.

In MySQL databases, the data is naturally split across different tables. Complex queries necessitate joining across several tables. This makes partitioning the database across different computers difficult. NoSQL databases emerged to fill this gap.

In this chapter, you will learn to interact with MongoDB, an open source database that offers high performance and can be distributed easily. MongoDB is one of the more popular NoSQL databases with a strong community. It offers a reasonable balance of speed and flexibility, making it a natural alternative to SQL for storing large datasets with uncertain query requirements, as might happen in data science. Many of the concepts and recipes in this chapter will apply to other NoSQL databases.

MongoDB

MongoDB is a *document-oriented* database. It contains collections of documents. Each document is a JSON-like object:

```
{
    _id: ObjectId("558e846730044ede70743be9"),
    name: "Gandalf",
    age: 2000,
    pseudonyms: [ "Mithrandir", "Olorin", "Greyhame" ],
    possessions: [
        { name: "Glamdring", type: "sword" },
        { name: "Narya", type: "ring" }
    ]
}
```

Just as in JSON, a document is a set of key-value pairs, where the values can be strings, numbers, Booleans, dates, arrays, or subdocuments. Documents are grouped in collections, and collections are grouped in databases.

You might be thinking that this is not very different from SQL: a document is similar to a row and a collection corresponds to a table. There are two important differences:

- The values in documents can be simple values, arrays, subdocuments, or arrays of subdocuments. This lets us encode one-to-many and many-to-many relationships in a single collection. For instance, consider the wizard collection. In SQL, if we wanted to store pseudonyms for each wizard, we would have to use a separate `wizard2pseudonym` table with a row for each wizard-pseudonym pair. In MongoDB, we can just use an array. In practice, this means that we can normally use a single document to represent an entity (a customer, transaction, or wizard, for instance). In SQL, we would normally have to join across several tables to retrieve all the information on a specific entity.

- MongoDB is *schemaless*. Documents in a collection can have varying sets of fields with different types for the same field across different documents. In practice, MongoDB collections have a loose schema enforced either client side or by convention: most documents will have a subset of the same fields, and fields will, in general, contain the same data type. Having a flexible schema makes adjusting the data structure easy as there is no need for time-consuming `ALTER TABLE` statements. The downside is that there is no easy way of enforcing our flexible schema on the database side.

Note the `_id` field: this is a unique key. MongoDB will generate one automatically if we insert a document without an `_id` field.

This chapter gives recipes for interacting with a MongoDB database from Scala, including maintaining type safety and best practices. We will not cover advanced MongoDB functionality (such as aggregation or distributing the database). We will assume that you have MongoDB installed on your computer (`http://docs.mongodb.org/manual/installation/`). It will also help to have a very basic knowledge of MongoDB (we discuss some references at the end of this chapter, but any basic tutorial available online will be sufficient for the needs of this chapter).

Connecting to MongoDB with Casbah

The official MongoDB driver for Scala is called **Casbah**. Rather than a fully-fledged driver, Casbah wraps the Java Mongo driver, providing a more functional interface. There are other MongoDB drivers for Scala, which we will discuss briefly at the end of this chapter. For now, we will stick to Casbah.

Let's start by adding Casbah to our `build.sbt` file:

```
scalaVersion := "2.11.7"

libraryDependencies += "org.mongodb" %% "casbah" % "3.0.0"
```

Casbah also expects `slf4j` bindings (a Scala logging framework) to be available, so let's also add `slf4j-nop`:

```
libraryDependencies += "org.slf4j" % "slf4j-nop" % "1.7.12"
```

We can now start an SBT console and import Casbah in the Scala shell:

```
$ sbt console
scala> import com.mongodb.casbah.Imports._
import com.mongodb.casbah.Imports._


scala> val client = MongoClient()
client: com.mongodb.casbah.MongoClient = com.mongodb.casbah.
MongoClient@4ac17318
```

This connects to a MongoDB server on the default host (`localhost`) and default port (`27017`). To connect to a different server, pass the host and port as arguments to `MongoClient`:

```
scala> val client = MongoClient("192.168.1.1", 27017)
client: com.mongodb.casbah.MongoClient = com.mongodb.casbah.
MongoClient@584c6b02
```

Note that creating a client is a lazy operation: it does not attempt to connect to the server until it needs to. This means that if you enter the wrong URL or password, you will not know about it until you try and access documents on the server.

Once we have a connection to the server, accessing a database is as simple as using the client's `apply` method. For instance, to access the `github` database:

```scala
scala> val db = client("github")
db: com.mongodb.casbah.MongoDB = DB{name='github'}
```

We can then access the `"users"` collection:

```scala
scala> val coll = db("users")
coll: com.mongodb.casbah.MongoCollection = users
```

Connecting with authentication

MongoDB supports several different authentication mechanisms. In this section, we will assume that your server is using the **SCRAM-SHA-1** mechanism, but you should find adapting the code to a different type of authentication straightforward.

The easiest way of authenticating is to pass `username` and `password` in the URI when connecting:

```scala
scala> val username = "USER"
username: String = USER


scala> val password = "PASSWORD"
password: String = PASSWORD


scala> val uri = MongoClientURI(
  s"mongodb://$username:$password@localhost/?authMechanism=SCRAM-SHA-1"
)
uri: MongoClientURI = mongodb://USER:PASSWORD@
localhost/?authMechanism=SCRAM-SHA-1


scala> val mongoClient = MongoClient(uri)
client: com.mongodb.casbah.MongoClient = com.mongodb.casbah.
MongoClient@4ac17318
```

In general, you will not want to put your password in plain text in the code. You can either prompt for a password on the command line or pass it through environment variables, as we did with the GitHub OAuth token in *Chapter 7, Web APIs*. The following code snippet demonstrates how to pass credentials through the environment:

```scala
// Credentials.scala

import com.mongodb.casbah.Imports._

object Credentials extends App {

  val username = sys.env.getOrElse("MONGOUSER",
    throw new IllegalStateException(
      "Need a MONGOUSER variable in the environment")
  )
  val password = sys.env.getOrElse("MONGOPASSWORD",
    throw new IllegalStateException(
      "Need a MONGOPASSWORD variable in the environment")
  )

  val host = "127.0.0.1"
  val port = 27017

  val uri = s"mongodb:
    //$username:$password@$host:$port/?authMechanism=SCRAM-SHA-1"

  val client = MongoClient(MongoClientURI(uri))
}
```

You can run it through SBT as follows:

```
$ MONGOUSER="pascal" MONGOPASSWORD="scalarulez" sbt
> runMain Credentials
```

Inserting documents

Let's insert some documents into our newly created database. We want to store information about GitHub users, using the following document structure:

```
{
    id: <mongodb object id>,
    login: "pbugnion",
    github_id: 1392879,
    repos: [
        {
            name: "scikit-monaco",
            id: 14821551,
            language: "Python"
        },
        {
            name: "contactpp",
            id: 20448325,
            language: "Python"
        }
    ]
}
```

Casbah provides a DBObject class to represent MongoDB documents (and subdocuments) in Scala. Let's start by creating a DBObject instance for each repository subdocument:

```
scala> val repo1 = DBObject("name" -> "scikit-monaco", "id" -> 14821551,
"language" -> "Python")
repo1: DBObject = { "name" : "scikit-monaco" , "id" : 14821551,
"language" : "Python"}
```

As you can see, a DBObject is just a list of key-value pairs, where the keys are strings. The values have compile-time type AnyRef, but Casbah will fail (at runtime) if you try to add a value that cannot be serialized.

We can also create DBObject instances from lists of key-value pairs directly. This is particularly useful when converting from a Scala map to a DBObject:

```
scala> val fields:Map[String, Any] = Map(
  "name" -> "contactpp",
  "id" -> 20448325,
  "language" -> "Python"
)
```

```
Map[String, Any] = Map(name -> contactpp, id -> 20448325, language ->
Python)
```

```
scala> val repo2 = DBObject(fields.toList)
```

```
repo2: dDBObject = { "name" : "contactpp" , "id" : 20448325, "language" :
"Python"}
```

The `DBObject` class provides many of the same methods as a map. For instance, we can address individual fields:

```
scala> repo1("name")
```

```
AnyRef = scikit-monaco
```

We can construct a new object by adding a field to an existing object:

```
scala> repo1 + ("fork" -> true)
```

```
mutable.Map[String,Any] = { "name" : "scikit-monaco" , "id" : 14821551,
"language" : "python", "fork" : true}
```

Note the return type: `mutable.Map[String,Any]`. Rather than implementing methods such as + directly, Casbah adds them to `DBObject` by providing an implicit conversion to and from `mutable.Map`.

New `DBObject` instances can also be created by concatenating two existing instances:

```
scala> repo1 ++ DBObject(
  "locs" -> 6342,
  "description" -> "Python library for Monte Carlo integration"
)
```

```
DBObject = { "name" : "scikit-monaco" , "id" : 14821551, "language" :
"Python", "locs" : 6342 , "description" : "Python library for Monte Carlo
integration"}
```

`DBObject` instances can then be inserted into a collection using the += operator. Let's insert our first document into the `user` collection:

```
scala> val userDocument = DBObject(
  "login" -> "pbugnion",
  "github_id" -> 1392879,
  "repos" -> List(repo1, repo2)
)
```

```
userDocument: DBObject = { "login" : "pbugnion" , ... }

scala> val coll = MongoClient()("github")("users")
coll: com.mongodb.casbah.MongoCollection = users

scala> coll += userDocument
com.mongodb.casbah.TypeImports.WriteResult = WriteResult{, n=0,
updateOfExisting=false, upsertedId=null}
```

A database containing a single document is a bit boring, so let's add a few more documents queried directly from the GitHub API. You learned how to query the GitHub API in the previous chapter, so we won't dwell on how to do this here.

In the code examples for this chapter, we have provided a class called `GitHubUserIterator` that queries the GitHub API (specifically the `/users` endpoint) for user documents, converts them to a case class, and offers them as an iterator. You will find the class in the code examples for this chapter (available on GitHub at `https://github.com/pbugnion/s4ds/tree/master/chap08`) in the `GitHubUserIterator.scala` file. The easiest way to have access to the class is to open an SBT console in the directory of the code examples for this chapter. The API then fetches users in increasing order of their login ID:

```
scala> val it = new GitHubUserIterator
it: GitHubUserIterator = non-empty iterator

scala> it.next // Fetch the first user
User = User(mojombo,1,List(Repo(...
```

`GitHubUserIterator` returns instances of the `User` case class, defined as follows:

```
// User.scala
case class User(login:String, id:Long, repos:List[Repo])

// Repo.scala
case class Repo(name:String, id:Long, language:String)
```

Let's write a short program to fetch 500 users and insert them into the MongoDB database. We will need to authenticate with the GitHub API to retrieve these users. The constructor for `GitHubUserIterator` takes the GitHub OAuth token as an optional argument. We will inject the token through the environment, as we did in the previous chapter.

We first give the entire code listing before breaking it down—if you are typing this out, you will need to copy `GitHubUserIterator.scala` from the code examples for this chapter to the directory in which you are running this to access the `GitHubUserIterator` class. The class relies on `scalaj-http` and `json4s`, so either copy the `build.sbt` file from the code examples or specify those packages as dependencies in your `build.sbt` file.

```scala
// InsertUsers.scala

import com.mongodb.casbah.Imports._

object InsertUsers {

  /** Function for reading GitHub token from environment. */
  lazy val token:Option[String] = sys.env.get("GHTOKEN") orElse {
    println("No token found: continuing without authentication")
    None
  }

  /** Transform a Repo instance to a DBObject */
  def repoToDBObject(repo:Repo):DBObject = DBObject(
    "github_id" -> repo.id,
    "name" -> repo.name,
    "language" -> repo.language
  )

  /** Transform a User instance to a DBObject */
  def userToDBObject(user:User):DBObject = DBObject(
    "github_id" -> user.id,
    "login" -> user.login,
    "repos" -> user.repos.map(repoToDBObject)
  )

  /** Insert a list of users into a collection. */
  def insertUsers(coll:MongoCollection)(users:Iterable[User]) {
    users.foreach { user => coll += userToDBObject(user) }
  }

  /**  Fetch users from GitHub and passes them to `inserter` */
  def ingestUsers(nusers:Int)(inserter:Iterable[User] => Unit) {
    val it = new GitHubUserIterator(token)
    val users = it.take(nusers).toList
    inserter(users)
```

```
    }

    def main(args:Array[String]) {
      val coll = MongoClient()("github")("users")
      val nusers = 500
      coll.dropCollection()
      val inserter = insertUsers(coll)_
      ingestUsers(inserter)(nusers)
    }

  }
```

Before diving into the details of how this program works, let's run it through SBT. You will want to query the API with authentication to avoid hitting the rate limit. Recall that we need to set the GHTOKEN environment variable:

```
$ GHTOKEN="e83638..." sbt
```

```
$ runMain InsertUsers
```

The program will take about five minutes to run (depending on your Internet connection). To verify that the program works, we can query the number of documents in the github database:

```
$ mongo github --quiet --eval "db.users.count()"
```

```
500
```

Let's break the code down. We first load the OAuth token to authenticate with the GithHub API. The token is stored as an environment variable, GHTOKEN. The token variable is a lazy val, so the token is loaded only when we formulate the first request to the API. We have already used this pattern in *Chapter 7, Web APIs*.

We then define two methods to transform from classes in the domain model to DBObject instances:

```
    def repoToDBObject(repo:Repo):DBObject = ...
    def userToDBObject(user:User):DBObject = ...
```

Armed with these two methods, we can add users to our MongoDB collection easily:

```
    def insertUsers(coll:MongoCollection)(users:Iterable[User]) {
      users.foreach { user => coll += userToDBObject(user) }
    }
```

We used currying to split the arguments of insertUsers. This lets us use insertUsers as a function factory:

```
    val inserter = insertUsers(coll)_
```

This creates a new method, `inserter`, with signature `Iterable[User] => Unit` that inserts users into `coll`. To see how this might come in useful, let's write a function to wrap the whole data ingestion process. This is how a first attempt at this function could look:

```
def ingestUsers(nusers:Int)(inserter:Iterable[User] => Unit) {
  val it = new GitHubUserIterator(token)
  val users = it.take(nusers).toList
  inserter(users)
}
```

Notice how `ingestUsers` takes a method that specifies how the list of users is inserted into the database as its second argument. This function encapsulates the entire code specific to insertion into a MongoDB collection. If we decide, at some later date, that we hate MongoDB and must insert the documents into a SQL database or write them to a flat file, all we need to do is pass a different `inserter` function to `ingestUsers`. The rest of the code remains the same. This demonstrates the increased flexibility afforded by using higher-order functions: we can easily build a framework and let the client code plug in the components that it needs.

The `ingestUsers` method, as defined previously, has one problem: if the `nusers` value is large, it will consume a lot of memory in constructing the entire list of users. A better solution would be to break it down into batches: we fetch a batch of users from the API, insert them into the database, and move on to the next batch. This allows us to control memory usage by changing the batch size. It is also more fault tolerant: if the program crashes, we can just restart from the last successfully inserted batch.

The `.grouped` method, available on all iterables, is useful for batching. It returns an iterator over fragments of the original iterable:

```
scala> val it = (0 to 10)
it: Range.Inclusive = Range(0, 1, 2, 3, 4, 5, 6, 7, 8, 9, 10)


scala> it.grouped(3).foreach { println } // In batches of 3
Vector(0, 1, 2)
Vector(3, 4, 5)
Vector(6, 7, 8)
Vector(9, 10)
```

Let's rewrite our `ingestUsers` method to use batches. We will also add a progress report after each batch in order to give the user some feedback:

```
/** Fetch users from GitHub and pass them to `inserter` */
def ingestUsers(nusers:Int)(inserter:Iterable[User] => Unit) {
```

```scala
    val batchSize = 100
    val it = new GitHubUserIterator(token)
    print("Inserted #users: ")
    it.take(nusers).grouped(batchSize).zipWithIndex.foreach {
      case (users, batchNumber) =>
        print(s"${batchNumber*batchSize} ")
        inserter(users)
    }
    println()
}
```

Let's look at the highlighted line more closely. We start from the user iterator, `it`. We then take the first `nusers`. This returns an `Iterator[User]` that, instead of happily churning through every user in the GitHub database, will terminate after `nusers`. We then group this iterator into batches of 100 users. The `.grouped` method returns `Iterator[Iterator[User]]`. We then zip each batch with its index so that we know which batch we are currently processing (we use this in the `print` statement). The `.zipWithIndex` method returns `Iterator[(Iterator[User], Int)]`. We unpack this tuple in the loop using a case statement that binds `users` to `Iterator[User]` and `batchNumber` to the index. Let's run this through SBT:

```
$ GHTOKEN="2502761..." sbt
> runMain InsertUsers
[info] Running InsertUsers
Inserted #users: 0 100 200 300 400
[success] Total time: 215 s, completed 01-Nov-2015 18:44:30
```

Extracting objects from the database

We now have a database populated with a few users. Let's query this database from the REPL:

```scala
scala> import com.mongodb.casbah.Imports._
import com.mongodb.casbah.Imports._


scala> val collection = MongoClient()("github")("users")
MongoCollection = users


scala> val maybeUser = collection.findOne
Option[collection.T] = Some({ "_id" : { "$oid" :
"562e922546f953739c43df02"} , "github_id" : 1 , "login" : "mojombo" ,
"repos" : ...
```

The `findOne` method returns a single `DBObject` object wrapped in an option, unless the collection is empty, in which case it returns `None`. We must therefore use the `get` method to extract the object:

```
scala> val user = maybeUser.get
collection.T = { "_id" : { "$oid" : "562e922546f953739c43df02"} ,
"github_id" : 1 , "login" : "mojombo" , "repos" : ...
```

As you learned earlier in this chapter, `DBObject` is a map-like object with keys of type `String` and values of type `AnyRef`:

```
scala> user("login")
AnyRef = mojombo
```

In general, we want to restore compile-time type information as early as possible when importing objects from the database: we do not want to pass `AnyRef`s around when we can be more specific. We can use the `getAs` method to extract a field and cast it to a specific type:

```
scala> user.getAs[String]("login")
Option[String] = Some(mojombo)
```

If the field is missing in the document or if the value cannot be cast, `getAs` will return `None`:

```
scala> user.getAs[Int]("login")
Option[Int] = None
```

The astute reader may note that the interface provided by `getAs[T]` is similar to the `read[T]` method that we defined on a JDBC result set in *Chapter 5*, *Scala and SQL through JDBC*.

If `getAs` fails (for instance, because the field is missing), we can use the `orElse` partial function to recover:

```
scala> val loginName = user.getAs[String]("login") orElse {
  println("No login field found. Falling back to 'name'")
  user.getAs[String]("name")
}
loginName: Option[String] = Some(mojombo)
```

The `getAsOrElse` method allows us to substitute a default value if the cast fails:

```
scala> user.getAsOrElse[Int]("id", 5)
Int = 1392879
```

Note that we can also use `getAsOrElse` to throw an exception:

```scala
scala> user.getAsOrElse[String]("name",
  throw new IllegalArgumentException(
    "Missing value for name")
)
java.lang.IllegalArgumentException: Missing value for name
...
```

Arrays embedded in documents can be cast to `List[T]` objects, where `T` is the type of elements in the array:

```scala
scala> user.getAsOrElse[List[DBObject]]("repos",
  List.empty[DBObject])
List[DBObject] = List({ "github_id" : 26899533 , "name" :
"30daysoflaptops.github.io" ...
```

Retrieving a single document at a time is not very useful. To retrieve all the documents in a collection, use the `.find` method:

```scala
scala> val userIterator = collection.find()
userIterator: collection.CursorType = non-empty iterator
```

This returns an iterator of `DBObject`s. To actually fetch the documents from the database, you need to materialize the iterator by transforming it into a collection, using, for instance, `.toList`:

```scala
scala> val userList = userIterator.toList
List[DBObject] = List({ "_id" : { "$oid": ...
```

Let's bring all of this together. We will write a toy program that prints the average number of repositories per user in our collection. The code works by fetching every document in the collection, extracting the number of repositories from each document, and then averaging over these:

```scala
// RepoNumber.scala

import com.mongodb.casbah.Imports._

object RepoNumber {

  /** Extract the number of repos from a DBObject
    * representing a user.
    */
  def extractNumber(obj:DBObject):Option[Int] = {
```

```scala
    val repos = obj.getAs[List[DBObject]]("repos") orElse {
      println("Could not find or parse 'repos' field")
      None
    }
    repos.map { _.size }
  }

  val collection = MongoClient()("github")("users")

  def main(args:Array[String]) {
    val userIterator = collection.find()

    // Convert from documents to Option[Int]
    val repoNumbers = userIterator.map { extractNumber }

    // Convert from Option[Int] to Int
    val wellFormattedNumbers = repoNumbers.collect {
      case Some(v) => v
    }.toList

    // Calculate summary statistics
    val sum = wellFormattedNumbers.reduce { _ + _ }
    val count = wellFormattedNumbers.size

    if (count == 0) {
      println("No repos found")
    }
    else {
      val mean = sum.toDouble / count.toDouble
      println(s"Total number of users with repos: $count")
      println(s"Total number of repos: $sum")
      println(s"Mean number of repos: $mean")
    }
  }
}
```

Let's run this through SBT:

```
> runMain RepoNumber
Total number of users with repos: 500
Total number of repos: 9649
Mean number of repos: 19.298
```

The code starts with the extractNumber function, which extracts the number of repositories from each DBObject. The return value is None if the document does not contain the repos field.

The main body of the code starts by creating an iterator over DBObjects in the collection. This iterator is then mapped through the extractNumber function, which transforms it into an iterator of Option[Int]. We then run .collect on this iterator to collect all the values that are not None, converting from Option[Int] to Int in the process. Only then do we materialize the iterator to a list using .toList. The resulting list, wellFormattedNumbers, has the List[Int] type. We then just take the mean of this list and print it to screen.

Note that, besides the extractNumber function, none of this program deals with Casbah-specific types: the iterator returned by .find() is just a Scala iterator. This makes Casbah straightforward to use: the only data type that you need to familiarize yourself with is DBObject (compare this with JDBC's ResultSet, which we had to explicitly wrap in a stream, for instance).

Complex queries

We now know how to convert DBObject instances to custom Scala classes. In this section, you will learn how to construct queries that only return a subset of the documents in the collection.

In the previous section, you learned to retrieve all the documents in a collection as follows:

```scala
scala> val objs = collection.find().toList
List[DBobject] = List({ "_id" : { "$oid" : "56365cec46f9534fae8ffd7f"}
,...
```

The collection.find() method returns an iterator over all the documents in the collection. By calling .toList on this iterator, we materialize it to a list.

We can customize which documents are returned by passing a query document to the .find method. For instance, we can retrieve documents for a specific login name:

```scala
scala> val query = DBObject("login" -> "mojombo")
query: DBObject = { "login" : "mojombo"}


scala> val objs = collection.find(query).toList
List[DBobject] = List({ "_id" : { "$oid" : "562e922546f953739c43df02"} ,
"login" : "mojombo",...
```

MongoDB queries are expressed as `DBObject` instances. Keys in the `DBObject` correspond to fields in the collection's documents, and the values are expressions controlling the allowed values of this field. Thus, `DBObject("login" -> "mojombo")` will select all the documents for which the `login` field is `mojombo`. Using a `DBObject` instance to represent a query might seem a little obscure, but it will quickly make sense if you read the MongoDB documentation (`https://docs.mongodb.org/manual/core/crud-introduction/`): queries are themselves just JSON objects in MongoDB. Thus, the fact that the query in Casbah is represented as a `DBObject` is consistent with other MongoDB client implementations. It also allows someone familiar with MongoDB to start writing Casbah queries in no time.

MongoDB supports more complex queries. For instance, to query everyone with `"github_id"` between 20 and 30, we can write the following query:

```scala
scala> val query = DBObject("github_id" ->
  DBObject("$gte" -> 20, "$lt" -> 30))
query: DBObject = { "github_id" : { "$gte" : 20 , "$lt" : 30}}
```

```scala
scala> collection.find(query).toList
List[com.mongodb.casbah.Imports.DBObject] = List({ "_id" : { "$oid" :
"562e922546f953739c43df0f"} , "github_id" : 23 , "login" : "takeo" , ...
```

We limit the range of values that `github_id` can take with `DBObject("$gte" -> 20, "$lt" -> 30)`. The `"$gte"` string indicates that `github_id` must be greater or equal to 20. Similarly, `"$lt"` denotes the *less than* operator. To get a full list of operators that you can use when querying, consult the MongoDB reference documentation (`http://docs.mongodb.org/manual/reference/operator/query/`).

So far, we have only looked at queries on top-level fields. Casbah also lets us query fields in subdocuments and arrays using the *dot* notation. In the context of array values, this will return all the documents for which at least one value in the array matches the query. For instance, to retrieve all users who have a repository whose main language is Scala:

```scala
scala> val query = DBObject("repos.language" -> "Scala")
query: DBObject = { "repos.language" : "Scala"}
```

```scala
scala> collection.find(query).toList
List[DBObject] = List({ "_id" : { "$oid" : "5635da4446f953234ca634df"},
"login" : "kevinclark"...
```

Casbah query DSL

Using DBObject instances to express queries can be very verbose and somewhat difficult to read. Casbah provides a DSL to express queries much more succinctly. For instance, to get all the documents with the github_id field between 20 and 30, we would write the following:

```scala
scala> collection.find("github_id" $gte 20 $lt 30).toList
List[com.mongodb.casbah.Imports.DBObject] = List({ "_id" : { "$oid" :
"562e922546f953739c43df0f"} , "github_id" : 23 , "login" : "takeo" ,
"repos" : ...
```

The operators provided by the DSL will automatically construct DBObject instances. Using the DSL operators as much as possible generally leads to much more readable and maintainable code.

Going into the full details of the query DSL is beyond the scope of this chapter. You should find it quite easy to use. For a full list of the operators supported by the DSL, refer to the Casbah documentation at http://mongodb.github.io/casbah/3.0/reference/query_dsl/. We summarize the most important operators here:

Operators	Description
"login" $eq "mojombo"	This selects documents whose login field is exactly mojombo
"login" $ne "mojombo"	This selects documents whose login field is not mojombo
"github_id" $gt 1 $lt 20	This selects documents with github_id greater than 1 and less than 20
"github_id" $gte 1 $lte 20	This selects documents with github_id greater than or equal to 1 and less than or equal to 20
"login" $in ("mojombo", "defunkt")	The login field is either mojombo or defunkt
"login" $nin ("mojombo", "defunkt")	The login field is not mojombo or defunkt
"login" $regex "^moj.*"	The login field matches the particular regular expression
"login" $exists true	The login field exists
$or("login" $eq "mojombo", "github_id" $gte 22)	Either the login field is mojombo or the github_id field is greater or equal to 22
$and("login" $eq "mojombo", "github_id" $gte 22)	The login field is mojombo and the github_id field is greater or equal to 22

We can also use the *dot* notation to query arrays and subdocuments. For instance, the following query will count all the users who have a repository in Scala:

```scala
scala> collection.find("repos.language" $eq "Scala").size
Int = 30
```

Custom type serialization

So far, we have only tried to serialize and deserialize simple types. What if we wanted to decode the language field in the repository array to an enumeration rather than a string? We might, for instance, define the following enumeration:

```scala
scala> object Language extends Enumeration {
  val Scala, Java, JavaScript = Value
}
defined object Language
```

Casbah lets us define custom serializers tied to a specific Scala type: we can inform Casbah that whenever it encounters an instance of the `Language.Value` type in a `DBObject`, the instance should be passed through a custom transformer that will convert it to, for instance, a string, before writing it to the database.

To define a custom serializer, we need to define a class that extends the `Transformer` trait. This trait exposes a single method, `transform(o:AnyRef):AnyRef`. Let's define a `LanguageTransformer` trait that transforms from `Language.Value` to `String`:

```scala
scala> import org.bson.{BSON, Transformer}
import org.bson.{BSON, Transformer}

scala> trait LanguageTransformer extends Transformer {
  def transform(o:AnyRef):AnyRef = o match {
    case l:Language.Value => l.toString
    case _ => o
  }
}
defined trait LanguageTransformer
```

We now need to register the trait to be used whenever an instance of type `Language.Value` needs to be decoded. We can do this using the `addEncodingHook` method:

```scala
scala> BSON.addEncodingHook(
  classOf[Language.Value], new LanguageTransformer {})
```

We can now construct DBObject instances containing values of the Language enumeration:

```scala
scala> val repoObj = DBObject(
  "github_id" -> 1234L,
  "language" -> Language.Scala
)
repoObj: DBObject = { "github_id" : 1234 , "language" : "Scala"}
```

What about the reverse? How do we tell Casbah to read the "language" field as Language.Value? This is not possible with custom deserializers: "Scala" is now stored as a string in the database. Thus, when it comes to deserialization, "Scala" is no different from, say, "mojombo". We thus lose type information when "Scala" is serialized.

Thus, while custom encoding hooks are useful for serialization, they are much less useful when deserializing. A cleaner, more consistent alternative to customize both serialization and deserialization is to use *type classes*. We have already covered how to use these extensively in *Chapter 5, Scala and SQL through JDBC*, in the context of serializing to and from SQL. The procedure here would be very similar:

1. Define a MongoReader[T] type class with a read(v:Any):T method.

2. Define concrete implementations of MongoReader in the MongoReader companion object for all types of interest, such as String, Language.Value.

3. Enrich DBObject with a read[T:MongoReader] method using the *pimp my library* pattern.

For instance, the implementation of MongoReader for Language.Value would be as follows:

```scala
implicit object LanguageReader extends MongoReader[Language.Value] {
  def read(v:Any):Language.Value = v match {
    case s:String => Language.withName(s)
  }
}
```

We could then do the same with a `MongoWriter` type class. Using type classes is an idiomatic and extensible approach to custom serialization and deserialization.

We provide a complete example of type classes in the code examples associated with this chapter (in the `typeclass` directory).

Beyond Casbah

We have only considered Casbah in this chapter. There are, however, other drivers for MongoDB.

ReactiveMongo is a driver that focusses on asynchronous read and writes to and from the database. All queries return a future, forcing asynchronous behavior. This fits in well with data streams or web applications.

Salat sits at a higher level than Casbah and aims to provide easy serialization and deserialization of case classes.

A full list of drivers is available at `https://docs.mongodb.org/ecosystem/drivers/scala/`.

Summary

In this chapter, you learned how to interact with a MongoDB database. By weaving the constructs learned in the previous chapter—pulling information from a web API—with those learned in this chapter, we can now build a concurrent, reactive program for data ingestion.

In the next chapter, you will learn to build distributed, concurrent structures with greater flexibility using Akka actors.

References

MongoDB: The Definitive Guide, by *Kristina Chodorow*, is a good introduction to MongoDB. It does not cover interacting with MongoDB in Scala at all, but Casbah is intuitive enough for anyone familiar with MongoDB.

Similarly, the MongoDB documentation (`https://docs.mongodb.org/manual/`) provides an in-depth discussion of MongoDB.

Casbah itself is well-documented (`http://mongodb.github.io/casbah/3.0/`). There is a *Getting Started* guide that is somewhat similar to this chapter and a complete reference guide that will fill in the gaps left by this chapter.

This gist, `https://gist.github.com/switzer/4218526`, implements type classes to serialize and deserialize objects in the domain model to `DBObject`s. The premise is a little different from the suggested usage of type classes in this chapter: we are converting from Scala types to `AnyRef` to be used as values in `DBObject`. However, the two approaches are complementary: one could imagine a set of type classes to convert from `User` or `Repo` to `DBObject` and another to convert from `Language.Value` to `AnyRef`.

9
Concurrency with Akka

Much of this book focusses on taking advantage of multicore and distributed architectures. In *Chapter 4, Parallel Collections and Futures*, you learned how to use parallel collections to distribute batch processing problems over several threads and how to perform asynchronous computations using futures. In *Chapter 7, Web APIs*, we applied this knowledge to query the GitHub API with several concurrent threads.

Concurrency abstractions such as futures and parallel collections simplify the enormous complexity of concurrent programming by limiting what you can do. Parallel collections, for instance, force you to phrase your parallelization problem as a sequence of pure functions on collections.

Actors offer a different way of thinking about concurrency. Actors are very good at encapsulating *state*. Managing state shared between different threads of execution is probably the most challenging part of developing concurrent applications, and, as we will discover in this chapter, actors make it manageable.

GitHub follower graph

In the previous two chapters, we explored the GitHub API, learning how to query the API and parse the results using *json-4s*.

Let's imagine that we want to extract the GitHub follower graph: we want a program that will start from a particular user, extract this user followers, and then extract their followers until we tell it to stop. The catch is that we don't know ahead of time what URLs we need to fetch: when we download the login names of a particular user's followers, we need to verify whether we have fetched these users previously. If not, we add them to a queue of users whose followers we need to fetch. Algorithm aficionados might recognize this as *breadth-first search*.

Let's outline how we might write this in a single-threaded way. The central components are a set of visited users and queue of future users to visit:

```
val seedUser = "odersky" // the origin of the network

// Users whose URLs need to be fetched
val queue = mutable.Queue(seedUser)

// set of users that we have already fetched
// (to avoid re-fetching them)
val fetchedUsers = mutable.Set.empty[String]

while (queue.nonEmpty) {
  val user = queue.dequeue
  if (!fetchedUsers(user)) {
    val followers = fetchFollowersForUser(user)
    followers foreach { follower =>
      // add the follower to queue of people whose
      // followers we want to find.
      queue += follower
    }
    fetchedUsers += user
  }
}
```

Here, the `fetchFollowersForUser` method has signature `String =>
Iterable[String]` and is responsible for taking a login name, transforming it into a URL in the GitHub API, querying the API, and extracting a list of followers from the response. We will not implement it here, but you can find a complete example in the `chap09/single_threaded` directory of the code examples for this book (`https://github.com/pbugnion/s4ds`). You should have all the tools to implement this yourself if you have read *Chapter 7, Web APIs*.

While this works, it will be painfully slow. The bottleneck is clearly the `fetchFollowersForUser` method, in particular, the part that queries the GitHub API. This program does not lend itself to the concurrency constructs that we have seen earlier in the book because we need to protect the state of the program, embodied by the user queue and set of fetched users, from race conditions. Note that it is not just a matter of making the queue and set thread-safe. We must also keep the two synchronized.

Actors offer an elegant abstraction to encapsulate state. They are lightweight objects that each perform a single task (possibly repeatedly) and communicate with each other by passing messages. The internal state of an actor can only be changed from within the actor itself. Importantly, actors only process messages one at a time, effectively preventing race conditions.

By hiding program state inside actors, we can reason about the program more effectively: if a bug is introduced that makes this state inconsistent, the culprit will be localized entirely in that actor.

Actors as people

In the previous section, you learned that an actor encapsulates state, interacting with the outside world through messages. Actors make concurrent programming more intuitive because they behave a little bit like an ideal workforce.

Let's think of an actor system representing a start-up with five people. There's Chris, the CEO, and Mark, who's in charge of marketing. Then there's Sally, who heads the engineering team. Sally has two minions, Bob and Kevin. As every good organization needs an organizational chart, refer to the following diagram:

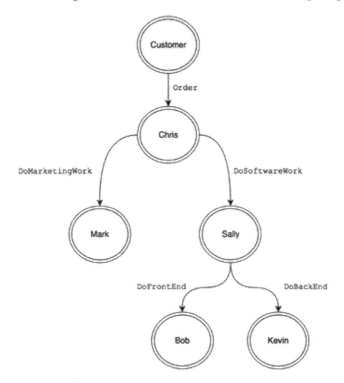

Let's say that Chris receives an order. He will look at the order, decide whether it is something that he can process himself, and if not, he will forward it to Mark or Sally. Let's assume that the order asks for a small program so Bob forwards the order to Sally. Sally is very busy working on a backlog of orders so she cannot process the order message straightaway, and it will just sit in her mailbox for a short while. When she finally gets round to processing the order, she might decide to split the order into several parts, some of which she will give to Kevin and some to Bob.

As Bob and Kevin complete items, they will send messages back to Sally to inform her. When every part of the order is fulfilled, Sally will aggregate the parts together and message either the customer directly or Chris with the results.

The task of keeping track of which jobs must be fulfilled to complete the order rests with Sally. When she receives messages from Bob and Kevin, she must update her list of tasks in progress and check whether every task related to this order is complete. This sort of coordination would be more challenging with traditional *synchronize* blocks: every access to the list of tasks in progress and to the list of completed tasks would need to be synchronized. By embedding this logic in Sally, who can only process a single message at a time, we can be sure that there will not be race conditions.

Our start-up works well because each person is responsible for doing a single thing: Chris either delegates to Mark or Sally, Sally breaks up orders into several parts and assigns them to Bob and Kevin, and Bob and Kevin fulfill each part. You might think "hold on, all the logic is embedded in Bob and Kevin, the employees at the bottom of the ladder who do all the actual work". Actors, unlike employees, are cheap, so if the logic embedded in an actor gets too complicated, it is easy to introduce additional layers of delegation until tasks get simple enough.

The employees in our start-up refuse to multitask. When they get a piece of work, they process it completely and then move on to the next task. This means that they cannot get muddled by the complexities of multitasking. Actors, by processing a single message at a time, greatly reduce the scope for introducing concurrency errors such as race conditions.

More importantly, by offering an abstraction that programmers can intuitively understand—that of human workers—Akka makes reasoning about concurrency easier.

Hello world with Akka

Let's install Akka. We add it as a dependency to our `build.sbt` file:

```
scalaVersion := "2.11.7"

libraryDependencies += "com.typesafe.akka" %% "akka-actor" %
  "2.4.0"
```

We can now import Akka as follows:

```
import akka.actor._
```

For our first foray into the world of actors, we will build an actor that echoes every message it receives. The code examples for this section are in a directory called `chap09/hello_akka` in the sample code provided with this book (`https://github.com/pbugnion/s4ds`):

```
// EchoActor.scala
import akka.actor._

class EchoActor extends Actor with ActorLogging {
  def receive = {
    case msg:String =>
      Thread.sleep(500)
      log.info(s"Received '$msg'")
  }
}
```

Let's pick this example apart, starting with the constructor. Our actor class must extend `Actor`. We also add `ActorLogging`, a utility trait that adds the `log` attribute.

The `Echo` actor exposes a single method, `receive`. This is the actor's only way of communicating with the external world. To be useful, all actors must expose a `receive` method. The `receive` method is a partial function, typically implemented with multiple `case` statements. When an actor starts processing a message, it will match it against every `case` statement until it finds one that matches. It will then execute the corresponding block.

Our echo actor accepts a single type of message, a plain string. When this message gets processed, the actor waits for half a second and then echoes the message to the log file.

Let's instantiate a couple of Echo actors and send them messages:

```scala
// HelloAkka.scala

import akka.actor._

object HelloAkka extends App {

  // We need an actor system before we can
  // instantiate actors
  val system = ActorSystem("HelloActors")

  // instantiate our two actors
  val echo1 = system.actorOf(Props[EchoActor], name="echo1")
  val echo2 = system.actorOf(Props[EchoActor], name="echo2")

  // Send them messages. We do this using the "!" operator
  echo1 ! "hello echo1"
  echo2 ! "hello echo2"
  echo1 ! "bye bye"

  // Give the actors time to process their messages,
  // then shut the system down to terminate the program
  Thread.sleep(500)
  system.shutdown
}
```

Running this gives us the following output:

```
[INFO] [07/19/2015 17:15:23.954] [HelloActor-akka.actor.default-
dispatcher-2] [akka://HelloActor/user/echo1] Received 'hello echo1'
[INFO] [07/19/2015 17:15:23.954] [HelloActor-akka.actor.default-
dispatcher-3] [akka://HelloActor/user/echo2] Received 'hello echo2'
[INFO] [07/19/2015 17:15:24.955] [HelloActor-akka.actor.default-
dispatcher-2] [akka://HelloActor/user/echo1] Received 'bye bye'
```

Note that the echo1 and echo2 actors are clearly acting concurrently: hello echo1 and hello echo2 are logged at the same time. The second message, passed to echo1, gets processed after the actor has finished processing hello echo1.

There are a few different things to note:

- To start instantiating actors, we must first create an actor system. There is typically a single actor system per application.

- The way in which we instantiate actors looks a little strange. Instead of calling the constructor, we create an actor properties object, `Props[T]`. We then ask the actor system to create an actor with these properties. In fact, we never instantiate actors with `new`: they are either created by calling the `actorOf` method in the actor system or a similar method from within another actor (more on this later).

We never call an actor's methods from outside that actor. The only way to interact with the actor is to send messages to it. We do this using the *tell* operator, `!`. There is thus no way to mess with an actor's internals from outside that actor (or at least, Akka makes it difficult to mess with an actor's internals).

Case classes as messages

In our "hello world" example, we constructed an actor that is expected to receive a string as message. Any object can be passed as a message, provided it is immutable. It is very common to use case classes to represent messages. This is better than using strings because of the additional type safety: the compiler will catch a typo in a case class but not in a string.

Let's rewrite our `EchoActor` to accept instances of case classes as messages. We will make it accept two different messages: `EchoMessage(message)` and `EchoHello`, which just echoes a default message. The examples for this section and the next are in the `chap09/hello_akka_case_classes` directory in the sample code provided with this book (`https://github.com/pbugnion/s4ds`).

A common Akka pattern is to define the messages that an actor can receive in the actor's companion object:

```
// EchoActor.scala

object EchoActor {
  case object EchoHello
  case class EchoMessage(msg:String)
}
```

Let's change the actor definition to accept these messages:

```
class EchoActor extends Actor with ActorLogging {
  import EchoActor._  // import the message definitions
  def receive = {
    case EchoHello => log.info("hello")
    case EchoMessage(s) => log.info(s)
  }
}
```

We can now send `EchoHello` and `EchoMessage` to our actors:

```
echo1 ! EchoActor.EchoHello
echo2 ! EchoActor.EchoMessage("We're learning Akka.")
```

Actor construction

Actor construction is a common source of difficulty for people new to Akka. Unlike (most) ordinary objects, you never instantiate actors explicitly. You would never write, for instance, `val echo = new EchoActor`. In fact, if you try this, Akka raises an exception.

Creating actors in Akka is a two-step process: you first create a `Props` object, which encapsulates the properties needed to construct an actor. The way to construct a `Props` object differs depending on whether the actor takes constructor arguments. If the constructor takes no arguments, we simply pass the actor class as a type parameter to `Props`:

```
val echoProps = Props[EchoActor]
```

If we have an actor whose constructor does take arguments, we must pass these as additional arguments when defining the `Props` object. Let's consider the following actor, for instance:

```
class TestActor(a:String, b:Int) extends Actor { ... }
```

We pass the constructor arguments to the `Props` object as follows:

```
val testProps = Props(classOf[TestActor], "hello", 2)
```

The `Props` instance just embodies the configuration for creating an actor. It does not actually create anything. To create an actor, we pass the `Props` instance to the `system.actorOf` method, defined on the `ActorSystem` instance:

```
val system = ActorSystem("HelloActors")
val echo1 = system.actorOf(echoProps, name="hello-1")
```

The `name` parameter is optional but is useful for logging and error messages. The value returned by `.actorOf` is not the actor itself: it is a *reference* to the actor (it helps to think of it as an address that the actor lives at) and has the `ActorRef` type. `ActorRef` is immutable, but it can be serialized and duplicated without affecting the underlying actor.

There is another way to create actors besides calling `actorOf` on the actor system: each actor exposes a `context.actorOf` method that takes a `Props` instance as its argument. The context is only accessible from within the actor:

```
class TestParentActor extends Actor {
  val echoChild = context.actorOf(echoProps, name="hello-child")
  ...
}
```

The difference between an actor created from the actor system and an actor created from another actor's context lies in the actor hierarchy: each actor has a parent. Any actor created within another actor's context will have that actor as its parent. An actor created by the actor system has a predefined actor, called the *user guardian*, as its parent. We will understand the importance of the actor hierarchy when we study the actor lifecycle at the end of this chapter.

A very common idiom is to define a `props` method in an actor's companion object that acts as a factory method for `Props` instances for that actor. Let's amend the `EchoActor` companion object:

```
object EchoActor {
  def props:Props = Props[EchoActor]

  // message case class definitions here
}
```

We can then instantiate the actor as follows:

```
val echoActor = system.actorOf(EchoActor.props)
```

Anatomy of an actor

Before diving into a full-blown application, let's look at the different components of the actor framework and how they fit together:

- **Mailbox**: A mailbox is basically a queue. Each actor has its own mailbox. When you send a message to an actor, the message lands in its mailbox and does nothing until the actor takes it off the queue and passes it through its `receive` method.

- **Messages**: Messages make synchronization between actors possible. A message can have any type with the sole requirement that it should be immutable. In general, it is better to use case classes or case objects to gain the compiler's help in checking message types.

- **Actor reference**: When we create an actor using `val echo1 = system.actorOf(Props[EchoActor])`, `echo1` has type `ActorRef`. An `ActorRef` is a proxy for an actor and is what the rest of the world interacts with: when you send a message, you send it to the `ActorRef`, not to the actor directly. In fact, you can never obtain a handle to an actor directly in Akka. An actor can obtain an `ActorRef` for itself using the `.self` method.

- **Actor context**: Each actor has a `context` attribute through which you can access methods to create or access other actors and find information about the outside world. We have already seen how to create new actors with `context.actorOf(props)`. We can also obtain a reference to an actor's parent through `context.parent`. An actor can also stop another actor with `context.stop(actorRef)`, where `actorRef` is a reference to the actor that we want to stop.

- **Dispatcher**: The dispatcher is the machine that actually executes the code in an actor. The default dispatcher uses a fork/join thread pool. Akka lets us use different dispatchers for different actors. Tweaking the dispatcher can be useful to optimize the performance and give priority to certain actors. The dispatcher that an actor runs on is accessible through `context.dispatcher`. Dispatchers implement the `ExecutionContext` interface so they can be used to run futures.

Follower network crawler

The end game for this chapter is to build a crawler to explore GitHub's follower graph. We have already outlined how we can do this in a single-threaded manner earlier in this chapter. Let's design an actor system to do this concurrently.

The moving parts in the code are the data structures managing which users have been fetched or are being fetched. These need to be encapsulated in an actor to avoid race conditions arising from multiple actors trying to change them concurrently. We will therefore create a *fetcher manager* actor whose job is to keep track of which users have been fetched and which users we are going to fetch next.

The part of the code that is likely to be a bottleneck is querying the GitHub API. We therefore want to be able to scale the number of workers doing this concurrently. We will create a pool of *fetchers*, actors responsible for querying the API for the followers of a particular user. Finally, we will create an actor whose responsibility is to interpret the API's response. This actor will forward its interpretation of the response to another actor who will extract the followers and give them to the fetcher manager.

This is what the architecture of the program will look like:

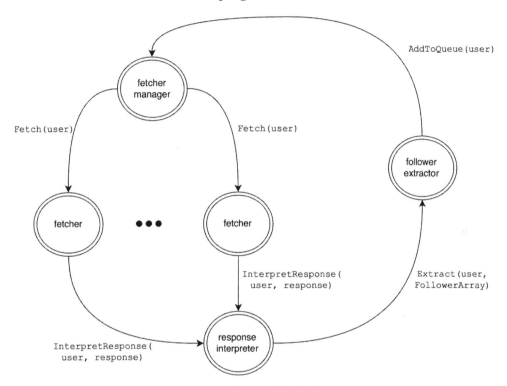

Actor system for our GitHub API crawler

Each actor in our program performs a single task: fetchers just query the GitHub API and the queue manager just distributes work to the fetchers. Akka best practice dictates giving actors as narrow an area of responsibility as possible. This enables better granularity when scaling out (for instance, by adding more fetcher actors, we just parallelize the bottleneck) and better resilience: if an actor fails, it will only affect his area of responsibility. We will explore actor failure later on in this chapter.

We will build the app in several steps, exploring the Akka toolkit as we write the program. Let's start with the build.sbt file. Besides Akka, we will mark scalaj-http and json4s as dependencies:

```
// build.sbt
scalaVersion := "2.11.7"

libraryDependencies ++= Seq(
  "org.json4s" %% "json4s-native" % "3.2.10",
  "org.scalaj" %% "scalaj-http" % "1.1.4",
  "com.typesafe.akka" %% "akka-actor" % "2.3.12"
)
```

Fetcher actors

The workhorse of our application is the fetcher, the actor responsible for fetching the follower details from GitHub. In the first instance, our actor will accept a single message, Fetch(user). It will fetch the followers corresponding to user and log the response to screen. We will use the recipes developed in *Chapter 7, Web APIs*, to query the GitHub API with an OAuth token. We will inject the token through the actor constructor.

Let's start with the companion object. This will contain the definition of the Fetch(user) message and two factory methods to create the Props instances. You can find the code examples for this section in the chap09/fetchers_alone directory in the sample code provided with this book (https://github.com/pbugnion/s4ds):

```
// Fetcher.scala
import akka.actor._
import scalaj.http._
import scala.concurrent.Future

object Fetcher {
  // message definitions
  case class Fetch(login:String)

  // Props factory definitions
  def props(token:Option[String]):Props =
    Props(classOf[Fetcher], token)
  def props():Props = Props(classOf[Fetcher], None)
}
```

Let's now define the fetcher itself. We will wrap the call to the GitHub API in a future. This avoids a single slow request blocking the actor. When our actor receives a `Fetch` request, it wraps this request into a future, sends it off, and can then process the next message. Let's go ahead and implement our actor:

```scala
// Fetcher.scala
class Fetcher(val token:Option[String])
extends Actor with ActorLogging {
  import Fetcher._ // import message definition

  // We will need an execution context for the future.
  // Recall that the dispatcher doubles up as execution
  // context.
  import context.dispatcher

  def receive = {
    case Fetch(login) => fetchUrl(login)
  }

  private def fetchUrl(login:String) {
    val unauthorizedRequest = Http(
      s"https://api.github.com/users/$login/followers")
    val authorizedRequest = token.map { t =>
      unauthorizedRequest.header("Authorization", s"token $t")
    }

    // Prepare the request: try to use the authorized request
    // if a token was given, and fall back on an unauthorized
    // request
    val request = authorizedRequest.getOrElse(unauthorizedRequest)

    // Fetch from github
    val response = Future { request.asString }
    response.onComplete { r =>
      log.info(s"Response from $login: $r")
    }
  }

}
```

Let's instantiate an actor system and four fetchers to check whether our actor is working as expected. We will read the GitHub token from the environment, as described in *Chapter 7, Web APIs*, then create four actors and ask each one to fetch the followers of a particular GitHub user. We wait five seconds for the requests to get completed, and then shut the system down:

```scala
// FetcherDemo.scala
import akka.actor._

object FetcherDemo extends App {
  import Fetcher._ // Import the messages

  val system = ActorSystem("fetchers")

  // Read the github token if present.
  val token = sys.env.get("GHTOKEN")

  val fetchers = (0 until 4).map { i =>
    system.actorOf(Fetcher.props(token))
  }

  fetchers(0) ! Fetch("odersky")
  fetchers(1) ! Fetch("derekwyatt")
  fetchers(2) ! Fetch("rkuhn")
  fetchers(3) ! Fetch("tototoshi")

  Thread.sleep(5000) // Wait for API calls to finish
  system.shutdown // Shut system down

}
```

Let's run the code through SBT:

```
$ GHTOKEN="2502761..." sbt run

[INFO] [11/08/2015 16:28:06.500] [fetchers-akka.actor.default-
dispatcher-2] [akka://fetchers/user/$d] Response from tototoshi: Success
(HttpResponse([{"login":"akr4","id":10892,"avatar_url":"https://avatars.
githubusercontent.com/u/10892?v=3","gravatar_id":""...
```

Notice how we explicitly need to shut the actor system down using `system.shutdown`. The program hangs until the system is shut down. However, shutting down the system will stop all the actors, so we need to make sure that they have finished working. We do this by inserting a call to `Thread.sleep`.

Using `Thread.sleep` to wait until the API calls have finished to shut down the actor system is a little crude. A better approach could be to let the actors signal back to the system that they have completed their task. We will see examples of this pattern later when we implement the *fetcher manager* actor.

Akka includes a feature-rich *scheduler* to schedule events. We can use the scheduler to replace the call to `Thread.sleep` by scheduling a system shutdown five seconds in the future. This is preferable as the scheduler does not block the calling thread, unlike `Thread.sleep`. To use the scheduler, we need to import a global execution context and the duration module:

```
// FetcherDemoWithScheduler.scala

import scala.concurrent.ExecutionContext.Implicits.global
import scala.concurrent.duration._
```

We can then schedule a system shutdown by replacing our call to `Thread.sleep` with the following:

```
system.scheduler.scheduleOnce(5.seconds) { system.shutdown }
```

Besides `scheduleOnce`, the scheduler also exposes a `schedule` method that lets you schedule events to happen regularly (every two seconds, for instance). This is useful for heartbeat checks or monitoring systems. For more information, read the API documentation on the scheduler available at `http://doc.akka.io/docs/akka/snapshot/scala/scheduler.html`.

Note that we are actually cheating a little bit here by not fetching every follower. The response to the follower's query is actually paginated, so we would need to fetch several pages to fetch all the followers. Adding logic to the actor to do this is not terribly complicated. We will ignore this for now and assume that users are capped at 100 followers each.

Routing

In the previous example, we created four fetchers and dispatched messages to them, one after the other. We have a pool of identical actors among which we distribute tasks. Manually routing the messages to the right actor to maximize the utilization of our pool is painful and error-prone. Fortunately, Akka provides us with several routing strategies that we can use to distribute work among our pool of actors. Let's rewrite the previous example with automatic routing. You can find the code examples for this section in the chap09/fetchers_routing directory in the sample code provided with this book (https://github.com/pbugnion/s4ds). We will reuse the same definition of Fetchers and its companion object as we did in the previous section.

Let's start by importing the routing package:

```
// FetcherDemo.scala
import akka.routing._
```

A *router* is an actor that forwards the messages that it receives to its children. The easiest way to define a pool of actors is to tell Akka to create a router and pass it a Props object for its children. The router will then manage the creation of the workers directly. In our example (we will only comment on the parts that differ from the previous example in the text, but you can find the full code in the fetchers_routing directory with the examples for this chapter), we replace the custom Fetcher creation code with the following:

```
// FetcherDemo.scala

// Create a router with 4 workers of props Fetcher.props()
val router = system.actorOf(
  RoundRobinPool(4).props(Fetcher.props(token))
)
```

We can then send the fetch messages directly to the router. The router will route the messages to the children in a round-robin manner:

```
List("odersky", "derekwyatt", "rkuhn", "tototoshi").foreach {
  login => router ! Fetch(login)
}
```

We used a round-robin router in this example. Akka offers many different types of routers, including routers with dynamic pool size, to cater to different types of load balancing. Head over to the Akka documentation for a list of all the available routers, at http://doc.akka.io/docs/akka/snapshot/scala/routing.html.

Message passing between actors

Merely logging the API response is not very useful. To traverse the follower graph, we must perform the following:

- Check the return code of the response to make sure that the GitHub API was happy with our request
- Parse the response as JSON
- Extract the login names of the followers and, if we have not fetched them already, push them into the queue

You learned how to do all these things in *Chapter 7*, *Web APIs*, but not in the context of actors.

We could just add the additional processing steps to the `receive` method of our `Fetcher` actor: we could add further transformations to the API response by future composition. However, having actors do several different things, and possibly failing in several different ways, is an anti-pattern: when we learn about managing the actor life cycle, we will see that it becomes much more difficult to reason about our actor systems if the actors contain several bits of logic.

We will therefore use a pipeline of three different actors:

- The fetchers, which we have already encountered, are responsible just for fetching a URL from GitHub. They will fail if the URL is badly formatted or they cannot access the GitHub API.

- The response interpreter is responsible for taking the response from the GitHub API and parsing it to JSON. If it fails at any step, it will just log the error (in a real application, we might take different corrective actions depending on the type of failure). If it manages to extract JSON successfully, it will pass the JSON array to the follower extractor.

- The follower extractor will extract the followers from the JSON array and pass them on to the queue of users whose followers we need to fetch.

We have already built the fetchers, though we will need to modify them to forward the API response to the response interpreter rather than just logging it.

You can find the code examples for this section in the `chap09/all_workers` directory in the sample code provided with this book (`https://github.com/pbugnion/s4ds`).The first step is to modify the fetchers so that, instead of logging the response, they forward the response to the response interpreter. To be able to forward the response to the response interpreter, the fetchers will need a reference to this actor. We will just pass the reference to the response interpreter through the fetcher constructor, which is now:

```scala
// Fetcher.scala
class Fetcher(
  val token:Option[String],
  val responseInterpreter:ActorRef)
extends Actor with ActorLogging {
  ...
}
```

We must also modify the `Props` factory method in the companion object:

```scala
// Fetcher.scala
def props(
  token:Option[String], responseInterpreter:ActorRef
):Props = Props(classOf[Fetcher], token, responseInterpreter)
```

We must also modify the `receive` method to forward the HTTP response to the interpreter rather than just logging it:

```scala
// Fetcher.scala
class Fetcher(...) extends Actor with ActorLogging {
  ...
  def receive = {
    case Fetch(login) => fetchFollowers(login)
  }

  private def fetchFollowers(login:String) {
    val unauthorizedRequest = Http(
      s"https://api.github.com/users/$login/followers")
    val authorizedRequest = token.map { t =>
      unauthorizedRequest.header("Authorization", s"token $t")
    }

    val request = authorizedRequest.getOrElse(unauthorizedRequest)
    val response = Future { request.asString }

    // Wrap the response in an InterpretResponse message and
    // forward it to the interpreter.
```

```
    response.onComplete { r =>
      responseInterpreter !
        ResponseInterpreter.InterpretResponse(login, r)
    }
  }
}
```

The *response interpreter* takes the response, decides if it is valid, parses it to JSON, and forwards it to a follower extractor. The response interpreter will need a reference to the follower extractor, which we will pass in the constructor.

Let's start by defining the `ResponseInterpreter` companion. It will just contain the definition of the messages that the response interpreter can receive and a factory to create a `Props` object to help with instantiation:

```
// ResponseInterpreter.scala
import akka.actor._
import scala.util._

import scalaj.http._
import org.json4s._
import org.json4s.native.JsonMethods._

object ResponseInterpreter {

  // Messages
  case class InterpretResponse(
    login:String, response:Try[HttpResponse[String]]
  )

  // Props factory
  def props(followerExtractor:ActorRef) =
    Props(classOf[ResponseInterpreter], followerExtractor)
}
```

The body of `ResponseInterpreter` should feel familiar: when the actor receives a message giving it a response to interpret, it parses it to JSON using the techniques that you learned in *Chapter 7, Web APIs*. If we parse the response successfully, we forward the parsed JSON to the follower extractor. If we fail to parse the response (possibly because it was badly formatted), we just log the error. We could recover from this in other ways, for instance, by re-adding this login to the queue manager to be fetched again:

```
// ResponseInterpreter.scala
class ResponseInterpreter(followerExtractor:ActorRef)
```

```scala
extends Actor with ActorLogging {
  // Import the message definitions
  import ResponseInterpreter._

  def receive = {
    case InterpretResponse(login, r) => interpret(login, r)
  }

  // If the query was successful, extract the JSON response
  // and pass it onto the follower extractor.
  // If the query failed, or is badly formatted, throw an error
  // We should also be checking error codes here.
  private def interpret(
    login:String, response:Try[HttpResponse[String]]
  ) = response match {
    case Success(r) => responseToJson(r.body) match {
      case Success(jsonResponse) =>
        followerExtractor ! FollowerExtractor.Extract(
          login, jsonResponse)
      case Failure(e) =>
        log.error(
          s"Error parsing response to JSON for $login: $e")
    }
    case Failure(e) => log.error(
      s"Error fetching URL for $login: $e")
  }

  // Try and parse the response body as JSON.
  // If successful, coerce the `JValue` to a `JArray`.
  private def responseToJson(responseBody:String):Try[JArray] = {
    val jvalue = Try { parse(responseBody) }
    jvalue.flatMap {
      case a:JArray => Success(a)
      case _ => Failure(new IllegalStateException(
        "Incorrectly formatted JSON: not an array"))
    }
  }
}
```

We now have two-thirds of our worker actors. The last link is the follower extractor. This actor's job is simple: it takes the JArray passed to it by the response interpreter and converts it to a list of followers. For now, we will just log this list, but when we build our fetcher manager, the follower extractor will send messages asking the manager to add the followers to its queue of logins to fetch.

As before, the companion just defines the messages that this actor can receive and a Props factory method:

```scala
// FollowerExtractor.scala
import akka.actor._

import org.json4s._
import org.json4s.native.JsonMethods._

object FollowerExtractor {

  // Messages
  case class Extract(login:String, jsonResponse:JArray)

  // Props factory method
  def props = Props[FollowerExtractor]
}
```

The `FollowerExtractor` class receives `Extract` messages containing a `JArray` of information representing a follower. It extracts the `login` field and logs it:

```scala
class FollowerExtractor extends Actor with ActorLogging {
  import FollowerExtractor._
  def receive = {
    case Extract(login, followerArray) => {
      val followers = extractFollowers(followerArray)
      log.info(s"$login -> ${followers.mkString(", ")}")
    }
  }

  def extractFollowers(followerArray:JArray) = for {
    JObject(follower) <- followerArray
    JField("login", JString(login)) <- follower
  } yield login
}
```

Let's write a new `main` method to exercise all our actors:

```scala
// FetchNetwork.scala

import akka.actor._
import akka.routing._
import scala.concurrent.ExecutionContext.Implicits.global
```

```scala
import scala.concurrent.duration._

object FetchNetwork extends App {

  import Fetcher._ // Import messages and factory method

  // Get token if exists
  val token = sys.env.get("GHTOKEN")

  val system = ActorSystem("fetchers")

  // Instantiate actors
  val followerExtractor = system.actorOf(FollowerExtractor.props)
  val responseInterpreter =
    system.actorOf(ResponseInterpreter.props(followerExtractor))

  val router = system.actorOf(RoundRobinPool(4).props(
    Fetcher.props(token, responseInterpreter))
  )

  List("odersky", "derekwyatt", "rkuhn", "tototoshi") foreach {
    login => router ! Fetch(login)
  }

  // schedule a shutdown
  system.scheduler.scheduleOnce(5.seconds) { system.shutdown }

}
```

Let's run this through SBT:

```
$ GHTOKEN="2502761d..." sbt run

[INFO] [11/05/2015 20:09:37.048] [fetchers-akka.actor.default-
dispatcher-3] [akka://fetchers/user/$a] derekwyatt -> adulteratedjedi,
joonas, Psycojoker, trapd00r, tyru, ...

[INFO] [11/05/2015 20:09:37.050] [fetchers-akka.actor.default-
dispatcher-3] [akka://fetchers/user/$a] tototoshi -> akr4, yuroyoro,
seratch, yyuu, ...

[INFO] [11/05/2015 20:09:37.051] [fetchers-akka.actor.default-
dispatcher-3] [akka://fetchers/user/$a] odersky -> misto, gkossakowski,
mushtaq, ...

[INFO] [11/05/2015 20:09:37.052] [fetchers-akka.actor.default-
dispatcher-3] [akka://fetchers/user/$a] rkuhn -> arnbak, uzoice, jond3k,
TimothyKlim, relrod, ...
```

Queue control and the pull pattern

We have now defined the three worker actors in our crawler application. The next step is to define the manager. The *fetcher manager* is responsible for keeping a queue of logins to fetch as well as a set of login names that we have already seen in order to avoid fetching the same logins more than once.

A first attempt might involve building an actor that keeps a set of users that we have already seen and just dispatches it to a round-robin router for fetchers when it is given a new user to fetch. The problem with this approach is that the number of messages in the fetchers' mailboxes would accumulate quickly: for each API query, we are likely to get tens of followers, each of which is likely to make it back to a fetcher's inbox. This gives us very little control over the amount of work piling up.

The first problem that this is likely to cause involves the GitHub API rate limit: even with authentication, we are limited to 5,000 requests per hour. It would be useful to stop queries as soon as we hit this threshold. We cannot be responsive if each fetcher has a backlog of hundreds of users that they need to fetch.

A better alternative is to use a *pull* system: the fetchers request work from a central queue when they find themselves idle. Pull systems are common in Akka when we have a producer that produces work faster than consumers can process it (refer to `http://www.michaelpollmeier.com/akka-work-pulling-pattern/`).

Conversations between the manager and fetchers will proceed as follows:

- If the manager goes from a state of having no work to having work, it sends a `WorkAvailable` message to all the fetchers.

- Whenever a fetcher receives a `WorkAvailable` message or when it completes an item of work, it sends a `GiveMeWork` message to the queue manager.

- When the queue manager receives a `GiveMeWork` message, it ignores the request if no work is available or it is throttled. If it has work, it sends a `Fetch(user)` message to the actor.

Let's start by modifying our fetcher. You can find the code examples for this section in the `chap09/ghub_crawler` directory in the sample code provided with this book (`https://github.com/pbugnion/s4ds`). We will pass a reference to the fetcher manager through the constructor. We need to change the companion object to add the `WorkAvailable` message and the `props` factory to include the reference to the manager:

```
// Fecther.scala
object Fetcher {
  case class Fetch(url:String)
```

```
    case object WorkAvailable

    def props(
      token:Option[String],
      fetcherManager:ActorRef,
      responseInterpreter:ActorRef):Props =
        Props(classOf[Fetcher],
          token, fetcherManager, responseInterpreter)
}
```

We also need to change the `receive` method so that it queries the `FetcherManager` asking for more work once it's done processing a request or when it receives a `WorkAvailable` message.

This is the final version of the fetchers:

```
class Fetcher(
  val token:Option[String],
  val fetcherManager:ActorRef,
  val responseInterpreter:ActorRef)
extends Actor with ActorLogging {
  import Fetcher._
  import context.dispatcher

  def receive = {
    case Fetch(login) => fetchFollowers(login)
    case WorkAvailable =>
      fetcherManager ! FetcherManager.GiveMeWork
  }

  private def fetchFollowers(login:String) {
    val unauthorizedRequest = Http(
      s"https://api.github.com/users/$login/followers")
    val authorizedRequest = token.map { t =>
      unauthorizedRequest.header("Authorization", s"token $t")
    }
    val request = authorizedRequest.getOrElse(unauthorizedRequest)
    val response = Future { request.asString }

    response.onComplete { r =>
      responseInterpreter !
        ResponseInterpreter.InterpretResponse(login, r)
      fetcherManager ! FetcherManager.GiveMeWork
    }
  }

}
```

Now that we have a working definition of the fetchers, let's build the
`FetcherManager`. This is the most complex actor that we have built so far, and,
before we dive into building it, we need to learn a bit more about the components of
the Akka toolkit.

Accessing the sender of a message

When our fetcher manager receives a `GiveMeWork` request, we will need to send
work back to the correct fetcher. We can access the actor who sent a message
using the `sender` method, which is a method of `Actor` that returns the `ActorRef`
corresponding to the actor who sent the message currently being processed. The
`case` statement corresponding to `GiveMeWork` in the fetcher manager is therefore:

```
def receive = {
  case GiveMeWork =>
    login = // get next login to fetch
    sender ! Fetcher.Fetch(login)
  ...
}
```

As `sender` is a *method*, its return value will change for every new incoming message.
It should therefore only be used synchronously with the `receive` method. In
particular, using it in a future is dangerous:

```
def receive = {
  case DoSomeWork =>
    val work = Future { Thread.sleep(20000) ; 5 }
    work.onComplete { result =>
      sender ! Complete(result) // NO!
    }
}
```

The problem is that when the future is completed 20 seconds after the message is
processed, the actor will, in all likelihood, be processing a different message so the
return value of `sender` will have changed. We will thus send the `Complete` message
to a completely different actor.

If you need to reply to a message outside of the `receive` method, such as when a future completes, you should bind the value of the current sender to a variable:

```
def receive = {
  case DoSomeWork =>
    // bind the current value of sender to a val
    val requestor = sender
    val work = Future { Thread.sleep(20000) ; 5 }
    work.onComplete { result => requestor ! Complete(result) }
}
```

Stateful actors

The behavior of the fetcher manager depends on whether it has work to give out to the fetchers:

- If it has work to give, it needs to respond to `GiveMeWork` messages with a `Fetcher.Fetch` message

- If it does not have work, it must ignore the `GiveMeWork` messages and, if work gets added, it must send a `WorkAvailable` message to the fetchers

Encoding the notion of state is straightforward in Akka. We specify different `receive` methods and switch from one to the other depending on the state. We will define the following `receive` methods for our fetcher manager, corresponding to each of the states:

```
// receive method when the queue is empty
def receiveWhileEmpty: Receive = {
    ...
}

// receive method when the queue is not empty
def receiveWhileNotEmpty: Receive = {
    ...
}
```

Note that we must define the return type of the receive methods as `Receive`. To switch the actor from one method to the other, we can use `context.become(methodName)`. Thus, for instance, when the last login name is popped off the queue, we can transition to using the `receiveWhileEmpty` method with `context.become(receiveWhileEmpty)`. We set the initial state by assigning `receiveWhileEmpty` to the `receive` method:

```
def receive = receiveWhileEmpty
```

Follower network crawler

We are now ready to code up the remaining pieces of our network crawler. The largest missing piece is the fetcher manager. Let's start with the companion object. As with the worker actors, this just contains the definitions of the messages that the actor can receive and a factory to create the `Props` instance:

```scala
// FetcherManager.scala
import scala.collection.mutable
import akka.actor._

object FetcherManager {
  case class AddToQueue(login:String)
  case object GiveMeWork

  def props(token:Option[String], nFetchers:Int) =
    Props(classOf[FetcherManager], token, nFetchers)
}
```

The manager can receive two messages: `AddToQueue`, which tells it to add a username to the queue of users whose followers need to be fetched, and `GiveMeWork`, emitted by the fetchers when they are unemployed.

The manager will be responsible for launching the fetchers, response interpreter, and follower extractor, as well as maintaining an internal queue of usernames and a set of usernames that we have seen:

```scala
// FetcherManager.scala

class FetcherManager(val token:Option[String], val nFetchers:Int)
extends Actor with ActorLogging {

  import FetcherManager._

  // queue of usernames whose followers we need to fetch
  val fetchQueue = mutable.Queue.empty[String]

  // set of users we have already fetched.
  val fetchedUsers = mutable.Set.empty[String]

  // Instantiate worker actors
  val followerExtractor = context.actorOf(
    FollowerExtractor.props(self))
  val responseInterpreter = context.actorOf(
    ResponseInterpreter.props(followerExtractor))
```

```scala
    val fetchers = (0 until nFetchers).map { i =>
      context.actorOf(
        Fetcher.props(token, self, responseInterpreter))
    }

    // receive method when the actor has work:
    // If we receive additional work, we just push it onto the
    // queue.
    // If we receive a request for work from a Fetcher,
    // we pop an item off the queue. If that leaves the
    // queue empty, we transition to the 'receiveWhileEmpty'
    // method.
    def receiveWhileNotEmpty:Receive = {
      case AddToQueue(login) => queueIfNotFetched(login)
      case GiveMeWork =>
        val login = fetchQueue.dequeue
        // send a Fetch message back to the sender.
        // we can use the `sender` method to reply to a message
        sender ! Fetcher.Fetch(login)
        if (fetchQueue.isEmpty) {
          context.become(receiveWhileEmpty)
        }
    }

    // receive method when the actor has no work:
    // if we receive work, we add it onto the queue, transition
    // to a state where we have work, and notify the fetchers
    // that work is available.
    def receiveWhileEmpty:Receive = {
      case AddToQueue(login) =>
        queueIfNotFetched(login)
        context.become(receiveWhileNotEmpty)
        fetchers.foreach { _ ! Fetcher.WorkAvailable }
      case GiveMeWork => // do nothing
    }

    // Start with an empty queue.
    def receive = receiveWhileEmpty

    def queueIfNotFetched(login:String) {
      if (! fetchedUsers(login)) {
        log.info(s"Pushing $login onto queue")
        // or do something useful...
        fetchQueue += login
```

```
        fetchedUsers += login
      }
    }
  }
```

We now have a fetcher manager. The rest of the code can remain the same, apart from the follower extractor. Instead of logging followers names, it must send `AddToQueue` messages to the manager. We will pass a reference to the manager at construction time:

```scala
// FollowerExtractor.scala
import akka.actor._
import org.json4s._
import org.json4s.native.JsonMethods._

object FollowerExtractor {

  // messages
  case class Extract(login:String, jsonResponse:JArray)

  // props factory method
  def props(manager:ActorRef) =
    Props(classOf[FollowerExtractor], manager)
}

class FollowerExtractor(manager:ActorRef)
extends Actor with ActorLogging {
  import FollowerExtractor._

  def receive = {
    case Extract(login, followerArray) =>
      val followers = extractFollowers(followerArray)
      followers foreach { f =>
        manager ! FetcherManager.AddToQueue(f)
      }
  }

  def extractFollowers(followerArray:JArray) = for {
    JObject(follower) <- followerArray
    JField("login", JString(login)) <- follower
  } yield login

}
```

The `main` method running all this is remarkably simple as all the code to instantiate actors has been moved to the `FetcherManager`. We just need to instantiate the manager and give it the first node in the network, and it will do the rest:

```
// FetchNetwork.scala
import akka.actor._

object FetchNetwork extends App {

  // Get token if exists
  val token = sys.env.get("GHTOKEN")

  val system = ActorSystem("GithubFetcher")
  val manager = system.actorOf(FetcherManager.props(token, 2))
  manager ! FetcherManager.AddToQueue("odersky")

}
```

Notice how we do not attempt to shut down the actor system anymore. We will just let it run, crawling the network, until we stop it or hit the authentication limit. Let's run this through SBT:

```
$ GHTOKEN="2502761d..." sbt "runMain FetchNetwork"

[INFO] [11/06/2015 06:31:04.614] [GithubFetcher-akka.actor.default-
dispatcher-2] [akka://GithubFetcher/user/$a] Pushing odersky onto queue

[INFO] [11/06/2015 06:31:05.563] [GithubFetcher-akka.actor.default-
dispatcher-4] [akka://GithubFetcher/user/$a] Pushing misto onto
queueINFO] [11/06/2015 06:31:05.563] [GithubFetcher-akka.actor.default-
dispatcher-4] [akka://GithubFetcher/user/$a] Pushing gkossakowski onto
queue

^C
```

Our program does not actually do anything useful with the followers that it retrieves besides logging them. We could replace the `log.info` call to, for instance, store the nodes in a database or draw the graph to screen.

Fault tolerance

Real programs fail, and they fail in unpredictable ways. Akka, and the Scala community in general, favors planning explicitly for failure rather than trying to write infallible applications. A *fault tolerant* system is a system that can continue to operate when one or more of its components fails. The failure of an individual subsystem does not necessarily mean the failure of the application. How does this apply to Akka?

The actor model provides a natural unit to encapsulate failure: the actor. When an actor throws an exception while processing a message, the default behavior is for the actor to restart, but the exception does not leak out and affect the rest of the system. For instance, let's introduce an arbitrary failure in the response interpreter. We will modify the `receive` method to throw an exception when it is asked to interpret the response for `misto`, one of Martin Odersky's followers:

```
// ResponseInterpreter.scala
def receive = {
  case InterpretResponse("misto", r) =>
    throw new IllegalStateException("custom error")
  case InterpretResponse(login, r) => interpret(login, r)
}
```

If you rerun the code through SBT, you will notice that an error gets logged. The program does not crash, however. It just continues as normal:

```
[ERROR] [11/07/2015 12:05:58.938] [GithubFetcher-akka.actor.default-
dispatcher-2] [akka://GithubFetcher/user/$a/$b] custom error

java.lang.IllegalStateException: custom error

  at ResponseInterpreter$

   ...

[INFO] [11/07/2015 12:05:59.117] [GithubFetcher-akka.actor.default-
dispatcher-2] [akka://GithubFetcher/user/$a] Pushing samfoo onto queue
```

None of the followers of `misto` will get added to the queue: he never made it past the `ResponseInterpreter` stage. Let's step through what happens when the exception gets thrown:

- The interpreter is sent the `InterpretResponse("misto", ...)` message. This causes it to throw an exception and it dies. None of the other actors are affected by the exception.

- A fresh instance of the response interpreter is created with the same Props instance as the recently deceased actor.

- When the response interpreter has finished initializing, it gets bound to the same `ActorRef` as the deceased actor. This means that, as far as the rest of the system is concerned, nothing has changed.

- The mailbox is tied to `ActorRef` rather than the actor, so the new response interpreter will have the same mailbox as its predecessor, without the offending message.

Thus, if, for whatever reason, our crawler crashes when fetching or parsing the response for a user, the application will be minimally affected — we will just not fetch this user's followers.

Any internal state that an actor carries is lost when it restarts. Thus, if, for instance, the fetcher manager died, we would lose the current value of the queue and visited users. The risks associated with losing the internal state can be mitigated by the following:

- Adopting a different strategy for failure: we can, for instance, carry on processing messages without restarting the actor in the event of failure. Of course, this is of little use if the actor died because its internal state is inconsistent. In the next section, we will discuss how to change the failure recovery strategy.

- Backing up the internal state by writing it to disk periodically and loading from the backup on restart.

- Protecting actors that carry critical state by ensuring that all "risky" operations are delegated to other actors. In our crawler example, all the interactions with external services, such as querying the GitHub API and parsing the response, happen with actors that carry no internal state. As we saw in the previous example, if one of these actors dies, the application is minimally affected. By contrast, the precious fetcher manager is only allowed to interact with sanitized inputs. This is called the *error kernel* pattern: code likely to cause errors is delegated to kamikaze actors.

Custom supervisor strategies

The default strategy of restarting an actor on failure is not always what we want. In particular, for actors that carry a lot of data, we might want to resume processing after an exception rather than restarting the actor. Akka lets us customize this behavior by setting a *supervisor strategy* in the actor's supervisor.

Recall that all actors have parents, including the top-level actors, who are children of a special actor called the *user guardian*. By default, an actor's supervisor is his parent, and it is the supervisor who decides what happens to the actor on failure.

Thus, to change how an actor reacts to failure, you must set its parent's supervisor strategy. You do this by setting the `supervisorStrategy` attribute. The default strategy is equivalent to the following:

```
val supervisorStrategy = OneForOneStrategy() {
  case _:ActorInitializationException => Stop
  case _:ActorKilledException => Stop
  case _:DeathPactException => Stop
  case _:Exception => Restart
}
```

There are two components to a supervisor strategy:

- `OneForOneStrategy` determines that the strategy applies only to the actor that failed. By contrast, we can use `AllForOneStrategy`, which applies the same strategy to all the supervisees. If a single child fails, all the children will be restarted (or stopped or resumed).

- A partial function mapping `Throwables` to a `Directive`, which is an instruction on what to do in response to a failure. The default strategy, for instance, maps `ActorInitializationException` (which happens if the constructor fails) to the `Stop` directive and (almost all) other exceptions to `Restart`.

There are four directives:

- `Restart`: This destroys the faulty actor and restarts it, binding the newborn actor to the old `ActorRef`. This clears the internal state of the actor, which may be a good thing (the actor might have failed because of some internal inconsistency).

- `Resume`: The actor just moves on to processing the next message in its inbox.

- `Stop`: The actor stops and is not restarted. This is useful in throwaway actors that you use to complete a single operation: if this operation fails, the actor is not needed any more.

- `Escalate`: The supervisor itself rethrows the exception, hoping that its supervisor will know what to do with it.

A supervisor does not have access to which of its children failed. Thus, if an actor has children that might require different recovery strategies, it is best to create a set of intermediate supervisor actors to supervise the different groups of children.

As an example of setting the supervisor strategy, let's tweak the `FetcherManager` supervisor strategy to adopt an all-for-one strategy and stop its children when one of them fails. We start with the relevant imports:

```
import akka.actor.SupervisorStrategy._
```

Then, we just need to set the `supervisorStrategy` attribute in the `FetcherManager` definition:

```
class FetcherManager(...) extends Actor with ActorLogging {

  ...

  override val supervisorStrategy = AllForOneStrategy() {
    case _:ActorInitializationException => Stop
    case _:ActorKilledException => Stop
    case _:Exception => Stop
  }

  ...

}
```

If you run this through SBT, you will notice that when the code comes across the custom exception thrown by the response interpreter, the system halts. This is because all the actors apart from the fetcher manager are now defunct.

Life-cycle hooks

Akka lets us specify code that runs in response to specific events in an actor's life, through *life-cycle hooks*. Akka defines the following hooks:

- `preStart()`: This runs after the actor's constructor has finished but before it starts processing messages. This is useful to run initialization code that depends on the actor being fully constructed.

- `postStop()`: This runs when the actor dies after it has stopped processing messages. This is useful to run cleanup code before terminating the actor.

- `preRestart(reason: Throwable, message: Option[Any])`: This is called just after an actor receives an order to restart. The `preRestart` method has access to the exception that was thrown and to the offending message, allowing for corrective action. The default behavior of `preRestart` is to stop each child and then call `postStop`.

- `postRestart(reason:Throwable)`: This is called after an actor has restarted. The default behavior is to call `preStart()`.

Let's use system hooks to persist the state of `FetcherManager` between runs of the programs. You can find the code examples for this section in the `chap09/ghub_crawler_fault_tolerant` directory in the sample code provided with this book (`https://github.com/pbugnion/s4ds`). This will make the fetcher manager fault-tolerant. We will use `postStop` to write the current queue and set of visited users to text files and `preStart` to read these text files from the disk. Let's start by importing the libraries necessary to read and write files:

```scala
// FetcherManager.scala

import scala.io.Source
import scala.util._
import java.io._
```

We will store the names of the two text files in which we persist the state in the `FetcherManager` companion object (a better approach would be to store them in a configuration file):

```scala
// FetcherManager.scala
object FetcherManager {
  ...
  val fetchedUsersFileName = "fetched-users.txt"
  val fetchQueueFileName = "fetch-queue.txt"
}
```

In the `preStart` method, we load both the set of fetched users and the backlog of users to fetch from the text files, and in the `postStop` method, we overwrite these files with the new values of these data structures:

```scala
class FetcherManager(
  val token:Option[String], val nFetchers:Int
) extends Actor with ActorLogging {

  ...

  /** pre-start method: load saved state from text files */
  override def preStart {
    log.info("Running pre-start on fetcher manager")

    loadFetchedUsers
    log.info(
      s"Read ${fetchedUsers.size} visited users from source"
    )

    loadFetchQueue
```

```
    log.info(
      s"Read ${fetchQueue.size} users in queue from source"
    )

    // If the saved state contains a non-empty queue,
    // alert the fetchers so they can start working.
    if (fetchQueue.nonEmpty) {
      context.become(receiveWhileNotEmpty)
      fetchers.foreach { _ ! Fetcher.WorkAvailable }
    }

  }

  /** Dump the current state of the manager */
  override def postStop {
    log.info("Running post-stop on fetcher manager")
    saveFetchedUsers
    saveFetchQueue
  }

    /* Helper methods to load from and write to files */
  def loadFetchedUsers {
    val fetchedUsersSource = Try {
      Source.fromFile(fetchedUsersFileName)
    }
    fetchedUsersSource.foreach { s =>
      try s.getLines.foreach { l => fetchedUsers += l }
      finally s.close
    }
  }

  def loadFetchQueue {
    val fetchQueueSource = Try {
      Source.fromFile(fetchQueueFileName)
    }
    fetchQueueSource.foreach { s =>
      try s.getLines.foreach { l => fetchQueue += l }
      finally s.close
    }
  }

  def saveFetchedUsers {
    val fetchedUsersFile = new File(fetchedUsersFileName)
    val writer = new BufferedWriter(
```

```
      new FileWriter(fetchedUsersFile))
    fetchedUsers.foreach { user => writer.write(user + "\n") }
    writer.close()
  }

  def saveFetchQueue {
    val queueUsersFile = new File(fetchQueueFileName)
    val writer = new BufferedWriter(
      new FileWriter(queueUsersFile))
    fetchQueue.foreach { user => writer.write(user + "\n") }
    writer.close()
  }


  ...
}
```

Now that we save the state of the crawler when it shuts down, we can put a better termination condition for the program than simply interrupting the program once we get bored. In production, we might halt the crawler when we have enough names in a database, for instance. In this example, we will simply let the crawler run for 30 seconds and then shut it down.

Let's modify the main method:

```
// FetchNetwork.scala
import akka.actor._
import scala.concurrent.ExecutionContext.Implicits.global
import scala.concurrent.duration._

object FetchNetwork extends App {

  // Get token if exists
  val token = sys.env.get("GHTOKEN")

  val system = ActorSystem("GithubFetcher")
  val manager = system.actorOf(FetcherManager.props(token, 2))

  manager ! FetcherManager.AddToQueue("odersky")

  system.scheduler.scheduleOnce(30.seconds) { system.shutdown }

}
```

After 30 seconds, we just call `system.shutdown`, which stops all the actors recursively. This will stop the fetcher manager, calling the `postStop` life cycle hook. After one run of the program, I have 2,164 names in the `fetched-users.txt` file. Running it again increases this number to 3,728 users.

We could improve fault tolerance further by making the fetcher manager dump the data structures at regular intervals while the code runs. As writing to the disk (or to a database) carries a certain element of risk (What if the database server goes down or the disk is full?) it would be better to delegate writing the data structures to a custom actor rather than endangering the manager.

Our crawler has one minor problem: when the fetcher manager stops, it stops the fetcher actors, response interpreter, and follower extractor. However, none of the users currently going through these actors are stored. This also results in a small number of undelivered messages at the end of the code: if the response interpreter stops before a fetcher, the fetcher will try to deliver to a non-existent actor. This only accounts for a small number of users. To recover these login names, we can create a reaper actor whose job is to coordinate the killing of all the worker actors in the correct order and harvest their internal state. This pattern is documented in a blog post by *Derek Wyatt* (`http://letitcrash.com/post/30165507578/shutdown-patterns-in-akka-2`).

What we have not talked about

Akka is a very rich ecosystem, far too rich to do it justice in a single chapter. There are some important parts of the toolkit that you will need, but we have not covered them here. We will give brief descriptions, but you can refer to the Akka documentation for more details:

- The ask operator, `?`, offers an alternative to the tell operator, `!`, that we have used to send messages to actors. Unlike "tell", which just fires a message to an actor, the ask operator expects a response. This is useful when we need to ask actors questions rather than just telling them what to do. The ask pattern is documented at `http://doc.akka.io/docs/akka/snapshot/scala/actors.html#Ask__Send-And-Receive-Future`.

- Deathwatch allows actors to watch another actor and receive a message when it dies. This is useful for actors that might depend on another actor but not be its direct supervisor. This is documented at `http://doc.akka.io/docs/akka/snapshot/scala/actors.html#Lifecycle_Monitoring_aka_DeathWatch`.

- In our crawler, we passed references to actors explicitly through the constructor. We can also look up actors using the actor hierarchy with a syntax reminiscent of files in a filesystem at `http://doc.akka.io/docs/akka/snapshot/scala/actors.html#Identifying_Actors_via_Actor_Selection`.

- We briefly explored how to implement stateful actors with different receive methods and using `context.become` to switch between them. Akka offers a more powerful alternative, based on finite state machines, to encode a more complex set of states and transitions: `http://doc.akka.io/docs/akka/snapshot/scala/fsm.html`.

- We have not discussed distributing actor systems across several nodes in this chapter. The message passing architecture works well with distributed setups: `http://doc.akka.io/docs/akka/2.4.0/common/cluster.html`.

Summary

In this chapter, you learned how to weave actors together to tackle a difficult concurrent problem. More importantly, we saw how Akka's actor framework encourages us to think about concurrent problems in terms of many separate chunks of encapsulated mutable data, synchronized through message passing. Akka makes concurrent programming easier to reason about and more fun.

References

Derek Wyatt's book, *Akka Concurrency*, is a fantastic introduction to Akka. It should definitely be the first stop for anyone wanting to do serious Akka programming.

The **LET IT CRASH** blog (`http://letitcrash.com`) is the official Akka blog, and contains many examples of idioms and patterns to solve common issues.

10
Distributed Batch Processing with Spark

In *Chapter 4*, *Parallel Collections and Futures*, we discovered how to use parallel collections for "embarrassingly" parallel problems: problems that can be broken down into a series of tasks that require no (or very little) communication between the tasks.

Apache Spark provides behavior similar to Scala parallel collections (and much more), but, instead of distributing tasks across different CPUs on the same computer, it allows the tasks to be distributed across a computer cluster. This provides arbitrary horizontal scalability, since we can simply add more computers to the cluster.

In this chapter, we will learn the basics of Apache Spark and use it to explore a set of emails, extracting features with the view of building a spam filter. We will explore several ways of actually building a spam filter in *Chapter 12*, *Distributed Machine Learning with MLlib*.

Installing Spark

In previous chapters, we included dependencies by specifying them in a `build.sbt` file, and relying on SBT to fetch them from the Maven Central repositories. For Apache Spark, downloading the source code or pre-built binaries explicitly is more common, since Spark ships with many command line scripts that greatly facilitate launching jobs and interacting with a cluster.

Head over to `http://spark.apache.org/downloads.html` and download Spark 1.5.2, choosing the "pre-built for Hadoop 2.6 or later" package. You can also build Spark from source if you need customizations, but we will stick to the pre-built version since it requires no configuration.

Clicking **Download** will download a tarball, which you can unpack with the following command:

```
$ tar xzf spark-1.5.2-bin-hadoop2.6.tgz
```

This will create a spark-1.5.2-bin-hadoop2.6 directory. To verify that Spark works correctly, navigate to spark-1.5.2-bin-hadoop2.6/bin and launch the Spark shell using ./spark-shell. This is just a Scala shell with the Spark libraries loaded.

You may want to add the bin/ directory to your system path. This will let you call the scripts in that directory from anywhere on your system, without having to reference the full path. On Linux or Mac OS, you can add variables to the system path by entering the following line in your shell configuration file (.bash_profile on Mac OS, and .bashrc or .bash_profile on Linux):

```
export PATH=/path/to/spark/bin:$PATH
```

The changes will take effect in new shell sessions. On Windows (if you use PowerShell), you need to enter this line in the profile.ps1 file in the WindowsPowerShell folder in Documents:

```
$env:Path += ";C:\Program Files\GnuWin32\bin"
```

If this worked correctly, you should be able to open a Spark shell in any directory on your system by just typing spark-shell in a terminal.

Acquiring the example data

In this chapter, we will explore the Ling-Spam email dataset (The original dataset is described at http://csmining.org/index.php/ling-spam-datasets.html). Download the dataset from http://data.scala4datascience.com/ling-spam.tar.gz (or ling-spam.zip, depending on your preferred mode of compression), and unpack the contents to the directory containing the code examples for this chapter. The archive contains two directories, spam/ and ham/, containing the spam and legitimate emails, respectively.

Resilient distributed datasets

Spark expresses all computations as a sequence of transformations and actions on distributed collections, called **Resilient Distributed Datasets** (**RDD**). Let's explore how RDDs work with the Spark shell. Navigate to the examples directory and open a Spark shell as follows:

```
$ spark-shell

scala>
```

Let's start by loading an email in an RDD:

```
scala> val email = sc.textFile("ham/9-463msg1.txt")
email: rdd.RDD[String] = MapPartitionsRDD[1] at textFile
```

`email` is an RDD, with each element corresponding to a line in the input file. Notice how we created the RDD by calling the `textFile` method on an object called `sc`:

```
scala> sc
spark.SparkContext = org.apache.spark.SparkContext@459bf87c
```

`sc` is a `SparkContext` instance, an object representing the entry point to the Spark cluster (for now, just our local machine). When we start a Spark shell, a context is created and bound to the variable `sc` automatically.

Let's split the email into words using `flatMap`:

```
scala> val words = email.flatMap { line => line.split("\\s") }
words: rdd.RDD[String] = MapPartitionsRDD[2] at flatMap
```

This will feel natural if you are familiar with collections in Scala: the `email` RDD behaves just like a list of strings. Here, we split using the regular expression \s, denoting white space characters. Instead of using `flatMap` explicitly, we can also manipulate RDDs using Scala's syntactic sugar:

```
scala> val words = for {
  line <- email
  word <- line.split("\\s")
} yield word
words: rdd.RDD[String] = MapPartitionsRDD[3] at flatMap
```

Let's inspect the results. We can use `.take(n)` to extract the first *n* elements of an RDD:

```
scala> words.take(5)
Array[String] = Array(Subject:, tsd98, workshop, -, -)
```

We can also use `.count` to get the number of elements in an RDD:

```
scala> words.count
Long = 939
```

RDDs support many of the operations supported by collections. Let's use `filter` to remove punctuation from our email. We will remove all words that contain any non-alphanumeric character. We can do this by filtering out elements that match this *regular expression* anywhere in the word: `[^a-zA-Z0-9]`.

```
scala> val nonAlphaNumericPattern = "[^a-zA-Z0-9]".r
nonAlphaNumericPattern: Regex = [^a-zA-Z0-9]

scala> val filteredWords = words.filter {
  word => nonAlphaNumericPattern.findFirstIn(word) == None
}
filteredWords: rdd.RDD[String] = MapPartitionsRDD[4] at filter

scala> filteredWords.take(5)
Array[String] = Array(tsd98, workshop, 2nd, call, paper)

scala> filteredWords.count
Long = 627
```

In this example, we created an RDD from a text file. We can also create RDDs from Scala iterables using the `sc.parallelize` method available on a Spark context:

```
scala> val words = "the quick brown fox jumped over the dog".split(" ")
words: Array[String] = Array(the, quick, brown, fox, ...)

scala> val wordsRDD = sc.parallelize(words)
wordsRDD: RDD[String] = ParallelCollectionRDD[1] at parallelize at
<console>:23
```

This is useful for debugging and for trialling behavior in the shell. The counterpart to parallelize is the `.collect` method, which converts an RDD to a Scala array:

```
scala> val wordLengths = wordsRDD.map { _.length }
wordLengths: RDD[Int] = MapPartitionsRDD[2] at map at <console>:25


scala> wordLengths.collect
Array[Int] = Array(3, 5, 5, 3, 6, 4, 3, 3)
```

The `.collect` method requires the entire RDD to fit in memory on the master node. It is thus either used for debugging with a reduced dataset, or at the end of a pipeline that trims down a dataset.

As you can see, RDDs offer an API much like Scala iterables. The critical difference is that RDDs are *distributed* and *resilient*. Let's explore what this means in practice.

RDDs are immutable

You cannot change an RDD once it is created. All operations on RDDs either create new RDDs or other Scala objects.

RDDs are lazy

When you execute operations like map and filter on a Scala collection in the interactive shell, the REPL prints the values of the new collection to screen. The same isn't true of Spark RDDs. This is because operations on RDDs are lazy: they are only evaluated when needed.

Thus, when we write:

```
val email = sc.textFile(...)
val words = email.flatMap { line => line.split("\\s") }
```

We are creating an RDD, `words` that knows how to build itself from its parent RDD, `email`, which, in turn, knows that it needs to read a text file and split it into lines. However, none of the commands actually happen until we force the evaluation of the RDDs by calling an *action* to return a Scala object. This is most evident if we try to read from a non-existent text file:

```
scala> val inp = sc.textFile("nonexistent")
inp: rdd.RDD[String] = MapPartitionsRDD[5] at textFile
```

We can create the RDD without a hitch. We can even define further transformations on the RDD. The program crashes only when these transformations are finally evaluated:

```scala
scala> inp.count // number of lines
org.apache.hadoop.mapred.InvalidInputException: Input path does not
exist: file:/Users/pascal/...
```

The action `.count` is expected to return the number of elements in our RDD as an integer. Spark has no choice but to evaluate `inp`, which results in an exception.

Thus, it is probably more appropriate to think of an RDD as a pipeline of operations, rather than a more traditional collection.

RDDs know their lineage

RDDs can only be constructed from stable storage (for instance, by loading data from a file that is present on every node in the Spark cluster), or through a set of transformations based on other RDDs. Since RDDs are lazy, they need to know how to build themselves when needed. They do this by knowing who their parent RDD is, and what operation they need to apply to the parent. This is a well-defined process since the parent RDD is immutable.

The `toDebugString` method provides a diagram of how an RDD is constructed:

```scala
scala> filteredWords.toDebugString
(2) MapPartitionsRDD[6] at filter at <console>:27 []
 |  MapPartitionsRDD[3] at flatMap at <console>:23 []
 |  MapPartitionsRDD[1] at textFile at <console>:21 []
 |  ham/9-463msg1.txt HadoopRDD[0] at textFile at <console>:21 []
```

RDDs are resilient

If you run an application on a single computer, you generally don't need to worry about hardware failure in your application: if the computer fails, your application is doomed anyway.

Distributed architectures should, by contrast, be fault-tolerant: the failure of a single machine should not crash the entire application. Spark RDDs are built with fault tolerance in mind. Let's imagine that one of the worker nodes fails, causing the destruction of some of the data associated with an RDD. Since the Spark RDD knows how to build itself from its parent, there is no permanent data loss: the elements that were lost can just be re-computed when needed on another computer.

RDDs are distributed

When you construct an RDD, for instance from a text file, Spark will split the RDD into a number of partitions. Each partition will be entirely localized on a single machine (though there is, in general, more than one partition per machine).

Many transformations on RDDs can be executed on each partition independently. For instance, when performing a `.map` operation, a given element in the output RDD depends on a single element in the parent: data does not need to be moved between partitions. The same is true of `.flatMap` and `.filter` operations. This means that the partition in the RDD produced by one of these operations depends on a single partition in the parent RDD.

On the other hand, a `.distinct` transformation, which removes all duplicate elements from an RDD, requires the data in a given partition to be compared to the data in every other partition. This requires *shuffling* the data across the nodes. Shuffling, especially for large datasets, is an expensive operation and should be avoided if possible.

Transformations and actions on RDDs

The set of operations supported by an RDD can be split into two categories:

- **Transformations** create a new RDD from the current one. Transformations are lazy: they are not evaluated immediately.

- **Actions** force the evaluation of an RDD, and normally return a Scala object, rather than an RDD, or have some form of side-effect. Actions are evaluated immediately, triggering the execution of all the transformations that make up this RDD.

In the tables below, we give some examples of useful transformations and actions. For a full, up-to-date list, consult the Spark documentation (`http://spark.apache.org/docs/latest/programming-guide.html#rdd-operations`).

For the examples in these tables, we assume that you have created an RDD with:

```scala
scala> val rdd = sc.parallelize(List("quick", "brown", "quick", "dog"))
```

The following table lists common transformations on an RDD. Recall that transformations always generate a new RDD, and that they are lazy operations:

Transformation	Notes	Example (assuming rdd is { "quick", "brown", "quick", "dog" })
`rdd.map(func)`		`rdd.map { _.size } // => { 5, 5, 5, 3 }`
`rdd.filter(pred)`		`rdd.filter { _.length < 4 } // => { "dog" }`
`rdd.flatMap(func)`		`rdd.flatMap { _.toCharArray } // => { 'q', 'u', 'i', 'c', 'k', 'b', 'r', 'o' … }`
`rdd.distinct()`	Remove duplicate elements in RDD.	`rdd.distinct // => { "dog", "brown", "quick" }`
`rdd.pipe(command, [envVars])`	Pipe through an external program. RDD elements are written, line-by-line, to the process's `stdin`. The output is read from `stdout`.	`rdd.pipe("tr a-z A-Z") // => { "QUICK", "BROWN", "QUICK", "DOG" }`

The following table describes common actions on RDDs. Recall that actions always generate a Scala type or cause a side-effect, rather than creating a new RDD. Actions force the evaluation of the RDD, triggering the execution of the transformations underpinning the RDD.

Action	Nodes	Example (assuming rdd is { "quick", "brown", "quick", "dog" })
`rdd.first`	First element in the RDD.	`rdd.first // => quick`
`rdd.collect`	Transform the RDD to an array (the array must be able to fit in memory on the master node).	`rdd.collect // => Array[String] ("quick", "brown", "quick", "dog")`
`rdd.count`	Number of elements in the RDD.	`rdd.count // => 4`

Action	Nodes	Example (assuming rdd is { "quick", "brown", "quick", "dog" })
`rdd.countByValue`	Map of element to the number of times this element occurs. The map must fit on the master node.	`rdd.countByValue // =>` `Map(quick -> 2, brown ->` `1, dog -> 1)`
`rdd.take(n)`	Return an array of the first *n* elements in the RDD.	`rdd.take(2) // =>` `Array(quick, brown)`
`rdd.takeOrdered(n:Int) (implicit ordering: Ordering[T])`	Top *n* elements in the RDD according to the element's default ordering, or the ordering passed as second argument. See the Scala docs for `Ordering` for how to define custom comparison functions (`http://www.scala-lang.org/api/current/index.html#scala.math.Ordering`).	`rdd.takeOrdered(2) // =>` `Array(brown, dog)` `rdd.takeOrdered(2)` `(Ordering.by { _.size` `}) // => Array[String] =` `Array(dog, quick)`
`rdd.reduce(func)`	Reduce the RDD according to the specified function. Uses the first element in the RDD as the base. `func` should be commutative and associative.	`rdd.map { _.size }.reduce` `{ _ + _ } // => 18`

Action	Nodes	Example (assuming rdd is { "quick", "brown", "quick", "dog" })
rdd. aggregate(zeroValue) (seqOp, combOp)	Reduction for cases where the reduction function returns a value of type different to the RDD's type. In this case, we need to provide a function for reducing within a single partition (seqOp) and a function for combining the value of two partitions (combOp).	rdd.aggregate(0) (_ + _.size, _ + _) // => 18

Persisting RDDs

We have learned that RDDs only retain the sequence of operations needed to construct the elements, rather than the values themselves. This, of course, drastically reduces memory usage since we do not need to keep intermediate versions of our RDDs in memory. For instance, let's assume we want to trawl through transaction logs to identify all the transactions that occurred on a particular account:

```
val allTransactions = sc.textFile("transaction.log")
val interestingTransactions = allTransactions.filter {
  _.contains("Account: 123456")
}
```

The set of all transactions will be large, while the set of transactions on the account of interest will be much smaller. Spark's policy of remembering *how* to construct a dataset, rather than the dataset itself, means that we never have all the lines of our input file in memory at any one time.

There are two situations in which we may want to avoid re-computing the elements of an RDD every time we use it:

- For interactive use: we might have detected fraudulent behavior on account "123456", and we want to investigate how this might have arisen. We will probably want to perform many different exploratory calculations on this RDD, without having to re-read the entire log file every time. It therefore makes sense to persist interestingTransactions.

- When an algorithm re-uses an intermediate result, or a dataset. A canonical example is logistic regression. In logistic regression, we normally use an iterative algorithm to find the 'optimal' coefficients that minimize the loss function. At every step in our iterative algorithm, we must calculate the loss function and its gradient from the training set. We should avoid re-computing the training set (or re-loading it from an input file) if at all possible.

Spark provides a `.persist` method on RDDs to achieve this. By calling `.persist` on an RDD, we tell Spark to keep the dataset in memory next time it is computed.

```scala
scala> words.persist
rdd.RDD[String] = MapPartitionsRDD[3] at filter
```

Spark supports different levels of persistence, which you can tune by passing arguments to `.persist`:

```scala
scala> import org.apache.spark.storage.StorageLevel
import org.apache.spark.storage.StorageLevel


scala> interestingTransactions.persist(
  StorageLevel.MEMORY_AND_DISK)
rdd.RDD[String] = MapPartitionsRDD[3] at filter
```

Spark provides several persistence levels, including:

- `MEMORY_ONLY`: the default storage level. The RDD is stored in RAM. If the RDD is too big to fit in memory, parts of it will not persist, and will need to be re-computed on the fly.
- `MEMORY_AND_DISK`: As much of the RDD is stored in memory as possible. If the RDD is too big, it will spill over to disk. This is only worthwhile if the RDD is expensive to compute. Otherwise, re-computing it may be faster than reading from the disk.

If you persist several RDDs and run out of memory, Spark will clear the least recently used out of memory (either discarding them or saving them to disk, depending on the chosen persistence level). RDDs also expose an `unpersist` method to explicitly tell Spark than an RDD is not needed any more.

Persisting RDDs can have a drastic impact on performance. What and how to persist therefore becomes very important when tuning a Spark application. Finding the best persistence level generally requires some tinkering, benchmarking and experimentation. The Spark documentation provides guidelines on when to use which persistence level (`http://spark.apache.org/docs/latest/programming-guide.html#rdd-persistence`), as well as general tips on tuning memory usage (`http://spark.apache.org/docs/latest/tuning.html`).

Importantly, the `persist` method does not force the evaluation of the RDD. It just notifies the Spark engine that, next time the values in this RDD are computed, they should be saved rather than discarded.

Key-value RDDs

So far, we have only considered RDDs of Scala value types. RDDs of more complex data types support additional operations. Spark adds many operations for *key-value RDDs*: RDDs whose type parameter is a tuple `(K, V)`, for any type `K` and `V`.

Let's go back to our sample email:

```scala
scala> val email = sc.textFile("ham/9-463msg1.txt")
email: rdd.RDD[String] = MapPartitionsRDD[1] at textFile

scala> val words = email.flatMap { line => line.split("\\s") }
words: rdd.RDD[String] = MapPartitionsRDD[2] at flatMap
```

Let's persist the `words` RDD in memory to avoid having to re-read the `email` file from disk repeatedly:

```scala
scala> words.persist
```

To access key-value operations, we just need to apply a transformation to our RDD that creates key-value pairs. Let's use the words as keys. For now, we will just use 1 for every value:

```scala
scala> val wordsKeyValue = words.map { _ -> 1 }
wordsKeyValue: rdd.RDD[(String, Int)] = MapPartitionsRDD[32] at map

scala> wordsKeyValue.first
(String, Int) = (Subject:,1)
```

Key-value RDDs support several operations besides the core RDD operations. These are added through an implicit conversion, using the "pimp my library" pattern that we explored in *Chapter 5, Scala and SQL through JDBC*. These additional transformations fall into two broad categories: *by-key* transformations and *joins* between RDDs.

By-key transformations are operations that aggregate the values corresponding to the same key. For instance, we can count the number of times each word appears in our email using `reduceByKey`. This method takes all the values that belong to the same key and combines them using a user-supplied function:

```
scala> val wordCounts = wordsKeyValue.reduceByKey { _ + _ }
wordCounts: rdd.RDD[(String, Int)] = ShuffledRDD[35] at reduceByKey


scala> wordCounts.take(5).foreach { println }
(university,6)
(under,1)
(call,3)
(paper,2)
(chasm,2)
```

Note that `reduceByKey` requires (in general) shuffling the RDD, since not every occurrence of a given key will be in the same partition:

```
scala> wordCounts.toDebugString
(2) ShuffledRDD[36] at reduceByKey at <console>:30 []
 +-(2) MapPartitionsRDD[32] at map at <console>:28 []
    |  MapPartitionsRDD[7] at flatMap at <console>:23 []
    |      CachedPartitions: 2; MemorySize: 50.3 KB;
ExternalBlockStoreSize: 0.0 B; DiskSize: 0.0 B
    |  MapPartitionsRDD[3] at textFile at <console>:21 []
    |      CachedPartitions: 2; MemorySize: 5.1 KB;
ExternalBlockStoreSize: 0.0 B; DiskSize: 0.0 B
    |  ham/9-463msg1.txt HadoopRDD[2] at textFile at <console>:21 []
```

Note that key-value RDDs are not like Scala Maps: the same key can occur multiple times, and they do not support *O(1)* lookup. A key-value RDD can be transformed to a Scala map using the `.collectAsMap` action:

```
scala> wordCounts.collectAsMap
scala.collection.Map[String,Int] = Map(follow -> 2, famous -> 1...
```

This requires pulling the entire RDD onto the main Spark node. You therefore need to have enough memory on the main node to house the map. This is often the last stage in a pipeline that filters a large RDD to just the information that we need.

There are many by-key operations, which we describe in the table below. For the examples in the table, we assume that `rdd` is created as follows:

```scala
scala> val words = sc.parallelize(List("quick", "brown","quick", "dog"))
words: RDD[String] = ParallelCollectionRDD[25] at parallelize at
<console>:21


scala> val rdd = words.map { word => (word -> word.size) }
rdd: RDD[(String, Int)] = MapPartitionsRDD[26] at map at <console>:23


scala> rdd.collect
Array[(String, Int)] = Array((quick,5), (brown,5), (quick,5), (dog,3))
```

Transformation	Notes	Example (assumes rdd is { quick -> 5, brown -> 5, quick -> 5, dog -> 3 })
rdd.mapValues	Apply an operation to the values.	rdd.mapValues { _ * 2 } // => { quick -> 10, brown -> 10, quick -> 10, dog ->6 }
rdd.groupByKey	Return a key-value RDD in which values corresponding to the same key are grouped into iterables.	rdd.groupByKey // => { quick -> Iterable(5, 5), brown -> Iterable(5), dog -> Iterable(3) }
rdd. reduceByKey(func)	Return a key-value RDD in which values corresponding to the same key are combined using a user-supplied function.	rdd.reduceByKey { _ + _ } // => { quick -> 10, brown -> 5, dog -> 3 }
rdd.keys	Return an RDD of the keys.	rdd.keys // => { quick, brown, quick, dog }
rdd.values	Return an RDD of the values.	rdd.values // => { 5, 5, 5, 3 }

The second category of operations on key-value RDDs involves joining different RDDs together by key. This is somewhat similar to SQL joins, where the keys are the column being joined on. Let's load a spam email and apply the same transformations we applied to our ham email:

```scala
scala> val spamEmail = sc.textFile("spam/spmsgb17.txt")
spamEmail: org.apache.spark.rdd.RDD[String] = MapPartitionsRDD[52] at
textFile at <console>:24


scala> val spamWords = spamEmail.flatMap { _.split("\\s") }
spamWords: org.apache.spark.rdd.RDD[String] = MapPartitionsRDD[53] at
flatMap at <console>:26


scala> val spamWordCounts = spamWords.map {
  _ -> 1 }.reduceByKey { _ + _ }
spamWordsCount: org.apache.spark.rdd.RDD[(String, Int)] = ShuffledRDD[55]
at reduceByKey at <console>:30


scala> spamWordCounts.take(5).foreach { println }
(banner,3)
(package,14)
(call,1)
(country,2)
(offer,1)
```

Both `spamWordCounts` and `wordCounts` are key-value RDDs for which the keys correspond to unique words in the message, and the values are the number of times that word occurs. There will be some overlap in keys between `spamWordCounts` and `wordCounts`, since the emails will share many of the same words. Let's do an *inner join* between those two RDDs to get the words that occur in both emails:

```scala
scala> val commonWordCounts = wordCounts.join(spamWordCounts)
res93: rdd.RDD[(String, (Int, Int))] = MapPartitionsRDD[58] at join at
<console>:41


scala> commonWordCounts.take(5).foreach { println }
(call,(3,1))
(include,(6,2))
(minute,(2,1))
(form,(1,7))
((,(36,5))
```

The values in the RDD resulting from an inner join will be pairs. The first element in the pair is the value for that key in the first RDD, and the second element is the value for that key in the second RDD. Thus, the word *call* occurs three times in the legitimate email and once in the spam email.

Spark supports all four join types. For instance, let's perform a left join:

```scala
scala> val leftWordCounts = wordCounts.leftOuterJoin(spamWordCounts)
leftWordCounts: rdd.RDD[(String, (Int, Option[Int]))] =
MapPartitionsRDD[64] at leftOuterJoin at <console>:40


scala> leftWordCounts.take(5).foreach { println }
(call,(3,Some(1)))
(paper,(2,None))
(chasm,(2,None))
(antonio,(1,None))
(event,(3,None))
```

Notice that the second element in our pair has type `Option[Int]`, to accommodate keys absent in `spamWordCounts`. The word *paper*, for instance, occurs twice in the legitimate email and never in the spam email. In this case, it is more useful to have zeros to indicate absence, rather than `None`. Replacing `None` with a default value is simple with `getOrElse`:

```scala
scala> val defaultWordCounts = leftWordCounts.mapValues {
  case(leftValue, rightValue) => (leftValue, rightValue.getOrElse(0))
}
org.apache.spark.rdd.RDD[(String, (Int, Option[Int]))] =
MapPartitionsRDD[64] at leftOuterJoin at <console>:40


scala> defaultwordCounts.take(5).foreach { println }
(call,(3,1))
(paper,(2,0))
(chasm,(2,0))
(antonio,(1,0))
(event,(3,0))
```

The table below lists the most common joins on key-value RDDs:

Transformation	Result (assuming `rdd1` is { `quick -> 1, brown -> 2, quick -> 3, dog -> 4` } and `rdd2` is { `quick -> 78, brown -> 79, fox -> 80` })
`rdd1.join(rdd2)`	{ `quick -> (1, 78), quick -> (3, 78), brown -> (2, 79)` }
`rdd1.leftOuterJoin(rdd2)`	{ `dog -> (4, None), quick -> (1, Some(78)), quick -> (3, Some(78)), brown -> (2, Some(79))` }
`rdd1.rightOuterJoin(rdd2)`	{ `quick -> (Some(1), 78), quick -> (Some(3), 78), brown -> (Some(2), 79), fox -> (None, 80)` }
`rdd1.fullOuterJoin(rdd2)`	{ `dog -> (Some(4), None), quick -> (Some(1), Some(78)), quick -> (Some(3), Some(78)), brown -> (Some(2), Some(79)), fox -> (None, Some(80))` }

For a complete list of transformations, consult the API documentation for `PairRDDFunctions`, `http://spark.apache.org/docs/latest/api/scala/index.html#org.apache.spark.rdd.PairRDDFunctions`.

Double RDDs

In the previous section, we saw that Spark adds functionality to key-value RDDs through an implicit conversion. Similarly, Spark adds statistics functionality to RDDs of doubles. Let's extract the word frequencies for the ham message, and convert the values from integers to doubles:

```scala
scala> val counts = wordCounts.values.map { _.toDouble }
counts: rdd.RDD[Double] = MapPartitionsRDD[9] at map
```

We can then get summary statistics using the `.stats` action:

```scala
scala> counts.stats
org.apache.spark.util.StatCounter = (count: 397, mean: 2.365239, stdev: 5.740843, max: 72.000000, min: 1.000000)
```

Thus, the most common word appears 72 times. We can also use the `.histogram` action to get an idea of the distribution of values:

```scala
scala> counts.histogram(5)
(Array(1.0, 15.2, 29.4, 43.6, 57.8, 72.0),Array(391, 1, 3, 1, 1))
```

The `.histogram` method returns a pair of arrays. The first array indicates the bounds of the histogram bins, and the second is the count of elements in that bin. Thus, there are 391 words that appear less than 15.2 times. The distribution of words is very skewed, such that a histogram with regular-sized bin is not really appropriate. We can, instead, pass in custom bins by passing an array of bin edges to the `histogram` method. For instance, we might distribute the bins logarithmically:

```scala
scala> counts.histogram(Array(1.0, 2.0, 4.0, 8.0, 16.0, 32.0, 64.0, 128.0))
res13: Array[Long] = Array(264, 94, 22, 11, 1, 4, 1)
```

Building and running standalone programs

So far, we have interacted exclusively with Spark through the Spark shell. In the section that follows, we will build a standalone application and launch a Spark program either locally or on an EC2 cluster.

Running Spark applications locally

The first step is to write the `build.sbt` file, as you would if you were running a standard Scala script. The Spark binary that we downloaded needs to be run against Scala 2.10 (You need to compile Spark from source to run against Scala 2.11. This is not difficult to do, just follow the instructions on `http://spark.apache.org/docs/latest/building-spark.html#building-for-scala-211`).

```
// build.sbt file

name := "spam_mi"

scalaVersion := "2.10.5"

libraryDependencies ++= Seq(
  "org.apache.spark" %% "spark-core" % "1.4.1"
)
```

We then run `sbt package` to compile and build a jar of our program. The jar will be built in `target/scala-2.10/`, and called `spam_mi_2.10-0.1-SNAPSHOT.jar`. You can try this with the example code provided for this chapter.

We can then run the jar locally using the `spark-submit` shell script, available in the
`bin/` folder in the Spark installation directory:

```
$ spark-submit target/scala-2.10/spam_mi_2.10-0.1-SNAPSHOT.jar
... runs the program
```

The resources allocated to Spark can be controlled by passing arguments to `spark-submit`. Use `spark-submit --help` to see the full list of arguments.

If the Spark programs has dependencies (for instance, on other Maven packages),
it is easiest to bundle them into the application jar using the *SBT assembly* plugin.
Let's imagine that our application depends on breeze-viz. The `build.sbt` file now
looks like:

```
// build.sbt

name := "spam_mi"

scalaVersion := "2.10.5"

libraryDependencies ++= Seq(
  "org.apache.spark" %% "spark-core" % "1.5.2" % "provided",
  "org.scalanlp" %% "breeze" % "0.11.2",
  "org.scalanlp" %% "breeze-viz" % "0.11.2",
  "org.scalanlp" %% "breeze-natives" % "0.11.2"
)
```

SBT assembly is an SBT plugin that builds *fat* jars: jars that contain not only the
program itself, but all the dependencies for the program.

Note that we marked Spark as "provided" in the list of dependencies, which
means that Spark itself will not be included in the jar (it is provided by the Spark
environment anyway). To include the SBT assembly plugin, create a file called
`assembly.sbt` in the `project/` directory, with the following line:

```
addSbtPlugin("com.eed3si9n" % "sbt-assembly" % "0.14.0")
```

You will need to re-start SBT for the changes to take effect. You can then create the
assembly jar using the `assembly` command in SBT. This will create a jar called `spam_mi-assembly-0.1-SNAPSHOT.jar` in the `target/scala-2.10` directory. You can run
this jar using `spark-submit`.

Reducing logging output and Spark configuration

Spark is, by default, very verbose. The default log-level is set to INFO. To avoid missing important messages, it is useful to change the log settings to WARN. To change the default log level system-wide, go into the conf directory in the directory in which you installed Spark. You should find a file called log4j.properties. template. Rename this file to log4j.properties and look for the following line:

```
log4j.rootCategory=INFO, console
```

Change this line to:

```
log4j.rootCategory=WARN, console
```

There are several other configuration files in that directory that you can use to alter Spark's default behavior. For a full list of configuration options, head over to http://spark.apache.org/docs/latest/configuration.html.

Running Spark applications on EC2

Running Spark locally is useful for testing, but the whole point of using a distributed framework is to run programs harnessing the power of several different computers. We can set Spark up on any set of computers that can communicate with each other using HTTP. In general, we also need to set up a distributed file system like HDFS, so that we can share input files across the cluster. For the purpose of this example, we will set Spark up on an Amazon EC2 cluster.

Spark comes with a shell script, ec2/spark-ec2, for setting up an EC2 cluster and installing Spark. It will also install HDFS. You will need an account with Amazon Web Services (AWS) to follow these examples (https://aws.amazon.com). You will need the AWS access key and secret key, which you can access through the **Account / Security Credentials / Access Credentials** menu in the AWS web console. You need to make these available to the spark-ec2 script through environment variables. Inject them into your current session as follows:

```
$ export AWS_ACCESS_KEY_ID=ABCDEF...
$ export AWS_SECRET_ACCESS_KEY=2dEf...
```

You can also write these lines into the configuration script for your shell (your .bashrc file, or equivalent), to avoid having to re-enter them every time you run the setup-ec2 script. We discussed environment variables in *Chapter 6, Slick – A Functional Interface for SQL*.

You will also need to create a key pair by clicking on **Key Pairs** in the EC2 web console, creating a new key pair and downloading the certificate file. I will assume you named the key pair `test_ec2` and the certificate file `test_ec2.pem`. Make sure that the key pair is created in the *N*. Virginia region (by choosing the correct region in the upper right corner of the EC2 Management console), to avoid having to specify the region explicitly in the rest of this chapter. You will need to set access permissions on the certificate file to user-readable only:

```
$ chmod 400 test_ec2.pem
```

We are now ready to launch the cluster. Navigate to the `ec2` directory and run:

```
$ ./spark-ec2 -k test_ec2 -i ~/path/to/certificate/test_ec2.pem -s 2
launch test_cluster
```

This will create a cluster called `test_cluster` with a master and two slaves. The number of slaves is set through the `-s` command line argument. The cluster will take a while to start up, but you can verify that the instances are launching correctly by looking at the **Instances** window in the EC2 Management Console.

The setup script supports many options for customizing the type of instances, the number of hard drives and so on. You can explore these options by passing the `--help` command line option to `spark-ec2`.

The life cycle of the cluster can be controlled by passing different commands to the `spark-ec2` script, such as:

```
# shut down 'test_cluster'
$ ./spark-ec2 stop test_cluster

# start 'test_cluster'
$ ./spark-ec2 -i test_ec2.pem start test_cluster

# destroy 'test_cluster'
$ ./spark-ec2 destroy test_cluster
```

For more detail on using Spark on EC2, consult the official documentation at `http://spark.apache.org/docs/latest/ec2-scripts.html#running-applications`.

Spam filtering

Let's put all we've learned to good use and do some data exploration for our spam filter. We will use the Ling-Spam email dataset: http://csmining.org/index.php/ling-spam-datasets.html. The dataset contains 2412 ham emails and 481 spam emails, all of which were received by a mailing list on linguistics. We will extract the words that are most informative of whether an email is spam or ham.

The first steps in any natural language processing workflow are to remove stop words and lemmatization. Removing stop words involves filtering very common words such as *the*, *this* and so on. Lemmatization involves replacing different forms of the same word with a canonical form: both *colors* and *color* would be mapped to *color*, and *organize*, *organizing* and *organizes* would be mapped to *organize*. Removing stop words and lemmatization is very challenging, and beyond the scope of this book (if you do need to remove stop words and lemmatize a dataset, your go-to tool should be the Stanford NLP toolkit: http://nlp.stanford.edu/software/corenlp.shtml). Fortunately, the Ling-Spam e-mail dataset has been cleaned and lemmatized already (which is why the text in the emails looks strange).

When we do build the spam filter, we will use the presence of a particular word in an email as the feature for our model. We will use a *bag-of-words* approach: we consider which words appear in an email, but not the word order.

Intuitively, some words will be more important than others when deciding whether an email is spam. For instance, an email that contains *language* is likely to be ham, since the mailing list was for linguistics discussions, and *language* is a word unlikely to be used by spammers. Conversely, words which are common to both message types, for instance *hello*, are unlikely to be much use.

One way of quantifying the importance of a word in determining whether a message is spam is through the **Mutual Information** (**MI**). The mutual information is the gain in information about whether a message is ham or spam if we know that it contains a particular word. For instance, the presence of *language* in a particular email is very informative as to whether that email is spam or ham. Similarly, the presence of the word *dollar* is informative since it appears often in spam messages and only infrequently in ham messages. By contrast, the presence of the word *morning* is uninformative, since it is approximately equally common in both spam and ham messages. The formula for the mutual information between the presence of a particular word in an email, and whether that email is spam or ham is:

$$MI(word) = \sum_{\substack{wordPresent \in \{true,\, false\} \\ class \in \{spam,\, ham\}}} P(wordPresent, class) \cdot \log_2 \frac{P(wordPresent, class)}{P(wordPresent)P(class)}$$

where $P(wordPresent, class)$ is the joint probability of an email containing a particular word and being of that class (either ham or spam), $P(wordPresent)$ is the probability that a particular word is present in an email, and $P(class)$ is the probability that any email is of that class. The MI is commonly used in decision trees.

> The derivation of the expression for the mutual information is beyond the scope of this book. The interested reader is directed to *David MacKay's* excellent *Information Theory, Inference, and Learning Algorithms*, especially the chapter *Dependent Random Variables*.

A key component of our MI calculation is evaluating the probability that a word occurs in spam or ham messages. The best approximation to this probability, given our data set, is the fraction of messages a word appears in. Thus, for instance, if *language* appears in 40% of messages, we will assume that the probability $P(languagePresent)$ of language being present in any message is 0.4. Similarly, if 40% of the messages are ham, and *language* appears in 50% of those, we will assume that the probability of language being present in an email, and that email being ham is $P(languagePresent, ham) = 0.5 \times 0.4 = 0.2$.

Let's write a `wordFractionInFiles` function to calculate the fraction of messages in which each word appears, for all the words in a given corpus. Our function will take, as argument, a path with a shell wildcard identifying a set of files, such as `ham/*`, and it will return a key-value RDD, where the keys are words and the values are the probability that that word occurs in any of those files. We will put the function in an object called `MutualInformation`.

We first give the entire code listing for this function. Don't worry if this doesn't all make sense straight-away: we explain the tricky parts in more detail just after the code. You may find it useful to type some of these commands in the shell, replacing `fileGlob` with, for instance `"ham/*"`:

```scala
// MutualInformation.scala
import org.apache.spark.{ SparkConf, SparkContext }
import org.apache.spark.SparkContext._
import org.apache.spark.rdd.RDD

object MutualInformation extends App {

  def wordFractionInFiles(sc:SparkContext)(fileGlob:String)
  :(RDD[(String, Double)], Long) = {

    // A set of punctuation words that need to be filtered out.
    val wordsToOmit = Set[String](
      "", ".", ",", ":", "-", "\"", "'", ")",
```

```
      "(", "@", "/", "Subject:"
    )

    val messages = sc.wholeTextFiles(fileGlob)
    // wholeTextFiles generates a key-value RDD of
    // file name -> file content

    val nMessages = messages.count()

    // Split the content of each message into a Set of unique
    // words in that message, and generate a new RDD mapping:
    // message -> word
    val message2Word = messages.flatMapValues {
      mailBody => mailBody.split("\\s").toSet
    }


    val message2FilteredWords = message2Word.filter {
      case(email, word) => ! wordsToOmit(word)
    }

    val word2Message = message2FilteredWords.map { _.swap }

    // word -> number of messages it appears in.
    val word2NumberMessages = word2Message.mapValues {
      _ => 1
    }.reduceByKey { _ + _ }

    // word -> fraction of messages it appears in
    val pPresent = word2NumberMessages.mapValues {
      _ / nMessages.toDouble
    }

    (pPresent, nMessages)
  }
}
```

Let's play with this function in the Spark shell. To be able to access this function from the shell, we need to create a jar with the `MutualInformation` object. Write a `build.sbt` file similar to the one presented in the previous section and package the code into a jar using `sbt package`. Then, open a Spark shell with:

```
$ spark-shell --jars=target/scala-2.10/spam_mi_2.10-0.1-SNAPSHOT.jar
```

This will open a Spark shell with our newly created jar on the classpath. Let's run our `wordFractionInFiles` method on the `ham` emails:

```scala
scala> import MutualInformation._
import MutualInformation._


scala> val (fractions, nMessages) = wordFractionInFiles(sc)("ham/*")
fractions: org.apache.spark.rdd.RDD[(String, Double)] =
MapPartitionsRDD[13] at mapValues

nMessages: Long = 2412
```

Let's get a snapshot of the `fractions` RDD:

```scala
scala> fractions.take(5)
Array[(String, Double)] = Array((rule-base,0.002902155887230514), (re
union,4.1459369817578774E-4), (embarrasingly,4.1459369817578774E-4),
(mller,8.291873963515755E-4), (sapore,4.1459369817578774E-4))
```

It would be nice to see the words that come up most often in ham messages. We can use the `.takeOrdered` action to take the top values of an RDD, with a custom ordering. `.takeOrdered` expects, as its second argument, an instance of the type class `Ordering[T]`, where `T` is the type parameter of our RDD: `(String, Double)` in this case. `Ordering[T]` is a trait with a single `compare(a:T, b:T)` method describing how to compare `a` and `b`. The easiest way of creating an `Ordering[T]` is through the companion object's `by` method, which defines a key by which to compare the elements of our RDD.

We want to order the elements in our key-value RDD by the value and, since we want the most common words, rather than the least, we need to reverse that ordering:

```scala
scala> fractions.takeOrdered(5)(Ordering.by { - _._2 })
res0: Array[(String, Double)] = Array((language,0.6737147595356551),
(university,0.6048922056384743), (linguistic,0.5149253731343284),
(information,0.45480928689883915), ('s,0.4369817578772803))
```

Unsurprisingly, `language` is present in 67% of ham emails, `university` in 60% of ham emails and so on. A similar investigation on spam messages reveals that the exclamation mark character *!* is present in 83% of spam emails, *our* is present in 61% and *free* in 57%.

We are now in a position to start writing the body of our application to calculate the mutual information between each word and whether a message is spam or ham. We will put the body of the code in the `MutualInformation` object, which already contains the `wordFractionInFiles` method.

The first step is to create a Spark context:

```scala
// MutualInformation.scala
import org.apache.spark.{ SparkConf, SparkContext }
import org.apache.spark.SparkContext._
import org.apache.spark.rdd.RDD

object MutualInformation extends App {

  def wordFractionInFiles(sc:SparkContext)(fileGlob:String)
  :(RDD[(String, Double)], Long) = {
    ...
  }

  val conf = new SparkConf().setAppName("lingSpam")
  val sc = new SparkContext(conf)
```

Note that we did not need to do this when we were using the Spark shell because the shell comes with a pre-built context bound to the variable `sc`.

We can now calculate the conditional probabilities of a message containing a particular word given that it is *spam*, $P(wordPresent \mid spam)$. This is just the fraction of messages containing that word in the *spam* corpus. This, in turn, lets us infer the joint probability of a message containing a certain word and being *spam* $P(wordPresent, spam) = P(wordPresent \mid spam) \times P(spam)$. We will do this for all four combinations of classes: whether any given word is present or absent in a message, and whether that message is spam or ham:

```scala
/* Conditional probabilities RDD:
   word -> P(present | spam)
*/
val (pPresentGivenSpam, nSpam) = wordFractionInFiles(sc)("spam/*")
val pAbsentGivenSpam = pPresentGivenSpam.mapValues { 1.0 - _ }
val (pPresentGivenHam, nHam) = wordFractionInFiles(sc)("ham/*")
val pAbsentGivenHam = pPresentGivenHam.mapValues { 1.0 - _ }

// pSpam is the fraction of spam messages
val nMessages = nSpam + nHam
val pSpam = nSpam / nMessages.toDouble

// pHam is the fraction of ham messages
```

```
val pHam = 1.0 - pSpam

/* pPresentAndSpam is a key-value RDD of joint probabilities
   word -> P(word present, spam)
*/
val pPresentAndSpam = pPresentGivenSpam.mapValues {
  _ * pSpam
}
val pPresentAndHam = pPresentGivenHam.mapValues { _ * pHam }
val pAbsentAndSpam = pAbsentGivenSpam.mapValues { _ * pSpam }
val pAbsentAndHam = pAbsentGivenHam.mapValues { _ * pHam }
```

We will re-use these RDDs in several places in the calculation, so let's tell Spark to keep them in memory to avoid having to re-calculate them:

```
pPresentAndSpam.persist
pPresentAndHam.persist
pAbsentAndSpam.persist
pAbsentAndHam.persist
```

We now need to calculate the probabilities of words being present, $P(wordPresent)$. This is just the sum of pPresentAndSpam and pPresentAndHam, for each word. The tricky part is that not all words are present in both the ham and spam messages. We must therefore do a full outer join of those RDDs. This will give an RDD mapping each word to a pair of Option[Double] values. For words absent in either the ham or spam messages, we must use a default value. A sensible default is $P(wordPresent \mid spam) = (0.5 / nSpam) \times P(spam)$ for spam messages (a more rigorous approach would be to use *additive smoothing*). This implies that the word would appear once if the corpus was twice as large.

```
val pJoined = pPresentAndSpam.fullOuterJoin(pPresentAndHam)
val pJoinedDefault = pJoined.mapValues {
  case (presentAndSpam, presentAndHam) =>
    (presentAndSpam.getOrElse(0.5/nSpam * pSpam),
    presentAndHam.getOrElse(0.5/nHam * pHam))
}
```

Note that we could also have chosen 0 as the default value. This complicates the information gain calculation somewhat, since we cannot just take the log of a zero value, and it seems unlikely that a particular word has exactly zero probability of occurring in an email.

We can now construct an RDD mapping words to $P(wordPresent)$, the probability that a word exists in either a spam or a ham message:

```
val pPresent = pJoinedDefault.mapValues {
  case(presentAndHam, presentAndSpam) =>
    presentAndHam + presentAndSpam
}
pPresent.persist

val pAbsent = pPresent.mapValues { 1.0 - _ }
pAbsent.persist
```

We now have all the RDDs that we need to calculate the mutual information between the presence of a word in a message and whether it is ham or spam. We need to bring them all together using the equation for the mutual information outlined earlier.

We will start by defining a helper method that, given an RDD of joint probabilities $P(X, Y)$ and marginal probabilities $P(X)$ and $P(Y)$, calculates $P(X,Y) \times \log\left(\dfrac{P(X,Y)}{P(X)P(Y)}\right)$. Here, $P(X)$ could, for instance, be the probability of a word being present in a message $P(wordPresent)$ and $P(Y)$ would be the probability that that message is spam, $P(spam)$:

```
def miTerm(
  pXYs:RDD[(String, Double)],
  pXs:RDD[(String, Double)],
  pY: Double,
  default: Double // for words absent in PXY
):RDD[(String, Double)] =
  pXs.leftOuterJoin(pXYs).mapValues {
    case (pX, Some(pXY)) => pXY * math.log(pXY/(pX*pY))
    case (pX, None) => default * math.log(default/(pX*pY))
  }
```

We can use our function to calculate the four terms in the mutual information sum:

```
val miTerms = List(
  miTerm(pPresentAndSpam, pPresent, pSpam, 0.5/nSpam * pSpam),
  miTerm(pPresentAndHam, pPresent, pHam, 0.5/nHam * pHam),
  miTerm(pAbsentAndSpam, pAbsent, pSpam, 0.5/nSpam * pSpam),
  miTerm(pAbsentAndHam, pAbsent, pHam, 0.5/nHam * pHam)
)
```

Finally, we just need to sum those four terms together:

```scala
val mutualInformation = miTerms.reduce {
  (term1, term2) => term1.join(term2).mapValues {
    case (l, r) => l + r
  }
}
```

The RDD `mutualInformation` is a key-value RDD mapping each word to a measure of how informative the presence of that word is in discerning whether a message is spam or ham. Let's print out the twenty words that are most informative of whether a message is ham or spam:

```scala
mutualInformation.takeOrdered(20)(Ordering.by { - _._2 })
  .foreach { println }
```

Let's run this using `spark-submit`:

```
$ sbt package
$ spark-submit target/scala-2.10/spam_mi_2.10-0.1-SNAPSHOT.jar
(!,0.1479941771292119)
(language,0.14574624861510874)
(remove,0.11380645864246142)
(free,0.1073496947123657)
(university,0.10695975885487692)
(money,0.07531772498093084)
(click,0.06887598051593441)
(our,0.058950906866052394)
(today,0.05485248095680509)
(sell,0.05385519653184113)
(english,0.053509319455430575)
(business,0.05299311289740539)
(market,0.05248394151802276)
(product,0.05096229706182162)
(million,0.050233193237964546)
(linguistics,0.04990172586630499)
(internet,0.04974101556655623)
(company,0.04941817269989519)
(%,0.04890193809823071)
(save,0.04861393414892205)
```

Thus, we find that the presence of words like `language` or `free` or `!` carry the most information, because they are almost exclusively present in either just spam messages or just ham messages. A very simple classification algorithm could just take the top 10 (by mutual information) spam words, and the top 10 ham words and see whether a message contains more spam words or ham words. We will explore machine learning algorithms for classification in more depth in *Chapter 12, Distributed Machine Learning with MLlib*.

Lifting the hood

In the last section of this chapter, we will discuss, very briefly, how Spark works internally. For a more detailed discussion, see the *References* section at the end of the chapter.

When you open a Spark context, either explicitly or by launching the Spark shell, Spark starts a web UI with details of how the current task and past tasks have executed. Let's see this in action for the example mutual information program we wrote in the last section. To prevent the context from shutting down when the program completes, you can insert a call to `readLine` as the last line of the `main` method (after the call to `takeOrdered`). This expects input from the user, and will therefore pause program execution until you press *enter*.

To access the UI, point your browser to `127.0.0.1:4040`. If you have other instances of the Spark shell running, the port may be `4041`, or `4042` and so on.

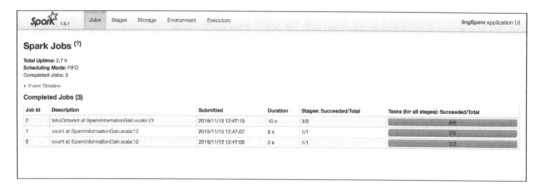

The first page of the UI tells us that our application contains three *jobs*. A job occurs as the result of an action. There are, indeed, three actions in our application: the first two are called within the `wordFractionInFiles` function:

```
val nMessages = messages.count()
```

The last job results from the call to `takeOrdered`, which forces the execution of the entire pipeline of RDD transformations that calculate the mutual information.

The web UI lets us delve deeper into each job. Click on the `takeOrdered` job in the job table. You will get taken to a page that describes the job in more detail:

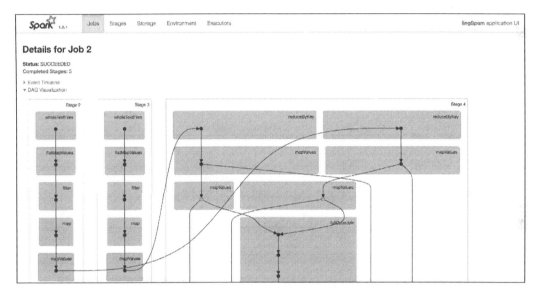

Of particular interest is the **DAG visualization** entry. This is a graph of the execution plan to fulfill the action, and provides a glimpse of the inner workings of Spark.

When you define a job by calling an action on an RDD, Spark looks at the RDD's lineage and constructs a graph mapping the dependencies: each RDD in the lineage is represented by a node, with directed edges going from this RDD's parent to itself. This type of graph is called a **directed acyclic graph (DAG)**, and is a data structure useful for dependency resolution. Let's explore the DAG for the `takeOrdered` job in our program using the web UI. The graph is quite complex, and it is therefore easy to get lost, so here is a simplified reproduction that only lists the RDDs bound to variable names in the program.

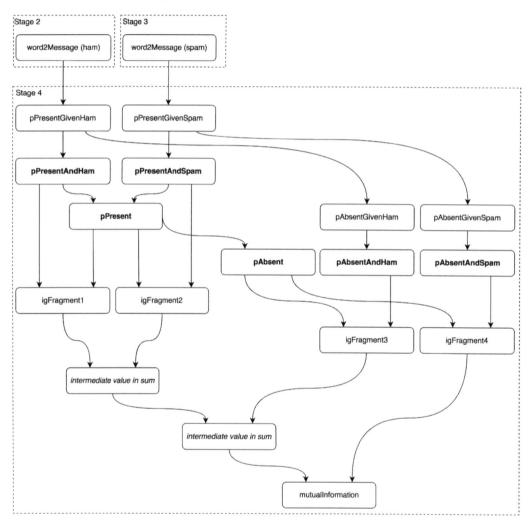

As you can see, at the bottom of the graph, we have the `mutualInformation` RDD. This is the RDD that we need to construct for our action. This RDD depends on the intermediate elements in the sum, `igFragment1`, `igFragment2`, and so on. We can work our way back through the list of dependencies until we reach the other end of the graph: RDDs that do not depend on other RDDs, only on external sources.

Once the graph is built, the Spark engines formulates a plan to execute the job. The plan starts with the RDDs that only have external dependencies (such as RDDs built by loading files from disk or fetching from a database) or RDDs that already have cached data. Each arrow along the graph is translated to a set of *tasks*, with each task applying a transformation to a partition of the data.

Tasks are grouped into *stages*. A stage consists of a set of tasks that can all be performed without needing an intermediate shuffle.

Data shuffling and partitions

To understand data shuffling in Spark, we first need to understand how data is partitioned in RDDs. When we create an RDD by, for instance, loading a file from HDFS, or reading a file in local storage, Spark has no control over what bits of data are distributed in which partitions. This becomes a problem for key-value RDDs: these often require knowing where occurrences of a particular key are, for instance to perform a join. If the key can occur anywhere in the RDD, we have to look through every partition to find the key.

To prevent this, Spark allows the definition of a *partitioner* on key-value RDDs. A partitioner is an attribute of the RDD that determines which partition a particular key lands in. When an RDD has a partitioner set, the location of a key is entirely determined by the partitioner, and not by the RDD's history, or the number of keys. Two different RDDs with the same partitioner will map the same key to the same partition.

Partitions impact performance through their effect on transformations. There are two types of transformations on key-value RDDs:

- Narrow transformations, like `mapValues`. In narrow transformations, the data to compute a partition in the child RDD resides on a single partition in the parent. The data processing for a narrow transformation can therefore be performed entirely locally, without needing to communicate data between nodes.

- Wide transformations, like `reduceByKey`. In wide transformations, the data to compute any single partition can reside on all the partitions in the parent. The RDD resulting from a wide transformation will, in general, have a partitioner set. For instance, the output of a `reduceByKey` transformation are hash-partitioned by default: the partition that a particular key ends up in is determined by `hash(key) % numPartitions`.

Thus, in our mutual information example, the RDDs `pPresentAndSpam` and `pPresentAndHam` will have the same partition structure since they both have the default hash partitioner. All descendent RDDs retain the same keys, all the way down to `mutualInformation`. The word `language`, for instance, will be in the same partition for each RDD.

Why does all this matter? If an RDD has a partitioner set, this partitioner is retained through all subsequent narrow transformations originating from this RDD. Let's go back to our mutual information example. The RDDs `pPresentGivenHam` and `pPresentGivenSpam` both originate from `reduceByKey` operations, and they both have string keys. They will therefore both have the same hash-partitioner (unless we explicitly set a different partitioner). This partitioner is retained as we construct `pPresentAndSpam` and `pPresentAndHam`. When we construct `pPresent`, we perform a full outer join of `pPresentAndSpam` and `pPresentAndHam`. Since both these RDDs have the same partitioner, the child RDD `pPresent` has narrow dependencies: we can just join the first partition of `pPresentAndSpam` with the first partition of `pPresentAndHam`, the second partition of `pPresentAndSpam` with the second partition of `pPresentAndHam` and so on, since any string key will be hashed to the same partition in both RDDs. By contrast, without partitioner, we would have to join the data in each partition of `pPresentAndSpam` with every partition of `pPresentAndSpam`. This would require sending data across the network to all the nodes holding `pPresentAndSpam`, a time-consuming exercise.

This process of having to send the data to construct a child RDD across the network, as a result of wide dependencies, is called *shuffling*. Much of the art of optimizing a Spark program involves reducing shuffling and, when shuffling is necessary, reducing the amount of shuffling.

Summary

In this chapter, we explored the basics of Spark and learned how to construct and manipulate RDDs. In the next chapter, we will learn about Spark SQL and DataFrames, a set of implicit conversions that allow us to manipulate RDDs in a manner similar to pandas DataFrames, and how to interact with different data sources using Spark.

Reference

- *Learning Spark*, by *Holden Karau, Andy Konwinski, Patrick Wendell*, and *Matei Zaharia, O'Reilly*, provides a much more complete introduction to Spark that this chapter can provide. I thoroughly recommend it.

- If you are interested in learning more about information theory, I recommend *David MacKay's* book *Information Theory, Inference, and Learning Algorithms*.

- *Information Retrieval*, by *Manning, Raghavan*, and *Schütze*, describes how to analyze textual data (including lemmatization and stemming). An online

- On the Ling-Spam dataset, and how to analyze it: `http://www.aueb.gr/users/ion/docs/ir_memory_based_antispam_filtering.pdf`.

- This blog post delves into the Spark Web UI in more detail. `https://databricks.com/blog/2015/06/22/understanding-your-spark-application-through-visualization.html`.

- This blog post, by *Sandy Ryza*, is the first in a two-part series discussing Spark internals, and how to leverage them to improve performance: `http://blog.cloudera.com/blog/2015/03/how-to-tune-your-apache-spark-jobs-part-1/`.

11
Spark SQL and DataFrames

In the previous chapter, we learned how to build a simple distributed application using Spark. The data that we used took the form of a set of e-mails stored as text files.

We learned that Spark was built around the concept of **resilient distributed datasets (RDDs)**. We explored several types of RDDs: simple RDDs of strings, key-value RDDs, and RDDs of doubles. In the case of key-value RDDs and RDDs of doubles, Spark added functionality beyond that of the simple RDDs through implicit conversions. There is one important type of RDD that we have not explored yet: **DataFrames** (previously called **SchemaRDD**). DataFrames allow the manipulation of objects significantly more complex than those we have explored to date.

A DataFrame is a distributed tabular data structure, and is therefore very useful for representing and manipulating structured data. In this chapter, we will first investigate DataFrames through the Spark shell, and then use the Ling-spam e-mail dataset, presented in the previous chapter, to see how DataFrames can be integrated in a machine learning pipeline.

DataFrames – a whirlwind introduction

Let's start by opening a Spark shell:

```
$ spark-shell
```

Let's imagine that we are interested in running analytics on a set of patients to estimate their overall health level. We have measured, for each patient, their height, weight, age, and whether they smoke.

We might represent the readings for each patient as a case class (you might wish to write some of this in a text editor and paste it into the Scala shell using `:paste`):

```scala
scala> case class PatientReadings(
  val patientId: Int,
  val heightCm: Int,
  val weightKg: Int,
  val age:Int,
  val isSmoker:Boolean
)

defined class PatientReadings
```

We would, typically, have many thousands of patients, possibly stored in a database or a CSV file. We will worry about how to interact with external sources later in this chapter. For now, let's just hard-code a few readings directly in the shell:

```scala
scala> val readings = List(
  PatientReadings(1, 175, 72, 43, false),
  PatientReadings(2, 182, 78, 28, true),
  PatientReadings(3, 164, 61, 41, false),
  PatientReadings(4, 161, 62, 43, true)
)

List[PatientReadings] = List(...
```

We can convert `readings` to an RDD by using `sc.parallelize`:

```scala
scala> val readingsRDD = sc.parallelize(readings)

readingsRDD: RDD[PatientReadings] = ParallelCollectionRDD[0] at
parallelize at <console>:25
```

Note that the type parameter of our RDD is `PatientReadings`. Let's convert the RDD to a DataFrame using the `.toDF` method:

```scala
scala> val readingsDF = readingsRDD.toDF

readingsDF: sql.DataFrame = [patientId: int, heightCm: int, weightKg:
int, age: int, isSmoker: boolean]
```

We have created a DataFrame where each row corresponds to the readings for a specific patient, and the columns correspond to the different features:

```
scala> readingsDF.show

+---------+--------+--------+---+--------+
|patientId|heightCm|weightKg|age|isSmoker|
+---------+--------+--------+---+--------+
|        1|     175|      72| 43|   false|
|        2|     182|      78| 28|    true|
|        3|     164|      61| 41|   false|
|        4|     161|      62| 43|    true|
+---------+--------+--------+---+--------+
```

The easiest way to create a DataFrame is to use the `toDF` method on an RDD. We can convert any `RDD[T]`, where `T` is a case class or a tuple, to a DataFrame. Spark will map each attribute of the case class to a column of the appropriate type in the DataFrame. It uses reflection to discover the names and types of the attributes. There are several other ways of constructing DataFrames, both from RDDs and from external sources, which we will explore later in this chapter.

DataFrames support many operations for manipulating the rows and columns. For instance, let's add a column for the **Body Mass Index (BMI)**. The BMI is a common way of aggregating *height* and *weight* to decide if someone is overweight or underweight. The formula for the BMI is:

$$BMI = weight\left(kg\right)/height\left(m\right)^2$$

Let's start by creating a column of the height in meters:

```
scala> val heightM = readingsDF("heightCm") / 100.0
heightM: sql.Column = (heightCm / 100.0)
```

`heightM` has data type `Column`, representing a column of data in a DataFrame. Columns support many arithmetic and comparison operators that apply element-wise across the column (similarly to Breeze vectors encountered in *Chapter 2, Manipulating Data with Breeze*). Operations on columns are lazy: the `heightM` column is not actually computed when defined. Let's now define a BMI column:

```
scala> val bmi = readingsDF("weightKg") / (heightM*heightM)
bmi: sql.Column = (weightKg / ((heightCm / 100.0) * (heightCm / 100.0)))
```

It would be useful to add the bmi column to our readings DataFrame. Since DataFrames, like RDDs, are immutable, we must define a new DataFrame that is identical to readingsDF, but with an additional column for the BMI. We can do this using the withColumn method, which takes, as its arguments, the name of the new column and a Column instance:

```
scala> val readingsWithBmiDF = readingsDF.withColumn("BMI", bmi)
readingsWithBmiDF: sql.DataFrame = [heightCm: int, weightKg: int, age:
int, isSmoker: boolean, BMI: double]
```

All the operations we have seen so far are *transformations*: they define a pipeline of operations that create new DataFrames. These transformations are executed when we call an **action**, such as show:

```
scala> readingsWithBmiDF.show
```

```
+---------+--------+--------+---+--------+------------------+
|patientId|heightCm|weightKg|age|isSmoker|               BMI|
+---------+--------+--------+---+--------+------------------+
|        1|     175|      72| 43|   false|23.510204081632654|
|        2|     182|      78| 28|    true| 23.54788069073783|
|        3|     164|      61| 41|   false|22.679952409280194|
|        4|     161|      62| 43|    true| 23.9188302920412|
+---------+--------+--------+---+--------+------------------+
```

Besides creating additional columns, DataFrames also support filtering rows that satisfy a certain predicate. For instance, we can select all smokers:

```
scala> readingsWithBmiDF.filter {
  readingsWithBmiDF("isSmoker")
}.show
```

```
+---------+--------+--------+---+--------+------------------+
|patientId|heightCm|weightKg|age|isSmoker|               BMI|
+---------+--------+--------+---+--------+------------------+
|        2|     182|      78| 28|    true|23.54788069073783|
|        4|     161|      62| 43|    true| 23.9188302920412|
+---------+--------+--------+---+--------+------------------+
```

Or, to select everyone who weighs more than 70 kgs:

```scala
scala> readingsWithBmiDF.filter {
  readingsWithBmiDF("weightKg") > 70
}.show
+---------+--------+--------+---+--------+------------------+
|patientId|heightCm|weightKg|age|isSmoker|               BMI|
+---------+--------+--------+---+--------+------------------+
|        1|     175|      72| 43|   false|23.510204081632654|
|        2|     182|      78| 28|    true| 23.54788069073783|
+---------+--------+--------+---+--------+------------------+
```

It can become cumbersome to keep repeating the DataFrame name in an expression. Spark defines the operator $ to refer to a column in the current DataFrame. Thus, the `filter` expression above could have been written more succinctly using:

```scala
scala> readingsWithBmiDF.filter { $"weightKg" > 70 }.show
+---------+--------+--------+---+--------+------------------+
|patientId|heightCm|weightKg|age|isSmoker|               BMI|
+---------+--------+--------+---+--------+------------------+
|        1|     175|      72| 43|   false|23.510204081632654|
|        2|     182|      78| 28|    true| 23.54788069073783|
+---------+--------+--------+---+--------+------------------+
```

The `.filter` method is overloaded. It accepts either a column of Boolean values, as above, or a string identifying a Boolean column in the current DataFrame. Thus, to filter our `readingsWithBmiDF` DataFrame to sub-select smokers, we could also have used the following:

```scala
scala> readingsWithBmiDF.filter("isSmoker").show
+---------+--------+--------+---+--------+------------------+
|patientId|heightCm|weightKg|age|isSmoker|               BMI|
+---------+--------+--------+---+--------+------------------+
|        2|     182|      78| 28|    true| 23.54788069073783|
|        4|     161|      62| 43|    true| 23.9188302920412|
+---------+--------+--------+---+--------+------------------+
```

When comparing for equality, you must compare columns with the special *triple-equals* operator:

```
scala> readingsWithBmiDF.filter { $"age" === 28 }.show
+---------+--------+--------+---+--------+-----------------+
|patientId|heightCm|weightKg|age|isSmoker|              BMI|
+---------+--------+--------+---+--------+-----------------+
|        2|     182|      78| 28|    true|23.54788069073783|
+---------+--------+--------+---+--------+-----------------+
```

Similarly, you must use `!==` to select rows that are not equal to a value:

```
scala> readingsWithBmiDF.filter { $"age" !== 28 }.show
+---------+--------+--------+---+--------+------------------+
|patientId|heightCm|weightKg|age|isSmoker|               BMI|
+---------+--------+--------+---+--------+------------------+
|        1|     175|      72| 43|   false|23.510204081632654|
|        3|     164|      61| 41|   false|22.679952409280194|
|        4|     161|      62| 43|    true| 23.9188302920412|
+---------+--------+--------+---+--------+------------------+
```

Aggregation operations

We have seen how to apply an operation to every row in a DataFrame to create a new column, and we have seen how to use filters to build new DataFrames with a sub-set of rows from the original DataFrame. The last set of operations on DataFrames is grouping operations, equivalent to the GROUP BY statement in SQL. Let's calculate the average BMI for smokers and non-smokers. We must first tell Spark to group the DataFrame by a column (the isSmoker column, in this case), and then apply an aggregation operation (averaging, in this case) to reduce each group:

```
scala> val smokingDF = readingsWithBmiDF.groupBy(
  "isSmoker").agg(avg("BMI"))
smokingDF: org.apache.spark.sql.DataFrame = [isSmoker: boolean, AVG(BMI):
double]
```

This has created a new DataFrame with two columns: the grouping column and the column over which we aggregated. Let's show this DataFrame:

```
scala> smokingDF.show
+--------+-------------------+
|isSmoker|           AVG(BMI)|
+--------+-------------------+
|    true|23.733355491389517|
|   false|23.095078245456424|
+--------+-------------------+
```

Besides averaging, there are several operators for performing the aggregation across each group. We outline some of the more important ones in the table below, but, for a full list, consult the *Aggregate functions* section of http://spark.apache.org/ docs/latest/api/scala/index.html#org.apache.spark.sql.functions$:

Operator	Notes
avg(column)	Group averages of the values in the specified column.
count(column)	Number of elements in each group in the specified column.
countDistinct(column, ...)	Number of distinct elements in each group. This can also accept multiple columns to return the count of unique elements across several columns.
first(column), last(column)	First/last element in each group
max(column), min(column)	Largest/smallest element in each group
sum(column)	Sum of the values in each group

Each aggregation operator takes either the name of a column, as a string, or an expression of type Column. The latter allows aggregation of compound expressions. If we wanted the average height, in meters, of the smokers and non-smokers in our sample, we could use:

```
scala> readingsDF.groupBy("isSmoker").agg {
  avg($"heightCm"/100.0)
}.show
+--------+----------------------+
|isSmoker|AVG((heightCm / 100.0))|
+--------+----------------------+
```

```
|    true|                1.715|
|   false|   1.6949999999999998|
+--------+---------------------+
```

We can also use compound expressions to define the column on which to group. For instance, to count the number of patients in each age group, increasing by decade, we can use:

```
scala> readingsDF.groupBy(floor($"age"/10)).agg(count("*")).show

+-----------------+--------+
|FLOOR((age / 10))|count(1)|
+-----------------+--------+
|              4.0|       3|
|              2.0|       1|
+-----------------+--------+
```

We have used the short-hand "*" to indicate a count over every column.

Joining DataFrames together

So far, we have only considered operations on a single DataFrame. Spark also offers SQL-like joins to combine DataFrames. Let's assume that we have another DataFrame mapping the patient id to a (systolic) blood pressure measurement. We will assume we have the data as a list of pairs mapping patient IDs to blood pressures:

```
scala> val bloodPressures = List((1 -> 110), (3 -> 100), (4 -> 125))
bloodPressures: List[(Int, Int)] = List((1,110), (3,100), (4,125))


scala> val bloodPressureRDD = sc.parallelize(bloodPressures)
res16: rdd.RDD[(Int, Int)] = ParallelCollectionRDD[74] at parallelize at
<console>:24
```

We can construct a DataFrame from this RDD of tuples. However, unlike when constructing DataFrames from RDDs of case classes, Spark cannot infer column names. We must therefore pass these explicitly to .toDF:

```
scala> val bloodPressureDF = bloodPressureRDD.toDF(
  "patientId", "bloodPressure")
bloodPressureDF: DataFrame = [patientId: int, bloodPressure: int]


scala> bloodPressureDF.show
```

```
+---------+-------------+
|patientId|bloodPressure|
+---------+-------------+
|        1|          110|
|        3|          100|
|        4|          125|
+---------+-------------+
```

Let's join `bloodPressureDF` with `readingsDF`, using the patient ID as the join key:

```
scala> readingsDF.join(bloodPressureDF,
  readingsDF("patientId") === bloodPressureDF("patientId")
).show
+---------+--------+--------+---+--------+--------+-------------+
|patientId|heightCm|weightKg|age|isSmoker|patientId|bloodPressure|
+---------+--------+--------+---+--------+--------+-------------+
|        1|     175|      72| 43|   false|        1|          110|
|        3|     164|      61| 41|   false|        3|          100|
|        4|     161|      62| 43|    true|        4|          125|
+---------+--------+--------+---+--------+--------+-------------+
```

This performs an *inner join*: only patient IDs present in both DataFrames are included in the result. The type of join can be passed as an extra argument to `join`. For instance, we can perform a *left join*:

```
scala> readingsDF.join(bloodPressureDF,
  readingsDF("patientId") === bloodPressureDF("patientId"),
  "leftouter"
).show
+---------+--------+--------+---+--------+--------+-------------+
|patientId|heightCm|weightKg|age|isSmoker|patientId|bloodPressure|
+---------+--------+--------+---+--------+--------+-------------+
|        1|     175|      72| 43|   false|        1|          110|
|        2|     182|      78| 28|    true|     null|         null|
|        3|     164|      61| 41|   false|        3|          100|
|        4|     161|      62| 43|    true|        4|          125|
+---------+--------+--------+---+--------+--------+-------------+
```

Possible join types are `inner`, `outer`, `leftouter`, `rightouter`, or `leftsemi`. These should all be familiar, apart from `leftsemi`, which corresponds to a *left semi join*. This is the same as an inner join, but only the columns on the left-hand side are retained after the join. It is thus a way to filter a DataFrame for rows which are present in another DataFrame.

Custom functions on DataFrames

So far, we have only used built-in functions to operate on DataFrame columns. While these are often sufficient, we sometimes need greater flexibility. Spark lets us apply custom transformations to every row through **user-defined functions** (UDFs). Let's assume that we want to use the equation that we derived in *Chapter 2, Manipulating Data with Breeze*, for the probability of a person being male, given their height and weight. We calculated that the decision boundary was given by:

$$f = -0.75 + 2.48 \times rescaledHeight + 2.23 \times rescaledWeight$$

Any person with $f > 0$ is more likely to be male than female, given their height and weight and the training set used for *Chapter 2, Manipulating Data with Breeze* (which was based on students, so is unlikely to be representative of the population as a whole). To convert from a height in centimeters to the normalized height, *rescaledHeight*, we can use this formula:

$$rescaledHeight = \frac{height - \langle height \rangle}{\sigma_{height}} = \frac{height - 171}{8.95}$$

Similarly, to convert a weight (in kilograms) to the normalized weight, *rescaledWeight*, we can use:

$$rescaledWeight = \frac{weight - \langle weight \rangle}{\sigma_{weight}} = \frac{weight - 65.7}{13.4}$$

The average and standard deviation of the *height* and *weight* are calculated from the training set. Let's write a Scala function that returns whether a person is more likely to be male, given their height and weight:

```scala
scala> def likelyMale(height:Int, weight:Int):Boolean = {
  val rescaledHeight = (height - 171.0)/8.95
```

```
  val rescaledWeight = (weight - 65.7)/13.4
  -0.75 + 2.48*rescaledHeight + 2.23*rescaledWeight > 0
}
```

To use this function on Spark DataFrames, we need to register it as a **user-defined function** (UDF). This transforms our function, which accepts integer arguments, into one that accepts column arguments:

```
scala> val likelyMaleUdf = sqlContext.udf.register(
  "likelyMaleUdf", likelyMale _)
likelyMaleUdf: org.apache.spark.sql.UserDefinedFunction = UserDefinedFunc
tion(<function2>,BooleanType,List())
```

To register a UDF, we must have access to a `sqlContext` instance. The SQL context provides the entry point for DataFrame operations. The Spark shell creates a SQL context at startup, bound to the variable `sqlContext`, and destroys it when the shell session is closed.

The first argument passed to the `register` function is the name of the UDF (we will use the UDF name later when we write SQL statements on the DataFrame, but you can ignore it for now). We can then use the UDF just like the built-in transformations included in Spark:

```
scala> val likelyMaleColumn = likelyMaleUdf(
  readingsDF("heightCm"), readingsDF("weightKg"))
likelyMaleColumn: org.apache.spark.sql.Column = UDF(heightCm,weightKg)

scala> readingsDF.withColumn("likelyMale", likelyMaleColumn).show
+---------+--------+--------+---+--------+---------+
|patientId|heightCm|weightKg|age|isSmoker|likelyMale|
+---------+--------+--------+---+--------+---------+
|        1|     175|      72| 43|   false|     true|
|        2|     182|      78| 28|    true|     true|
|        3|     164|      61| 41|   false|    false|
|        4|     161|      62| 43|    true|    false|
+---------+--------+--------+---+--------+---------+
```

As you can see, Spark applies the function underlying the UDF to every row in the DataFrame. We are not limited to using UDFs to create new columns. We can also use them in `filter` expressions. For instance, to select rows likely to correspond to women:

```scala
scala> readingsDF.filter(
  ! likelyMaleUdf($"heightCm", $"weightKg")
).show
+---------+--------+--------+---+--------+
|patientId|heightCm|weightKg|age|isSmoker|
+---------+--------+--------+---+--------+
|        3|     164|      61| 41|   false|
|        4|     161|      62| 43|    true|
+---------+--------+--------+---+--------+
```

Using UDFs lets us define arbitrary Scala functions to transform rows, giving tremendous additional power for data manipulation.

DataFrame immutability and persistence

DataFrames, like RDDs, are immutable. When you define a transformation on a DataFrame, this always creates a new DataFrame. The original DataFrame cannot be modified in place (this is notably different to pandas DataFrames, for instance).

Operations on DataFrames can be grouped into two: *transformations*, which result in the creation of a new DataFrame, and *actions*, which usually return a Scala type or have a side-effect. Methods like `filter` or `withColumn` are transformations, while methods like `show` or `head` are actions.

Transformations are lazy, much like transformations on RDDs. When you generate a new DataFrame by transforming an existing DataFrame, this results in the elaboration of an execution plan for creating the new DataFrame, but the data itself is not transformed immediately. You can access the execution plan with the `queryExecution` method.

When you call an action on a DataFrame, Spark processes the action as if it were a regular RDD: it implicitly builds a direct acyclic graph to resolve dependencies, processing the transformations needed to build the DataFrame on which the action was called.

Much like RDDs, we can persist DataFrames in memory or on disk:

```scala
scala> readingsDF.persist
readingsDF.type = [patientId: int, heightCm: int,...]
```

This works in the same way as persisting RDDs: next time the RDD is calculated, it will be kept in memory (provided there is enough space), rather than discarded. The level of persistence can also be set:

```scala
scala> import org.apache.spark.storage.StorageLevel
import org.apache.spark.storage.StorageLevel

scala> readingsDF.persist(StorageLevel.MEMORY_AND_DISK)
readingsDF.type = [patientId: int, heightCm: int, ...]
```

SQL statements on DataFrames

By now, you will have noticed that many operations on DataFrames are inspired by SQL operations. Additionally, Spark allows us to register DataFrames as tables and query them with SQL statements directly. We can therefore build a temporary database as part of the program flow.

Let's register `readingsDF` as a temporary table:

```scala
scala> readingsDF.registerTempTable("readings")
```

This registers a temporary table that can be used in SQL queries. Registering a temporary table relies on the presence of a SQL context. The temporary tables are destroyed when the SQL context is destroyed (when we close the shell, for instance).

Let's explore what we can do with our temporary tables and the SQL context. We can first get a list of all the tables currently registered with the context:

```scala
scala> sqlContext.tables
DataFrame = [tableName: string, isTemporary: boolean]
```

This returns a DataFrame. In general, all operations on a SQL context that return data return DataFrames:

```scala
scala> sqlContext.tables.show
+---------+-----------+
|tableName|isTemporary|
+---------+-----------+
| readings|       true|
+---------+-----------+
```

We can query this table by passing SQL statements to the SQL context:

```
scala> sqlContext.sql("SELECT * FROM readings").show

+---------+--------+--------+---+--------+
|patientId|heightCm|weightKg|age|isSmoker|
+---------+--------+--------+---+--------+
|        1|     175|      72| 43|   false|
|        2|     182|      78| 28|    true|
|        3|     164|      61| 41|   false|
|        4|     161|      62| 43|    true|
+---------+--------+--------+---+--------+
```

Any UDFs registered with the `sqlContext` are available through the name given to them when they were registered. We can therefore use them in SQL queries:

```
scala> sqlContext.sql("""
SELECT
  patientId,
  likelyMaleUdf(heightCm, weightKg) AS likelyMale
FROM readings
""").show

+---------+----------+
|patientId|likelyMale|
+---------+----------+
|        1|      true|
|        2|      true|
|        3|     false|
|        4|     false|
+---------+----------+
```

You might wonder why one would want to register DataFrames as temporary tables and run SQL queries on those tables, when the same functionality is available directly on DataFrames. The main reason is for interacting with external tools. Spark can run a SQL engine that exposes a JDBC interface, meaning that programs that know how to interact with a SQL database will be able to make use of the temporary tables.

We don't have the space to cover how to set up a distributed SQL engine in this book, but you can find details in the Spark documentation (http://spark.apache.org/docs/latest/sql-programming-guide.html#distributed-sql-engine).

Complex data types – arrays, maps, and structs

So far, all the elements in our DataFrames were simple types. DataFrames support three additional collection types: arrays, maps, and structs.

Structs

The first compound type that we will look at is the **struct**. A struct is similar to a case class: it stores a set of key-value pairs, with a fixed set of keys. If we convert an RDD of a case class containing nested case classes to a DataFrame, Spark will convert the nested objects to a struct.

Let's imagine that we want to serialize Lords of the Ring characters. We might use the following object model:

```
case class Weapon(name:String, weaponType:String)
case class LotrCharacter(name:String, val weapon:Weapon)
```

We want to create a DataFrame of `LotrCharacter` instances. Let's create some dummy data:

```
scala> val characters = List(
  LotrCharacter("Gandalf", Weapon("Glamdring", "sword")),
  LotrCharacter("Frodo", Weapon("Sting", "dagger")),
  LotrCharacter("Aragorn", Weapon("Anduril", "sword"))
)
characters: List[LotrCharacter] = List(LotrCharacter...

scala> val charactersDF = sc.parallelize(characters).toDF
charactersDF: DataFrame = [name: string, weapon: struct<name:string,weapo
nType:string>]

scala> charactersDF.printSchema
root
 |-- name: string (nullable = true)
 |-- weapon: struct (nullable = true)
 |    |-- name: string (nullable = true)
```

```
|    |-- weaponType: string (nullable = true)
```

```
scala> charactersDF.show
+-------+----------------+
|   name|          weapon|
+-------+----------------+
|Gandalf|[Glamdring,sword]|
|  Frodo|   [Sting,dagger]|
|Aragorn|   [Anduril,sword]|
+-------+----------------+
```

The weapon attribute in the case class was converted to a struct column in the DataFrame. To extract sub-fields from a struct, we can pass the field name to the column's .apply method:

```
scala> val weaponTypeColumn = charactersDF("weapon")("weaponType")
weaponTypeColumn: org.apache.spark.sql.Column = weapon[weaponType]
```

We can use this derived column just as we would any other column. For instance, let's filter our DataFrame to only contain characters who wield a sword:

```
scala> charactersDF.filter { weaponTypeColumn === "sword" }.show
+-------+----------------+
|   name|          weapon|
+-------+----------------+
|Gandalf|[Glamdring,sword]|
|Aragorn|   [Anduril,sword]|
+-------+----------------+
```

Arrays

Let's return to the earlier example, and assume that, besides height, weight, and age measurements, we also have phone numbers for our patients. Each patient might have zero, one, or more phone numbers. We will define a new case class and new dummy data:

```
scala> case class PatientNumbers(
  patientId:Int, phoneNumbers:List[String])
```

```
defined class PatientNumbers

scala> val numbers = List(
  PatientNumbers(1, List("07929123456")),
  PatientNumbers(2, List("07929432167", "07929234578")),
  PatientNumbers(3, List.empty),
  PatientNumbers(4, List("07927357862"))
)


scala> val numbersDF = sc.parallelize(numbers).toDF
numbersDF: org.apache.spark.sql.DataFrame = [patientId: int,
phoneNumbers: array<string>]
```

The List[String] array in our case class gets translated to an array<string>
data type:

```
scala> numbersDF.printSchema
root
 |-- patientId: integer (nullable = false)
 |-- phoneNumbers: array (nullable = true)
 |    |-- element: string (containsNull = true)
```

As with structs, we can construct a column for a specific index the array. For
instance, we can select the first element in each array:

```
scala> val bestNumberColumn = numbersDF("phoneNumbers")(0)
bestNumberColumn: org.apache.spark.sql.Column = phoneNumbers[0]


scala> numbersDF.withColumn("bestNumber", bestNumberColumn).show
+---------+--------------------+-----------+
|patientId|        phoneNumbers| bestNumber|
+---------+--------------------+-----------+
|        1|   List(07929123456)|07929123456|
|        2|List(07929432167,...|07929432167|
|        3|              List()|       null|
|        4|   List(07927357862)|07927357862|
+---------+--------------------+-----------+
```

Maps

The last compound data type is the map. Maps are similar to structs inasmuch as they store key-value pairs, but the set of keys is not fixed when the DataFrame is created. They can thus store arbitrary key-value pairs.

Scala maps will be converted to DataFrame maps when the DataFrame is constructed. They can then be queried in a manner similar to structs.

Interacting with data sources

A major challenge in data science or engineering is dealing with the wealth of input and output formats for persisting data. We might receive or send data as CSV files, JSON files, or through a SQL database, to name a few.

Spark provides a unified API for serializing and de-serializing DataFrames to and from different data sources.

JSON files

Spark supports loading data from JSON files, provided that each line in the JSON file corresponds to a single JSON object. Each object will be mapped to a DataFrame row. JSON arrays are mapped to arrays, and embedded objects are mapped to structs.

This section would be a little dry without some data, so let's generate some from the GitHub API. Unfortunately, the GitHub API does not return JSON formatted as a single object per line. The code repository for this chapter contains a script, `FetchData.scala` which will download and format JSON entries for Martin Odersky's repositories, saving the objects to a file named `odersky_repos.json` (go ahead and change the GitHub user in `FetchData.scala` if you want). You can also download a pre-constructed data file from `data.scala4datascience.com/odersky_repos.json`.

Let's dive into the Spark shell and load this data into a DataFrame. Reading from a JSON file is as simple as passing the file name to the `sqlContext.read.json` method:

```scala
scala> val df = sqlContext.read.json("odersky_repos.json")
df: DataFrame = [archive_url: string, assignees_url: ...]
```

Reading from a JSON file loads data as a DataFrame. Spark automatically infers the schema from the JSON documents. There are many columns in our DataFrame. Let's sub-select a few to get a more manageable DataFrame:

```scala
scala> val reposDF = df.select("name", "language", "fork", "owner")
reposDF: DataFrame = [name: string, language: string, ...]
```

```scala
scala> reposDF.show
+----------------+----------+-----+--------------------+
|            name|  language| fork|               owner|
+----------------+----------+-----+--------------------+
|           dotty|     Scala| true|[https://avatars....|
|        frontend|JavaScript| true|[https://avatars....|
|           scala|     Scala| true|[https://avatars....|
|       scala-dist|     Scala| true|[https://avatars....|
|scala.github.com|JavaScript| true|[https://avatars....|
|          scalax|     Scala|false|[https://avatars....|
|            sips|       CSS|false|[https://avatars....|
+----------------+----------+-----+--------------------+
```

Let's save the DataFrame back to JSON:

```scala
scala> reposDF.write.json("repos_short.json")
```

If you look at the files present in the directory in which you are running the Spark shell, you will notice a `repos_short.json` directory. Inside it, you will see files named `part-000000`, `part-000001`, and so on. When serializing JSON, each partition of the DataFrame is serialized independently. If you are running this on several machines, you will find parts of the serialized output on each computer.

You may, optionally, pass a `mode` argument to control how Spark deals with the case of an existing `repos_short.json` file:

```scala
scala> import org.apache.spark.sql.SaveMode
import org.apache.spark.sql.SaveMode
```

```scala
scala> reposDF.write.mode(
  SaveMode.Overwrite).json("repos_short.json")
```

Available save modes are `ErrorIfExists`, `Append` (only available for Parquet files), `Overwrite`, and `Ignore` (do not save if the file exists already).

Parquet files

Apache Parquet is a popular file format well-suited for storing tabular data. It is often used for serialization in the Hadoop ecosystem, since it allows for efficient extraction of specific columns and rows without having to read the entire file.

Serialization and deserialization of Parquet files is identical to JSON, with the substitution of `json` with `parquet`:

```scala
scala> reposDF.write.parquet("repos_short.parquet")


scala> val newDF = sqlContext.read.parquet("repos_short.parquet")
newDF: DataFrame = [name: string, language: string, fo...]


scala> newDF.show
+----------------+----------+-----+--------------------+
|            name|  language| fork|               owner|
+----------------+----------+-----+--------------------+
|           dotty|     Scala| true|[https://avatars....|
|        frontend|JavaScript| true|[https://avatars....|
|           scala|     Scala| true|[https://avatars....|
|      scala-dist|     Scala| true|[https://avatars....|
|scala.github.com|JavaScript| true|[https://avatars....|
|          scalax|     Scala|false|[https://avatars....|
|            sips|       CSS|false|[https://avatars....|
+----------------+----------+-----+--------------------+
```

In general, Parquet will be more space-efficient than JSON for storing large collections of objects. Parquet is also much more efficient at retrieving specific columns or rows, if the partition can be inferred from the row. Parquet is thus advantageous over JSON unless you need the output to be human-readable, or de-serializable by an external program.

Standalone programs

So far, we have been using Spark SQL and DataFrames through the Spark shell. To use it in standalone programs, you will need to create it explicitly, from a Spark context:

```scala
val conf = new SparkConf().setAppName("applicationName")
val sc = new SparkContext(conf)
val sqlContext = new org.apache.spark.sql.SQLContext(sc)
```

Additionally, importing the `implicits` object nested in `sqlContext` allows the conversions of RDDs to DataFrames:

```
import sqlContext.implicits._
```

We will use DataFrames extensively in the next chapter to manipulate data to get it ready for use with MLlib.

Summary

In this chapter, we explored Spark SQL and DataFrames. DataFrames add a rich layer of abstraction on top of Spark's core engine, greatly facilitating the manipulation of tabular data. Additionally, the source API allows the serialization and de-serialization of DataFrames from a rich variety of data files.

In the next chapter, we will build on our knowledge of Spark and DataFrames to build a spam filter using MLlib.

References

DataFrames are a relatively recent addition to Spark. There is thus still a dearth of literature and documentation. The first port of call should be the Scala docs, available at: `http://spark.apache.org/docs/latest/api/scala/index.html#org.apache.spark.sql.DataFrame`.

The Scaladocs for operations available on the DataFrame `Column` type can be found at: `http://spark.apache.org/docs/latest/api/scala/#org.apache.spark.sql.Column`.

There is also extensive documentation on the Parquet file format: `https://parquet.apache.org`.

12
Distributed Machine Learning with MLlib

Machine learning describes the construction of algorithms that make predictions from data. It is a core component of most data science pipelines, and is often seen to be the component adding the most value: the accuracy of the machine learning algorithm determines the success of the data science endeavor. It is also, arguably, the section of the data science pipeline that requires the most knowledge from fields beyond software engineering: a machine learning expert will be familiar, not just with algorithms, but also with statistics and with the business domain.

Choosing and tuning a machine learning algorithm to solve a particular problem involves significant exploratory analysis to try and determine which features are relevant, how features are correlated, whether there are outliers in the dataset, and so on. Designing suitable machine learning pipelines is difficult. Add on an additional layer of complexity resulting from the size of datasets and the need for scalability, and you have a real challenge.

MLlib helps mitigate this difficulty. MLlib is a component of Spark that provides machine learning algorithms on top of the core Spark libraries. It offers a set of learning algorithms that parallelize well over distributed datasets.

MLlib has evolved into two separate layers. MLlib itself contains the core algorithms, and **ml**, also called the *pipeline API*, defines an API for gluing algorithms together and provides a higher level of abstraction. The two libraries differ in the data types on which they operate: the original MLlib predates the introduction of DataFrames, and acts mainly on RDDs of feature vectors. The pipeline API operates on DataFrames.

In this chapter, we will study the newer pipeline API, diving into MLlib only when the functionality is missing from the pipeline API.

This chapter does not try to teach the machine learning fundamentals behind the algorithms that we present. We assume that the reader has a good enough grasp of machine learning tools and techniques to understand, at least superficially, what the algorithms presented here do, and we defer to better authors for in-depth explanations of the mechanics of statistical learning (we present several references at the end of the chapter).

MLlib is a rich library that is evolving rapidly. This chapter does not aim to give a complete overview of the library. We will work through the construction of a machine learning pipeline to train a spam filter, learning about the parts of MLlib that we need along the way. Having read this chapter, you will have an understanding of how the different parts of the library fit together, and can use the online documentation, or a more specialized book (see references at the end of this chapter) to learn about the parts of MLlib not covered here.

Introducing MLlib – Spam classification

Let's introduce MLlib with a concrete example. We will look at spam classification using the Ling-Spam dataset that we used in the *Chapter 10, Distributed Batch Processing with Spark*. We will create a spam filter that uses logistic regression to estimate the probability that a given message is spam.

We will run through examples using the Spark shell, but you will find an analogous program in `LogisticRegressionDemo.scala` among the examples for this chapter. If you have not installed Spark, refer to *Chapter 10, Distributed Batch Processing with Spark*, for installation instructions.

Let's start by loading the e-mails in the Ling-Spam dataset. If you have not done this for *Chapter 10, Distributed Batch Processing with Spark*, download the data from `data.scala4datascience.com/ling-spam.tar.gz` or `data.scala4datascience.com/ling-spam.zip`, depending on whether you want a `tar.gz` file or a `zip` file, and unpack the archive. This will create a `spam` directory and a `ham` directory containing spam and ham messages, respectively.

Let's use the `wholeTextFiles` method to load spam and ham e-mails:

```scala
scala> val spamText = sc.wholeTextFiles("spam/*")
spamText: RDD[(String, String)] = spam/...


scala> val hamText = sc.wholeTextFiles("ham/*")
hamText: RDD[(String, String)] = ham/...
```

The `wholeTextFiles` method creates a key-value RDD where the keys are the file names and the values are the contents of the files:

```scala
scala> spamText.first
(String, String) =
(file:spam/spmsga1.txt,"Subject: great part-time summer job! ...")


scala> spamText.count
Long = 481
```

The algorithms in the pipeline API work on DataFrames. We must therefore convert our key-value RDDs to DataFrames. We define a new case class, LabelledDocument, which contains a message text and a category label identifying whether a message is spam or ham:

```scala
scala> case class LabelledDocument(
  fileName:String,
  text:String,
  category:String
)
defined class LabelledDocument


scala> val spamDocuments = spamText.map {
  case (fileName, text) =>
    LabelledDocument(fileName, text, "spam")
}
spamDocuments: RDD[LabelledDocument] = MapPartitionsRDD[2] at map


scala> val hamDocuments = hamText.map {
  case (fileName, text) =>
    LabelledDocument(fileName, text, "ham")
}
hamDocuments: RDD[LabelledDocument] = MapPartitionsRDD[3] at map
```

To create models, we will need all the documents in a single DataFrame. Let's therefore take the union of our two LabelledDocument RDDs, and transform that to a DataFrame. The union method concatenates RDDs together:

```scala
scala> val allDocuments = spamDocuments.union(hamDocuments)
allDocuments: RDD[LabelledDocument] = UnionRDD[4] at union

scala> val documentsDF = allDocuments.toDF
documentsDF: DataFrame = [fileName: string, text: string, category:
string]
```

Let's do some basic checks to verify that we have loaded all the documents. We start by persisting the DataFrame in memory to avoid having to re-create it from the raw text files.

```scala
scala> documentsDF.persist
documentsDF.type = [fileName: string, text: string, category: string]

scala> documentsDF.show
+--------------------+--------------------+--------+
|            fileName|                text|category|
+--------------------+--------------------+--------+
|file:/Users/pasca...|Subject: great pa...|    spam|
|file:/Users/pasca...|Subject: auto ins...|    spam|
|file:/Users/pasca...|Subject: want bes...|    spam|
|file:/Users/pasca...|Subject: email 57...|    spam|
|file:/Users/pasca...|Subject: n't miss...|    spam|
|file:/Users/pasca...|Subject: amaze wo...|    spam|
|file:/Users/pasca...|Subject: help loa...|    spam|
|file:/Users/pasca...|Subject: beat irs...|    spam|
|file:/Users/pasca...|Subject: email 57...|    spam|
|file:/Users/pasca...|Subject: best , b...|    spam|
|                 ...|                    |        |
+--------------------+--------------------+--------+

scala> documentsDF.groupBy("category").agg(count("*")).show
+--------+--------+
|category|COUNT(1)|
+--------+--------+
```

```
|    spam|    481|
|     ham|   2412|
+--------+--------+
```

Let's now split the DataFrame into a training set and a test set. We will use the test set to validate the model that we build. For now, we will just use a single split, training the model on 70% of the data and testing it on the remaining 30%. In the next section, we will look at cross-validation, which provides more rigorous way to check the accuracy of our models.

We can achieve this 70-30 split using the DataFrame's `.randomSplit` method:

```scala
scala> val Array(trainDF, testDF) = documentsDF.randomSplit(
  Array(0.7, 0.3))
trainDF: DataFrame = [fileName: string, text: string, category: string]
testDF: DataFrame = [fileName: string, text: string, category: string]
```

The `.randomSplit` method takes an array of weights and returns an array of DataFrames, of approximately the size specified by the weights. For instance, we passed weights `0.7` and `0.3`, indicating that any given row has a 70% chance of ending up in `trainDF`, and a 30% chance of ending up in `testDF`. Note that this means the split DataFrames are not of fixed size: `trainDF` is approximately, but not exactly, 70% the size of `documentsDF`:

```scala
scala> trainDF.count / documentsDF.count.toDouble
Double = 0.7013480815762184
```

If you need a fixed size sample, use the DataFrame's `.sample` method to obtain `trainDF` and filter `documentDF` for rows not in `trainDF`.

We are now in a position to start using MLlib. Our attempt at classification will involve performing logistic regression on *term-frequency vectors*: we will count how often each word appears in each message, and use the frequency of occurrence as a feature. Before jumping into the code, let's take a step back and discuss the structure of machine learning pipelines.

Pipeline components

Pipelines consist of a set of components joined together such that the DataFrame produced by one component is used as input for the next component. The components available are split into two classes: *transformers* and *estimators*.

Transformers

Transformers transform one DataFrame into another, normally by appending one or more columns.

The first step in our spam classification algorithm is to split each message into an array of words. This is called **tokenization**. We can use the `Tokenizer` transformer, provided by MLlib:

```scala
scala> import org.apache.spark.ml.feature._
import org.apache.spark.ml.feature._


scala> val tokenizer = new Tokenizer()
tokenizer: org.apache.spark.ml.feature.Tokenizer = tok_75559f60e8cf
```

The behavior of transformers can be customized through getters and setters. The easiest way of obtaining a list of the parameters available is to call the `.explainParams` method:

```scala
scala> println(tokenizer.explainParams)
inputCol: input column name (undefined)
outputCol: output column name (default: tok_75559f60e8cf__output)
```

We see that the behavior of a `Tokenizer` instance can be customized using two parameters: `inputCol` and `outputCol`, describing the header of the column containing the input (the string to be tokenized) and the output (the array of words), respectively. We can set these parameters using the `setInputCol` and `setOutputCol` methods.

We set `inputCol` to `"text"`, since that is what the column is called in our training and test DataFrames. We will set `outputCol` to `"words"`:

```scala
scala> tokenizer.setInputCol("text").setOutputCol("words")
org.apache.spark.ml.feature.Tokenizer = tok_75559f60e8cf
```

In due course, we will integrate `tokenizer` into a pipeline, but, for now, let's just use it to transform the training DataFrame, to verify that it works correctly.

```scala
scala> val tokenizedDF = tokenizer.transform(trainDF)
tokenizedDF: DataFrame = [fileName: string, text: string, category:
string, words: array<string>]


scala> tokenizedDF.show
```

```
+---------------+---------------+--------+-------------------+
|      fileName |          text|category|              words|
+---------------+---------------+--------+-------------------+
|file:/Users...|Subject: auto...|    spam|[subject:, auto, ...|
|file:/Users...|Subject: want...|    spam|[subject:, want, ...|
|file:/Users...|Subject: n't ...|    spam|[subject:, n't, m...|
|file:/Users...|Subject: amaz...|    spam|[subject:, amaze,...|
|file:/Users...|Subject: help...|    spam|[subject:, help, ...|
|file:/Users...|Subject: beat...|    spam|[subject:, beat, ...|
|...                                                         |
+---------------+---------------+--------+-------------------+
```

The `tokenizer` transformer produces a new DataFrame with an additional column, `words`, containing an array of the words in the `text` column.

Clearly, we can use our `tokenizer` to transform any DataFrame with the correct schema. We could, for instance, use it on the test set. Much of machine learning involves calling the same (or a very similar) pipeline on different data sets. By providing the pipeline abstraction, MLlib facilitates reasoning about complex machine learning algorithms consisting of many cleaning, transformation, and modeling components.

The next step in our pipeline is to calculate the frequency of occurrence of each word in each message. We will eventually use these frequencies as features in our algorithm. We will use the `HashingTF` transformer to transform from arrays of words to word frequency vectors for each message.

The `HashingTF` transformer constructs a sparse vector of word frequencies from input iterables. Each element in the word array gets transformed to a hash code. This hash code is truncated to a value between *0* and a large number *n*, the total number of elements in the output vector. The term frequency vector is just the number of occurrences of the truncated hash.

Let's run through an example manually to understand how this works. We will calculate the term frequency vector for `Array("the", "dog", "jumped", "over", "the")`. Let's set *n*, the number of elements in the sparse output vector, to 16 for this example. The first step is to calculate the hash code for each element in our array. We can use the built-in ## method, which calculates a hash code for any object:

```
scala> val words = Array("the", "dog", "jumped", "over", "the")
words: Array[String] = Array(the, dog, jumped, over, the)


scala> val hashCodes = words.map { _.## }
hashCodes: Array[Int] = Array(114801, 99644, -1148867251, 3423444,
114801)
```

To transform the hash codes into valid vector indices, we take the modulo of each hash by the size of the vector (16, in this case):

```
scala> val indices = hashCodes.map { code => Math.abs(code % 16) }
indices: Array[Int] = Array(1, 12, 3, 4, 1)
```

We can then create a mapping from indices to the number of times that index appears:

```
scala> val indexFrequency = indices.groupBy(identity).mapValues {
  _.size.toDouble
}
indexFrequency: Map[Int,Double] = Map(4 -> 1.0, 1 -> 2.0, 3 -> 1.0, 12 ->
1.0)
```

Finally, we can convert this map to a sparse vector, where the value at each element in the vector is the frequency with which this particular index occurs:

```
scala> import org.apache.spark.mllib.linalg._
import org.apache.spark.mllib.linalg._


scala> val termFrequencies = Vectors.sparse(16, indexFrequency.toSeq)
termFrequencies: linalg.Vector = (16,[1,3,4,12],[2.0,1.0,1.0,1.0])
```

Note that the .toString output for a sparse vector consists of three elements: the total size of the vector, followed by two lists: the first is a series of indices, and the second is a series of values at those indices.

Using a sparse vector provides a compact and efficient way of representing the frequency of occurrence of words in the message, and is exactly how `HashingTF` works under the hood. The disadvantage is that the mapping from words to indices is not necessarily unique: truncating hash codes by the length of the vector will map different strings to the same index. This is known as a *collision*. The solution is to make *n* large enough that the frequency of collisions is minimized.

> `HashingTF` is similar to building a hash table (for example, a Scala map) whose keys are words and whose values are the number of times that word occurs in the message, with one important difference: it does not attempt to deal with hash collisions. Thus, if two words map to the same hash, they will have the wrong frequency. There are two advantages to using this algorithm over just constructing a hash table:
>
> - We do not have to maintain a list of distinct words in memory.
> - Each e-mail can be transformed to a vector independently of all others: we do not have to reduce over different partitions to get the set of keys in the map. This greatly eases applying this algorithm to each e-mail in a distributed manner, since we can apply the `HashingTF` transformation on each partition independently.
>
> The main disadvantage is that we must use machine learning algorithms that can take advantage of the sparse representation efficiently. This is the case with logistic regression, which we will use here.

As you might expect, the `HashingTF` transformer takes, as parameters, the input and output columns. It also takes a parameter defining the number of distinct hash buckets in the vector. Increasing the number of buckets decreases the number of collisions. In practice, a value between $2^{18} = 262144$ and $2^{20} = 1048576$ is recommended.

```scala
scala> val hashingTF = (new HashingTF()
  .setInputCol("words")
  .setOutputCol("features")
  .setNumFeatures(1048576))
hashingTF: org.apache.spark.ml.feature.HashingTF = hashingTF_3b78eca9595c


scala> val hashedDF = hashingTF.transform(tokenizedDF)
```

```
hashedDF: DataFrame = [fileName: string, text: string, category: string,
words: array<string>, features: vector]
```

```
scala> hashedDF.select("features").show
+--------------------+
|            features|
+--------------------+
|(1048576,[0,33,36...|
|(1048576,[0,36,40...|
|(1048576,[0,33,34...|
|(1048576,[0,33,36...|
|(1048576,[0,33,34...|
|(1048576,[0,33,34...|
+--------------------+
```

Each element in the `features` column is a sparse vector:

```
scala> import org.apache.spark.sql.Row
import org.apache.spark.sql.Row
```

```
scala> val firstRow = hashedDF.select("features").first
firstRow: org.apache.spark.sql.Row = ...
```

```
scala> val Row(v:Vector) = firstRow
v: Vector = (1048576,[0,33,36,37,...],[1.0,3.0,4.0,1.0,...])
```

We can thus interpret our vector as: the word that hashes to element 33 occurs three times, the word that hashes to element 36 occurs four times etc.

Estimators

We now have the features ready for logistic regression. The last step prior to running logistic regression is to create the target variable. We will transform the `category` column in our DataFrame to a binary 0/1 target column. Spark provides a `StringIndexer` class that replaces a set of strings in a column with doubles. A `StringIndexer` is not a transformer: it must first be 'fitted' to a set of categories to calculate the mapping from string to numeric value. This introduces the second class of components in the pipeline API: *estimators*.

Unlike a transformer, which works "out of the box", an estimator must be fitted to a DataFrame. For our string indexer, the fitting process involves obtaining the list of unique strings ("spam" and "ham") and mapping each of these to a double. The fitting process outputs a transformer which can be used on subsequent DataFrames.

```scala
scala> val indexer = (new StringIndexer()
  .setInputCol("category")
  .setOutputCol("label"))
indexer: org.apache.spark.ml.feature.StringIndexer = strIdx_16db03fd0546


scala> val indexTransform = indexer.fit(trainDF)
indexTransform: StringIndexerModel = strIdx_16db03fd0546
```

The transformer produced by the fitting process has a `labels` attribute describing the mapping it applies:

```scala
scala> indexTransform.labels
Array[String] = Array(ham, spam)
```

Each label will get mapped to its index in the array: thus, our transformer maps ham to 0 and spam to 1:

```scala
scala> val labelledDF = indexTransform.transform(hashedDF)
labelledDF: org.apache.spark.sql.DataFrame = [fileName: string, text:
string, category: string, words: array<string>, features: vector, label:
double]


scala> labelledDF.select("category", "label").distinct.show
+--------+-----+
|category|label|
+--------+-----+
|     ham|  0.0|
|    spam|  1.0|
+--------+-----+
```

We now have the feature vectors and classification labels in the correct format for logistic regression. The component for performing logistic regression is an estimator: it is fitted to a training DataFrame to create a trained model. The model can then be used to transform test DataFrames.

```scala
scala> import org.apache.spark.ml.classification.LogisticRegression
import org.apache.spark.ml.classification.LogisticRegression


scala> val classifier = new LogisticRegression().setMaxIter(50)
classifier: LogisticRegression = logreg_a5e921e7c1a1
```

The `LogisticRegression` estimator expects the feature column to be named `"features"` and the label column (the target) to be named `"label"`, by default. There is no need to set these explicitly, since they match the column names set by `hashingTF` and `indexer`. There are several parameters that can be set to control how logistic regression works:

```scala
scala> println(classifier.explainParams)
elasticNetParam: the ElasticNet mixing parameter, in range [0, 1]. For
alpha = 0, the penalty is an L2 penalty. For alpha = 1, it is an L1
penalty. (default: 0.0)

fitIntercept: whether to fit an intercept term (default: true)

labelCol: label column name (default: label)

maxIter: maximum number of iterations (>= 0) (default: 100, current: 50)

regParam: regularization parameter (>= 0) (default: 0.0)

threshold: threshold in binary classification prediction, in range [0, 1]
(default: 0.5)

tol: the convergence tolerance for iterative algorithms (default: 1.0E-6)
...
```

For now, we just set the `maxIter` parameter. We will look at the effect of other parameters, such as regularization, later on. Let's now fit the classifier to `labelledDF`:

```scala
scala> val trainedClassifier = classifier.fit(labelledDF)
trainedClassifier: LogisticRegressionModel = logreg_353d18f6a5f0
```

This produces a transformer that we can use on a DataFrame with a `features` column. The transformer appends a `prediction` column and a `probability` column. We can, for instance use `trainedClassifier` to transform `labelledDF`, the training set itself:

```scala
scala> val labelledDFWithPredictions = trainedClassifier.transform(
  labelledDF)
labelledDFWithPredictions: DataFrame = [fileName: string, ...


scala> labelledDFWithPredictions.select($"label", $"prediction").show
+-----+----------+
|label|prediction|
+-----+----------+
|  1.0|       1.0|
|  1.0|       1.0|
|  1.0|       1.0|
|  1.0|       1.0|
|  1.0|       1.0|
|  1.0|       1.0|
|  1.0|       1.0|
|  1.0|       1.0|
+-----+----------+
```

A quick way of checking the performance of our model is to just count the number of misclassified messages:

```scala
scala> labelledDFWithPredictions.filter {
  $"label" !== $"prediction"
}.count
Long = 1
```

In this case, logistic regression managed to correctly classify every message but one in the training set. This is perhaps unsurprising, given the large number of features and the relatively clear demarcation between the words used in spam and legitimate e-mails.

Of course, the real test of a model is not how well it performs on the training set, but how well it performs on a test set. To test this, we could just push the test DataFrame through the same stages that we used to train the model, replacing estimators with the fitted transformer that they produced. MLlib provides the *pipeline* abstraction to facilitate this: we wrap an ordered list of transformers and estimators in a pipeline. This pipeline is then fitted to a DataFrame corresponding to the training set. The fitting produces a `PipelineModel` instance, equivalent to the pipeline but with estimators replaced by transformers, as shown in this diagram:

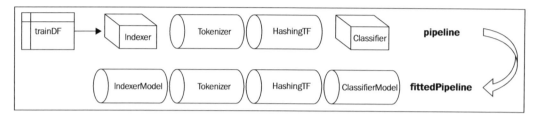

Let's construct the pipeline for our logistic regression spam filter:

```scala
scala> import org.apache.spark.ml.Pipeline
import org.apache.spark.ml.Pipeline


scala> val pipeline = new Pipeline().setStages(
  Array(indexer, tokenizer, hashingTF, classifier)
)
pipeline: Pipeline = pipeline_7488113e284d
```

Once the pipeline is defined, we fit it to the DataFrame holding the training set:

```scala
scala> val fittedPipeline = pipeline.fit(trainDF)
fittedPipeline: org.apache.spark.ml.PipelineModel = pipeline_089525c6f100
```

When fitting a pipeline to a DataFrame, estimators and transformers are treated differently:

- Transformers are applied to the DataFrame and copied, as is, into the pipeline model.

- Estimators are fitted to the DataFrame, producing a transformer. The transformer is then applied to the DataFrame, and appended to the pipeline model.

We can now apply the pipeline model to the test set:

```scala
scala> val testDFWithPredictions = fittedPipeline.transform(testDF)
testDFWithPredictions: DataFrame = [fileName: string, ...
```

This has added a `prediction` column to the DataFrame with the predictions of our logistic regression model. To measure the performance of our algorithm, we calculate the classification error on the test set:

```scala
scala> testDFWithPredictions.filter {
  $"label" !== $"prediction"
}.count
Long = 20
```

Thus, our naive logistic regression algorithm, with no model selection, or regularization, mis-classifies 2.3% of e-mails. You may, of course, get slightly different results, since the train-test split was random.

Let's save the training and test DataFrames, with predictions, as `parquet` files:

```scala
scala> import org.apache.spark.sql.SaveMode
import org.apache.spark.sql.SaveMode

scala> (labelledDFWithPredictions
  .select("fileName", "label", "prediction", "probability")
  .write.mode(SaveMode.Overwrite)
  .parquet("transformedTrain.parquet"))

scala> (testDFWithPredictions
  .select("fileName", "label", "prediction", "probability")
  .write.mode(SaveMode.Overwrite)
  .parquet("transformedTest.parquet"))
```

In spam classification, a false positive is considerably worse than a false negative: it is much worse to classify a legitimate message as spam, than it is to let a spam message through. To account for this, we could increase the threshold for classification: only messages that score, for instance, 0.7 or above would get classified as spam. This raises the obvious question of choosing the right threshold. One way to do this would be to investigate the false positive rate incurred in the test set for different thresholds, and choosing the lowest threshold to give us an acceptable false positive rate. A good way of visualizing this is to use ROC curves, which we will investigate in the next section.

Evaluation

Unfortunately, the functionality for evaluating model quality in the pipeline API remains limited, as of version 1.5.2. Logistic regression does output a summary containing several evaluation metrics (available through the `summary` attribute on the trained model), but these are calculated on the training set. In general, we want to evaluate the performance of the model both on the training set and on a separate test set. We will therefore dive down to the underlying MLlib layer to access evaluation metrics.

MLlib provides a module, `org.apache.spark.mllib.evaluation`, with a set of classes for assessing the quality of a model. We will use the `BinaryClassificationMetrics` class here, since spam classification is a binary classification problem. Other evaluation classes provide metrics for multi-class models, regression models and ranking models.

As in the previous section, we will illustrate the concepts in the shell, but you will find analogous code in the `ROC.scala` script in the code examples for this chapter. We will use *breeze-viz* to plot curves, so, when starting the shell, we must ensure that the relevant libraries are on the classpath. We will use SBT assembly, as described in *Chapter 10, Distributed Batch Processing with Spark* (specifically, the *Building and running standalone programs* section), to create a JAR with the required dependencies. We will then pass this JAR to the Spark shell, allowing us to import breeze-viz. Let's write a `build.sbt` file that declares a dependency on breeze-viz:

```
// build.sbt
name := "spam_filter"

scalaVersion := "2.10.5"

libraryDependencies ++= Seq(
```

```
"org.apache.spark" %% "spark-core" % "1.5.2" % "provided",
"org.apache.spark" %% "spark-mllib" % "1.5.2" % "provided",
"org.scalanlp" %% "breeze" % "0.11.2",
"org.scalanlp" %% "breeze-viz" % "0.11.2",
"org.scalanlp" %% "breeze-natives" % "0.11.2"
)
```

Package the dependencies into a jar with:

```
$ sbt assembly
```

This will create a jar called spam_filter-assembly-0.1-SNAPSHOT.jar in the target/scala-2.10/ directory. To include this jar in the Spark shell, re-start the shell with the --jars command line argument:

```
$ spark-shell --jars=target/scala-2.10/spam_filter-assembly-0.1-SNAPSHOT.jar
```

To verify that the packaging worked correctly, try to import breeze.plot:

```
scala> import breeze.plot._
import breeze.plot._
```

Let's load the test set, with predictions, which we created in the previous section and saved as a parquet file:

```
scala> val testDFWithPredictions = sqlContext.read.parquet(
  "transformedTest.parquet")
testDFWithPredictions: org.apache.spark.sql.DataFrame = [fileName:
string, label: double, prediction: double, probability: vector]
```

The BinaryClassificationMetrics object expects an RDD[(Double, Double)] object of pairs of scores (the probability assigned by the classifier that a particular e-mail is spam) and labels (whether an e-mail is actually spam). We can extract this RDD from our DataFrame:

```
scala> import org.apache.spark.mllib.linalg.Vector
import org.apache.spark.mllib.linalg.Vector

scala> import org.apache.spark.sql.Row
import org.apache.spark.sql.Row

scala> val scoresLabels = testDFWithPredictions.select(
```

```
  "probability", "label").map {
    case Row(probability:Vector, label:Double) =>
      (probability(1), label)
}
org.apache.spark.rdd.RDD[(Double, Double)] = MapPartitionsRDD[3] at map
at <console>:23


scala> scoresLabels.take(5).foreach(println)
(0.9999999967713409,1.0)
(0.9999983827108793,1.0)
(0.9982059900606365,1.0)
(0.9999790713978142,1.0)
(0.9999999999999272,1.0)
```

We can now construct the `BinaryClassificationMetrics` instance:

```
scala> import org.apache.spark.mllib.evaluation.
BinaryClassificationMetrics
import mllib.evaluation.BinaryClassificationMetrics


scala> val bm = new BinaryClassificationMetrics(scoresLabels)
bm: BinaryClassificationMetrics = mllib.evaluation.BinaryClassificationMe
trics@254ed9ba
```

The `BinaryClassificationMetrics` objects contain many useful metrics for evaluating the performance of a classification model. We will look at the **receiver operating characteristic (ROC)** curve.

ROC Curves

Imagine gradually decreasing, from 1.0, the probability threshold at which we assume a particular e-mail is spam. Clearly, when the threshold is set to 1.0, no e-mails will get classified as spam. This means that there will be no **false positives** (ham messages which we incorrectly classify as spam), but it also means that there will be no **true positives** (spam messages that we correctly identify as spam): all spam e-mails will be incorrectly identified as ham.

As we gradually lower the probability threshold at which we assume a particular e-mail is spam, our spam filter will, hopefully, start identifying a large fraction of e-mails as spam. The vast majority of these will, if our algorithm is well-designed, be real spam. Thus, our rate of true positives increases. As we gradually lower the threshold, we start classifying messages about which we are less sure of as spam. This will increase the number of messages correctly identified as spam, but it will also increase the number of false positives.

The ROC curve plots, for each threshold value, the fraction of true positives against the fraction of false positives. In the best case, the curve is always 1: this happens when all spam messages are given a score of 1.0, and all ham messages are given a score of 0.0. By contrast, the worst case happens when the curve is a diagonal *P(true positive) = P(false positive)*, which occurs when our algorithm does no better than random. In general, ROC curves fall somewhere in between, forming a convex shell above the diagonal. The deeper this shell, the better our algorithm.

(left) ROC curve for a model performing much better than random: the curve reaches very high true positive rates for a low false positive rate.

(middle) ROC curve for a model performing significantly better than random.

(right) ROC curve for a model performing only marginally better than random: the true positive rate is only marginally larger than the rate of false positives, for any given threshold, meaning that nearly half the examples are misclassified.

We can calculate an array of points on the ROC curve using the .roc method on our BinaryClassificationMetrics instance. This returns an RDD[(Double, Double)] of (*false positive, true positive*) fractions for each threshold value. We can collect this as an array:

```scala
scala> val rocArray = bm.roc.collect
rocArray: Array[(Double, Double)] = Array((0.0,0.0),
(0.0,0.16793893129770993), ...
```

Of course, an array of numbers is not very enlightening, so let's plot the ROC curve with breeze-viz. We start by transforming our array of pairs into two arrays, one of false positives and one of true positives:

```scala
scala> val falsePositives = rocArray.map { _._1 }
falsePositives: Array[Double] = Array(0.0, 0.0, 0.0, 0.0, 0.0, ...

scala> val truePositives = rocArray.map { _._2 }
truePositives: Array[Double] = Array(0.0, 0.16793893129770993,
0.19083969465...
```

Let's plot these two arrays:

```scala
scala> import breeze.plot._
import breeze.plot.

scala> val f = Figure()
f: breeze.plot.Figure = breeze.plot.Figure@3aa746cd

scala> val p = f.subplot(0)
p: breeze.plot.Plot = breeze.plot.Plot@5ed1438a

scala> p += plot(falsePositives, truePositives)
p += plot(falsePositives, truePositives)

scala> p.xlabel = "false positives"
p.xlabel: String = false positives

scala> p.ylabel = "true positives"
p.ylabel: String = true positives

scala> p.title = "ROC"
```

```
p.title: String = ROC
```

```
scala> f.refresh
```

The ROC curve hits *1.0* for a small value of x: that is, we retrieve all true positives at the cost of relatively few false positives. To visualize the curve more accurately, it is instructive to limit the range on the *x*-axis from *0* to *0.1*.

```
scala> p.xlim = (0.0, 0.1)
p.xlim: (Double, Double) = (0.0,0.1)
```

We also need to tell breeze-viz to use appropriate tick spacing, which requires going down to the JFreeChart layer underlying breeze-viz:

```
scala> import org.jfree.chart.axis.NumberTickUnit
import org.jfree.chart.axis.NumberTickUnit
```

```
scala> p.xaxis.setTickUnit(new NumberTickUnit(0.01))
```

```
scala> p.yaxis.setTickUnit(new NumberTickUnit(0.1))
```

We can now save the graph:

```
scala> f.saveas("roc.png")
```

This produces the following graph, stored in `roc.png`:

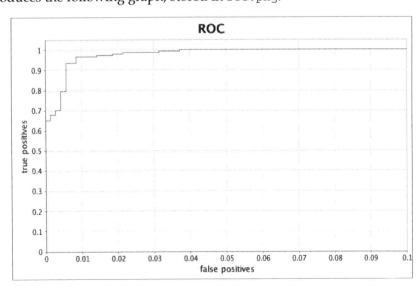

ROC curve for spam classification with logistic regression.
Note that we have limited the false positive axis at 0.1

By looking at the graph, we see that we can filter out 85% of spam without a single **false positive**. Of course, we would need a larger test set to really validate this assumption.

A graph is useful to really understand the behavior of a model. Sometimes, however, we just want to have a single measure of the quality of a model. The area under the ROC curve can be a good such metric:

```scala
scala> bm.areaUnderROC
res21: Double = 0.9983061235861147
```

This can be interpreted as follows: given any two messages randomly drawn from the test set, one of which is ham, and one of which is spam, there is a 99.8% probability that the model assigned a greater likelihood of spam to the spam message than to the ham message.

Other useful measures of model quality are the precision and recall for particular thresholds, or the F1 score. All of these are provided by the `BinaryClassificationMetrics` instance. The API documentation lists the methods available: `https://spark.apache.org/docs/latest/api/scala/index.html#org.apache.spark.mllib.evaluation.BinaryClassificationMetrics`.

Regularization in logistic regression

One of the dangers of machine learning is over-fitting: the algorithm captures not only the signal in the training set, but also the statistical noise that results from the finite size of the training set.

A way to mitigate over-fitting in logistic regression is to use regularization: we impose a penalty for large values of the parameters when optimizing. We can do this by adding a penalty to the cost function that is proportional to the magnitude of the parameters. Formally, we re-write the logistic regression cost function (described in *Chapter 2, Manipulating Data with Breeze*) as:

$$Cost(params) = Cost_{LR}(params) + \lambda \|params\|_n$$

where $Cost_{LR}$ is the normal logistic regression cost function:

$$Cost_{LR}(params) = \sum_i target_i \times (params \cdot training_i) - \log\left[\exp(params \cdot training_i) + 1\right]$$

Here, *params* is the vector of parameters, $training_i$ is the vector of features for the *ith* training example, and $target_i$ is *1* if the *i*th training example is spam, and *0* otherwise. This is identical to the logistic regression cost-function introduced in *Chapter 2, Manipulating data with Breeze*, apart from the addition of the regularization term $\lambda \|params\|_n$, the L_n norm of the parameter vector. The most common value of *n* is 2, in which case $\|params\|_2$ is just the magnitude of the parameter vector:

$$\|params\|_2 = \sqrt{\sum_i params_i^2}$$

The additional regularization term drives the algorithm to reduce the magnitude of the parameter vector. When using regularization, features must all have comparable magnitude. This is commonly achieved by normalizing the features. The logistic regression estimator provided by MLlib normalizes all features by default. This can be turned off with the setStandardization parameter.

Spark has two hyperparameters that can be tweaked to control regularization:

- The type of regularization, set with the elasticNetParam parameter. A value of 0 indicates L_2 regularization.

- The degree of regularization (λ in the cost function), set with the regParam parameter. A high value of the regularization parameter indicates a strong regularization. In general, the greater the danger of over-fitting, the larger the regularization parameter ought to be.

Let's create a new logistic regression instance that uses regularization:

```scala
scala> val lrWithRegularization = (new LogisticRegression()
  .setMaxIter(50))
lrWithRegularization: LogisticRegression = logreg_16b65b325526


scala> lrWithRegularization.setElasticNetParam(0)
lrWithRegularization.type = logreg_1e3584a59b3a
```

To choose the appropriate value of λ, we fit the pipeline to the training set and calculate the classification error on the test set for several values of λ. Further on in the chapter, we will learn about cross-validation in MLlib, which provides a much more rigorous way of choosing hyper-parameters.

```scala
scala> val lambdas = Array(0.0, 1.0E-12, 1.0E-10, 1.0E-8)
lambdas: Array[Double] = Array(0.0, 1.0E-12, 1.0E-10, 1.0E-8)


scala> lambdas foreach { lambda =>
  lrWithRegularization.setRegParam(lambda)
  val pipeline = new Pipeline().setStages(
    Array(indexer, tokenizer, hashingTF, lrWithRegularization))
  val model = pipeline.fit(trainDF)
  val transformedTest = model.transform(testDF)
  val classificationError = transformedTest.filter {
    $"prediction" !== $"label"
  }.count
  println(s"$lambda => $classificationError")
}
0 => 20
1.0E-12 => 20
1.0E-10 => 20
1.0E-8 => 23
```

For our example, we see that any attempt to add L_2 regularization leads to a decrease in classification accuracy.

Cross-validation and model selection

In the previous example, we validated our approach by withholding 30% of the data when training, and testing on this subset. This approach is not particularly rigorous: the exact result changes depending on the random train-test split. Furthermore, if we wanted to test several different hyperparameters (or different models) to choose the best one, we would, unwittingly, choose the model that best reflects the specific rows in our test set, rather than the population as a whole.

This can be overcome with *cross-validation*. We have already encountered cross-validation in *Chapter 4, Parallel Collections and Futures*. In that chapter, we used random subsample cross-validation, where we created the train-test split randomly.

In this chapter, we will use **k-fold cross-validation**: we split the training set into *k* parts (where, typically, *k* is *10* or *3*) and use *k-1* parts as the training set and the last as the test set. The train/test cycle is repeated *k* times, keeping a different part as test set each time.

Cross-validation is commonly used to choose the best set of hyperparameters for a model. To illustrate choosing suitable hyperparameters, we will go back to our regularized logistic regression example. Instead of intuiting the hyper-parameters ourselves, we will choose the hyper-parameters that give us the best cross-validation score.

We will explore setting both the regularization type (through `elasticNetParam`) and the degree of regularization (through `regParam`). A crude, but effective way to find good values of the parameters is to perform a grid search: we calculate the cross-validation score for every pair of values of the regularization parameters of interest.

We can build a grid of parameters using MLlib's `ParamGridBuilder`.

```scala
scala> import org.apache.spark.ml.tuning.{ParamGridBuilder,
CrossValidator}
import org.apache.spark.ml.tuning.{ParamGridBuilder, CrossValidator}


scala> val paramGridBuilder = new ParamGridBuilder()
paramGridBuilder: ParamGridBuilder = ParamGridBuilder@1dd694d0
```

To add hyper-parameters over which to optimize to the grid, we use the `addGrid` method:

```scala
scala> val lambdas = Array(0.0, 1.0E-12, 1.0E-10, 1.0E-8)
Array[Double] = Array(0.0, 1.0E-12, 1.0E-10, 1.0E-8)


scala> val elasticNetParams = Array(0.0, 1.0)
elasticNetParams: Array[Double] = Array(0.0, 1.0)


scala> paramGridBuilder.addGrid(
  lrWithRegularization.regParam, lambdas).addGrid(
  lrWithRegularization.elasticNetParam, elasticNetParams)
paramGridBuilder.type = ParamGridBuilder@1dd694d0
```

Once all the dimensions are added, we can just call the `build` method on the builder to build the grid:

```
scala> val paramGrid = paramGridBuilder.build
paramGrid: Array[org.apache.spark.ml.param.ParamMap] =
Array({
  logreg_f7dfb27bed7d-elasticNetParam: 0.0,
  logreg_f7dfb27bed7d-regParam: 0.0
}, {
  logreg_f7dfb27bed7d-elasticNetParam: 1.0,
  logreg_f7dfb27bed7d-regParam: 0.0
} ...)


scala> paramGrid.length
Int = 8
```

As we can see, the grid is just a one-dimensional array of sets of parameters to pass to the logistic regression model prior to fitting.

The next step in setting up the cross-validation pipeline is to define a metric for comparing model performance. Earlier in the chapter, we saw how to use `BinaryClassificationMetrics` to estimate the quality of a model. Unfortunately, the `BinaryClassificationMetrics` class is part of the core MLlib API, rather than the new pipeline API, and is thus not (easily) compatible. The pipeline API offers a `BinaryClassificationEvaluator` class instead. This class works directly on DataFrames, and thus fits perfectly into the pipeline API flow:

```
scala> import org.apache.spark.ml.evaluation.
BinaryClassificationEvaluator
import org.apache.spark.ml.evaluation.BinaryClassificationEvaluator


scala> val evaluator = new BinaryClassificationEvaluator()
evaluator: BinaryClassificationEvaluator = binEval_64b08538f1a2


scala> println(evaluator.explainParams)
labelCol: label column name (default: label)
metricName: metric name in evaluation (areaUnderROC|areaUnderPR)
(default: areaUnderROC)
rawPredictionCol: raw prediction (a.k.a. confidence) column name
(default: rawPrediction)
```

From the parameter list, we see that the `BinaryClassificationEvaluator` class supports two metrics: the area under the ROC curve, and the area under the precision-recall curve. It expects, as input, a DataFrame containing a `label` column (the model truth) and a `rawPrediction` column (the column containing the probability that an e-mail is spam or ham).

We now have all the parameters we need to run cross-validation. We first build the pipeline, and then pass the pipeline, the evaluator and the array of parameters over which to run the cross-validation to an instance of `CrossValidator`:

```scala
scala> val pipeline = new Pipeline().setStages(
  Array(indexer, tokenizer, hashingTF, lrWithRegularization))
pipeline: Pipeline = pipeline_3ed29f72a4cc


scala> val crossval = (new CrossValidator()
  .setEstimator(pipeline)
  .setEvaluator(evaluator)
  .setEstimatorParamMaps(paramGrid)
  .setNumFolds(3))
crossval: CrossValidator = cv_5ebfa1143a9d
```

We will now fit `crossval` to `trainDF`:

```scala
scala> val cvModel = crossval.fit(trainDF)
cvModel: CrossValidatorModel = cv_5ebfa1143a9d
```

This step can take a fairly long time (over an hour on a single machine). This creates a transformer, `cvModel`, corresponding to the logistic regression object with the parameters that best represent `trainDF`. We can use it to predict the classification error on the test DataFrame:

```scala
scala> cvModel.transform(testDF).filter {
  $"prediction" !== $"label"
}.count
Long = 20
```

Cross-validation has therefore resulted in a model that performs identically to the original, naive logistic regression model with no hyper-parameters. `cvModel` also contains a list of the evaluation score for each set of parameter in the parameter grid:

```scala
scala> cvModel.avgMetrics
Array[Double] = Array(0.996427805316161, ...)
```

The easiest way to relate this to the hyper-parameters is to zip it with `cvModel.getEstimatorParamMaps`. This gives us a list of (*hyperparameter values, cross-validation score*) pairs:

```scala
scala> val params2score = cvModel.getEstimatorParamMaps.zip(
  cvModel.avgMetrics)
Array[(ml.param.ParamMap,Double)] = Array(({
  logreg_8f107aabb304-elasticNetParam: 0.0,
  logreg_8f107aabb304-regParam: 0.0
},0.996427805316161),...
```

```scala
scala> params2score.foreach {
  case (params, score) =>
    val lambda = params(lrWithRegularization.regParam)
    val elasticNetParam = params(
      lrWithRegularization.elasticNetParam)
    val l2Orl1 = if(elasticNetParam == 0.0) "L2" else "L1"
    println(s"$l2Orl1, $lambda => $score")
}
L2, 0.0 => 0.996427805316161
L1, 0.0 => 0.996427805316161
L2, 1.0E-12 => 0.9964278053175655
L1, 1.0E-12 => 0.9961429402772803
L2, 1.0E-10 => 0.9964382546369551
L1, 1.0E-10 => 0.9962223090037103
L2, 1.0E-8 => 0.9964159754613495
L1, 1.0E-8 => 0.9891008277659763
```

The best set of hyper-parameters correspond to L_2 regularization with a regularization parameter of `1E-10`, though this only corresponds to a tiny improvement in AUC.

This completes our spam filter example. We have successfully trained a spam filter for this particular Ling-Spam dataset. To obtain better results, one could experiment with better feature extraction: we could remove stop words or use TF-IDF vectors, rather than just term frequency vectors as features, and we could add additional features like the length of messages, or even *n-grams*. We could also experiment with non-linear algorithms, such as random forest. All of these steps would be straightforward to add to the pipeline.

Beyond logistic regression

We have concentrated on logistic regression in this chapter, but MLlib offers many alternative algorithms that will capture non-linearity in the data more effectively. The consistency of the pipeline API makes it easy to try out different algorithms and see how they perform. The pipeline API offers decision trees, random forest and gradient boosted trees for classification, as well as a simple feed-forward neural network, which is still experimental. It offers lasso and ridge regression and decision trees for regression, as well as PCA for dimensionality reduction.

The lower level MLlib API also offers principal component analysis for dimensionality reduction, several clustering methods including *k*-means and latent Dirichlet allocation and recommender systems using alternating least squares.

Summary

MLlib tackles the challenge of devising scalable machine learning algorithms head-on. In this chapter, we used it to train a simple scalable spam filter. MLlib is a vast, rapidly evolving library. The best way to learn more about what it can offer is to try and port code that you might have written using another library (such as scikit-learn).

In the next chapter, we will look at how to build web APIs and interactive visualizations to share our results with the rest of the world.

References

The best reference is the online documentation, including:

- The pipeline API: `http://spark.apache.org/docs/latest/ml-features.html`

- A full list of transformers: `http://spark.apache.org/docs/latest/mllib-guide.html#sparkml-high-level-apis-for-ml-pipelines`

Advanced Analytics with Spark, by *Sandy Ryza, Uri Laserson, Sean Owen* and *Josh Wills* provides a detailed and up-to-date introduction to machine learning with Spark.

There are several books that introduce machine learning in more detail than we can here. We have mentioned *The Elements of Statistical Learning*, by *Friedman*, *Tibshirani* and *Hastie* several times in this book. It is one of the most complete introductions to the mathematical underpinnings of machine learning currently available.

Andrew Ng's Machine Learning course on `https://www.coursera.org/` provides a good introduction to machine learning. It uses Octave/MATLAB as the programming language, but should be straightforward to adapt to Breeze and Scala.

13
Web APIs with Play

In the first 12 chapters of this book, we introduced basic tools and libraries for anyone wanting to build data science applications: we learned how to interact with SQL and MongoDB databases, how to build fast batch processing applications using Spark, how to apply state-of-the-art machine learning algorithms using MLlib, and how to build modular concurrent applications in Akka.

In the last chapters of this book, we will branch out to look at a web framework: *Play*. You might wonder why a web framework would feature in a data science book; surely such topics are best left to software engineers or web developers. Data scientists, however, rarely exist in a vacuum. They often need to communicate results or insights to stakeholders. As compelling as an ROC curve may be to someone well versed in statistics, it may not carry as much weight with less technical people. Indeed, it can be much easier to sell insights when they are accompanied by an engaging visualization.

Many modern interactive data visualization applications are web applications running in a web browser. Often, these involve **D3.js**, a JavaScript library for building data-driven web pages. In this chapter and the next, we will look at integrating D3 with Scala.

Writing a web application is a complex endeavor. We will split this task over this chapter and the next. In this chapter, we will learn how to write a REST API that we can use as backend for our application, or query in its own right. In the next chapter, we will look at integrating front-end code with Play to query the API exposed by the backend and display it using D3. We assume at least a basic familiarity with HTTP in this chapter: you should have read *Chapter 7, Web APIs*, at least.

Many data scientists or aspiring data scientists are unlikely to be familiar with the inner workings of web technologies. Learning how to build complex websites or web APIs can be daunting. This chapter therefore starts with a general discussion of dynamic websites and the architecture of web applications. If you are already familiar with server-side programming and with web frameworks, you can easily skip over the first few sections.

Client-server applications

A website works through the interaction between two computers: the client and the server. If you enter the URL www.github.com/pbugnion/s4ds/graphs in a web browser, your browser queries one of the GitHub servers. The server will look though its database for information concerning the repository that you are interested in. It will serve this information as HTML, CSS, and JavaScript to your computer. Your browser is then responsible for interpreting this response in the correct way.

If you look at the URL in question, you will notice that there are several graphs on that page. Unplug your internet connection and you can still interact with the graphs. All the information necessary for interacting with the graphs was transferred, as JavaScript, when you loaded that webpage. When you play with the graphs, the CPU cycles necessary to make those changes happen are spent on *your* computer, not a GitHub server. The code is executed *client-side*. Conversely, when you request information about a new repository, that request is handled by a GitHub server. It is said to be handled *server-side*.

A web framework like Play can be used on the server. For client-side code, we can only use a language that the client browser will understand: HTML for the layout, CSS for the styling and JavaScript, or languages that can compile to JavaScript, for the logic.

Introduction to web frameworks

This section is a brief introduction to how modern web applications are designed. Go ahead and skip it if you already feel comfortable writing backend code.

Loosely, a web framework is a set of tools and code libraries for building web applications. To understand what a web framework provides, let's take a step back and think about what you would need to do if you did not have one.

You want to write a program that listens on port 80 and sends HTML (or JSON or XML) back to clients that request it. This is simple if you are serving the same file back to every client: just load the HTML from file when you start the server, and send it to clients who request it.

So far, so good. But what if you now want to customize the HTML based on the client request? You might choose to respond differently based on part of the URL that the client put in his browser, or based on specific elements in the HTTP request. For instance, the product page on amazon.com is different to the payment page. You need to write code to parse the URL and the request, and then route the request to the relevant handler.

You might now want to customize the HTML returned dynamically, based on specific elements of the request. The page for every product on amazon.com follows the same outline, but specific elements are different. It would be wasteful to store the entire HTML content for every product. A better way is to store the details for each product in a database and inject them into an HTML template when a client requests information on that product. You can do this with a *template processor*. Of course, writing a good template processor is difficult.

You might deploy your web framework and realize that it cannot handle the traffic directed to it. You decide that handlers responding to client requests should run asynchronously. You now have to deal with concurrency.

A web framework essentially provides the wires to bind everything together. Besides bundling an HTTP server, most frameworks will have a router that automatically routes a request, based on the URL, to the correct handler. In most cases, the handler will run asynchronously, giving you much better scalability. Many frameworks have a template processor that lets you write HTML (or sometimes JSON or XML) templates intuitively. Some web frameworks also provide functionality for accessing a database, for parsing JSON or XML, for formulating HTTP requests and for localization and internationalization.

Model-View-Controller architecture

Many web frameworks impose program architectures: it is difficult to provide wires to bind disparate components together without making some assumptions about what those components are. The **Model-View-Controller (MVC)** architecture is particularly popular on the Web, and it is the architecture the Play framework assumes. Let's look at each component in turn:

- The model is the data underlying the application. For example, I expect the application underlying GitHub has models for users, repositories, organizations, pull requests and so on. In the Play framework, a model is often an instance of a case class. The core responsibility of the model is to remember the current state of the application.

- Views are representations of a model or a set of models on the screen.

- The controller handles client interactions, possibly changing the model. For instance, if you *star* a project on GitHub, the controller will update the relevant models. Controllers normally carry very little application state: remembering things is the job of the models.

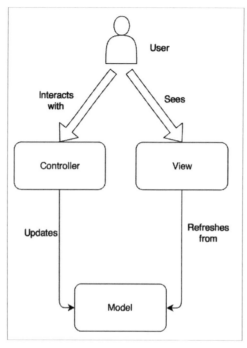

MVC architecture: the state of the application is provided by the model. The view provides a visual representation of the model to the user, and the controller handles logic: what to do when the user presses a button or submits a form.

The MVC framework works well because it decouples the user interface from the underlying data and structures the flow of actions: a controller can update the model state or the view, a model can send signals to the view to tell it to update, and the view merely displays that information. The model carries no information related to the user interface. This separation of concerns results in an easier mental model of information flow, better encapsulation and greater testability.

Single page applications

The client-server duality adds a degree of complication to the elegant MVC architecture. Where should the model reside? What about the controller? Traditionally, the model and the controller ran almost entirely on the server, which just pushed the relevant HTML view to the client.

The growth in client-side JavaScript frameworks, such AngularJS, has resulted in a gradual shift to putting more code in the client. Both the controller and a temporary version of the model typically run client-side. The server just functions as a web API: if, for instance, the user updates the model, the controller will send an HTTP request to the server informing it of the change.

It then makes sense to think of the program running server-side and the one running client-side as two separate applications: the server persists data in databases, for instance, and provides a programmatic interface to this data, usually as a web service returning JSON or XML data. The client-side program maintains its own model and controller, and polls the server whenever it needs a new model, or whenever it needs to inform the server that the persistent view of the model should be changed.

Taken to the extreme, this results in **Single-Page Applications**. In a single-page application, the first time the client requests a page from the server, he receives the HTML and the JavaScript necessary to build the framework for the entire application. If the client needs further data from the server, he will poll the server's API. This data is returned as JSON or XML.

This might seem a little complicated in the abstract, so let's think how the Amazon website might be structured as a single-page application. We will just concern ourselves with the products page here, since that's complicated enough. Let's imagine that you are on the home page, and you hit a link for a particular product. The application running on your computer knows how to display products, for instance through an HTML template. The JavaScript also has a prototype for the model, such as:

```
{
    product_id: undefined,
    product_name: undefined,
    product_price: undefined,
    ...
}
```

What it's currently missing is knowledge of what data to put in those fields for the product you have just selected: there is no way that information could have been sent to your computer when the website loaded, since there was no way to know what product you might click on (and sending information about every product would be prohibitively costly). So the Amazon client sends a request to the server for information on that product. The Amazon server replies with a JSON object (or maybe XML). The client then updates its model with that information. When the update is complete, an event is fired to update the view:

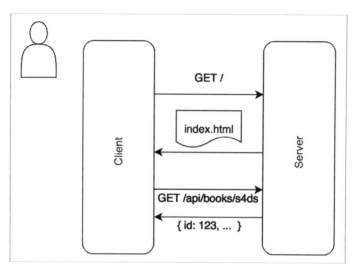

Client-server communications in a single-page application: when the client first accesses the website, it receives HTML, CSS and JavaScript files that contain the entire logic for the application. From then on, the client only uses the server as an API when it requests additional data. The application running in the user's web browser and the one running on the server are nearly independent. The only coupling is through the structure of the API exposed by the server.

Building an application

In this chapter and the next, we will build a single-page application that relies on an API written in Play. We will build a webpage that looks like this:

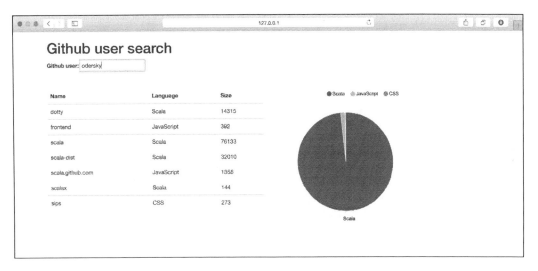

The user enters the name of someone on GitHub and can view a list of their repositories and a chart summarizing what language they use. You can find the application deployed at `app.scala4datascience.com`. Go ahead and give it a whirl.

To get a glimpse of the innards, type `app.scala4datascience.com/api/repos/odersky`. This returns a JSON object like:

```
[{"name":"dotty","language":"Scala","is_fork":true,"size":14653},
{"name":"frontend","language":"JavaScript","is_fork":true,"size":392},
{"name":"legacy-svn-scala","language":"Scala","is_
fork":true,"size":296706},
...
```

We will build the API in this chapter, and write the front-end code in the next chapter.

The Play framework

The Play framework is a web framework built on top of Akka. It has a proven track record in industry, and is thus a reliable choice for building scalable web applications.

Play is an *opinionated* web framework: it expects you to follow the MVC architecture, and it has a strong opinion about the tools you should be using. It comes bundled with its own JSON and XML parsers, with its own tools for accessing external APIs, and with recommendations for how to access databases.

Web applications are much more complex than the command line scripts we have been developing in this book, because there are many more components: the backend code, routing information, HTML templates, JavaScript files, images, and so on. The Play framework makes strong assumptions about the directory structure for your project. Building that structure from scratch is both mind-numbingly boring and easy to get wrong. Fortunately, we can use **Typesafe activators** to bootstrap the project (you can also download the code from the Git repository in `https://github.com/pbugnion/s4ds` but I encourage you to start the project from a basic activator structure and code along instead, using the finished version as an example).

Typesafe activator is a custom version of SBT that includes templates to get Scala programmers up and running quickly. To install activator, you can either download a JAR from `https://www.typesafe.com/activator/download`, or, on Mac OS, via homebrew:

```
$ brew install typesafe-activator
```

You can then launch the activator console from the terminal. If you downloaded activator:

```
$ ./path/to/activator/activator new
```

Or, if you installed via Homebrew:

```
$ activator new
```

This starts a new project in the current directory. It starts by asking what template you want to start with. Choose `play-scala`. It then asks for a name for your application. I chose `ghub-display`, but go ahead and be creative!

Let's explore the newly created project structure (I have only retained the most important files):

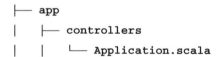

```
├── app
│   ├── controllers
│   │   └── Application.scala
```

```
|   └── views
|       ├── main.scala.html
|       └── index.scala.html
├── build.sbt
├── conf
|   ├── application.conf
|   └── routes
├── project
|   ├── build.properties
|   └── plugins.sbt
├── public
|   ├── images
|   |   └── favicon.png
|   ├── javascripts
|   |   └── hello.js
|   └── stylesheets
|       └── main.css
└── test
    ├── ApplicationSpec.scala
    └── IntegrationSpec.scala
```

Let's run the app:

```
$ ./activator
[ghub-display] $ run
```

Head over to your browser and navigate to the URL 127.0.0.1:9000/. The page may take a few seconds to load. Once it is loaded, you should see a default page that says **Your application is ready**.

Before we modify anything, let's walk through how this happens. When you ask your browser to take you to 127.0.0.1:9000/, your browser sends an HTTP request to the server listening at that address (in this case, the Netty server bundled with Play). The request is a GET request for the route /. The Play framework looks in conf/routes to see if it has a route satisfying /:

```
$ cat conf/routes
# Home page
GET     /                           controllers.Application.index
...
```

We see that the `conf/routes` file does contain the route / for GET requests. The second part of that line, `controllers.Application.index`, is the name of a Scala function to handle that route (more on that in a moment). Let's experiment. Change the route end-point to `/hello`. Refresh your browser without changing the URL. This will trigger recompilation of the application. You should now see an error page:

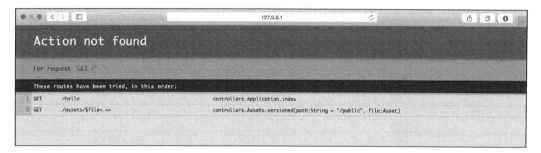

The error page tells you that the app does not have an action for the route / any more. If you navigate to `127.0.0.1:9000/hello`, you should see the landing page again.

Besides learning a little of how routing works, we have also learned two things about developing Play applications:

- In development mode, code gets recompiled when you refresh your browser and there have been code changes
- Compilation and runtime errors get propagated to the web page

Let's change the route back to /. There is a lot more to say on routing, but it can wait till we start building our application.

The `conf/routes` file tells the Play framework to use the method `controllers.Application.index` to handle requests to /. Let's look at the `Application.scala` file in `app/controllers`, where the `index` method is defined:

```
// app/controllers/Application.scala
package controllers

import play.api._
import play.api.mvc._

class Application extends Controller {

  def index = Action {
    Ok(views.html.index("Your new application is ready."))
  }

}
```

We see that `controllers.Application.index` refers to the method `index` in the class `Application`. This method has return type `Action`. An `Action` is just a function that maps HTTP requests to responses. Before explaining this in more detail, let's change the action to:

```
def index = Action {
  Ok("hello, world")
}
```

Refresh your browser and you should see the landing page replaced with `"hello world"`. By having our action return `Ok("hello, world")`, we are asking Play to return an HTTP response with status code 200 (indicating that the request was successful) and the body `"hello world"`.

Let's go back to the original content of `index`:

```
Action {
  Ok(views.html.index("Your new application is ready."))
}
```

We can see that this calls the method `views.html.index`. This might appear strange, because there is no `views` package anywhere. However, if you look at the `app/views` directory, you will notice two files: `index.scala.html` and `main.scala.html`. These are templates, which, at compile time, get transformed into Scala functions. Let's have a look at `main.scala.html`:

```
// app/views/main.scala.html
@(title: String)(content: Html)

<!DOCTYPE html>

<html lang="en">
    <head>
        <title>@title</title>
        <!-- not so important stuff -->
    </head>
    <body>
        @content
    </body>
</html>
```

At compile time, this template is compiled to a function `main(title:String)` `(content:Html)` in the package `views.html`. Notice that the function package and name comes from the template file name, and the function arguments come from the first line of the template. The template contains embedded @title and @content values, which get filled in by the arguments to the function. Let's experiment with this in a Scala console:

```
$ activator console
scala> import views.html._
import views.html._

scala> val title = "hello"
title: String = hello

scala> val content = new play.twirl.api.Html("<b>World</b>")
content: play.twirl.api.Html = <b>World</b>

scala> main(title)(content)
res8: play.twirl.api.HtmlFormat.Appendable =
<!DOCTYPE html>

<html lang="en">
    <head>
        <title>hello</title>
        <!-- not so important stuff -->
    </head>
    <body>
        <b>World</b>
    </body>
</html>
```

We can call `views.html.main`, just like we would call a normal Scala function. The arguments we pass in get embedded in the correct place, as defined by the template in `views/main.scala.html`.

This concludes our introductory tour of Play. Let's briefly go over what we have learnt: when a request reaches the Play server, the server reads the URL and the HTTP verb and checks that these exist in its `conf/routes` file. It will then pass the request to the `Action` defined by the controller for that route. This `Action` returns an HTTP response that gets fed back to the browser. In constructing the response, the `Action` may make use of a template, which, as far as it is concerned is just a function `(arguments list) => String` or `(arguments list) => HTML`.

Dynamic routing

Routing, as we saw, is the mapping of HTTP requests to Scala handlers. Routes are stored in `conf/routes`. A route is defined by an HTTP verb, followed by the end-point, followed by a Scala function:

```
// verb    // end-point              // Scala handler
GET         /                        controllers.Application.index
```

We learnt to add new routes by just adding lines to the `routes` file. We are not limited to static routes, however. The Play framework lets us include wild cards in routes. The value of the wild card can be passed as an argument to the controller. To see how this works, let's create a controller that takes the name of a person as argument. In the `Application` object in `app.controllers`, add:

```
// app/controllers/Application.scala

class Application extends Controller {

  ...

  def hello(name:String) = Action {
    Ok(s"hello, $name")
  }
}
```

We can now define a route handled by this controller:

```
// conf/routes
GET    /hello/:name              controllers.Application.hello(name)
```

If you now point your browser to `127.0.0.1:9000/hello/Jim`, you will see **hello, Jim** appear on the screen.

Any string between : and the following / is treated as a wild card: it will match any combination of characters. The value of the wild card can be passed to the controller. Note that the wild card can appear anywhere in the URL, and there can be more than one wild card. The following are all valid route definitions, for instance:

```
GET /hello/person-:name        controllers.Application.hello(name)
// ... matches /hello/person-Jim

GET /hello/:name/picture  controllers.Application.pictureFor(name)
// ... matches /hello/Jim/picture

GET /hello/:first/:last controllers.Application.hello(first, last)
// ... matches /hello/john/doe
```

There are many other options for selecting routes and passing arguments to the controller. Consult the documentation for the Play framework for a full discussion on the routing possibilities: `https://www.playframework.com/documentation/2.4.x/ScalaRouting`.

URL design

It is generally considered best practice to leave the URL as simple as possible. The URL should reflect the hierarchical structure of the information of the website, rather than the underlying implementation. GitHub is a very good example of this: its URLs make intuitive sense. For instance, the URL for the repository for this book is:

`https://github.com/pbugnion/s4ds`

To access the issues page for that repository, add `/issues` to the route. To access the first issue, add `/1` to that route. These are called **semantic URLs** (`https://en.wikipedia.org/wiki/Semantic_URL`).

Actions

We have talked about routes, and how to pass parameters to controllers. Let's now talk about what we can do with the controller.

The method defined in the route must return a `play.api.mvc.Action` instance. The `Action` type is a thin wrapper around the type `Request[A] => Result`, where `Request[A]` identifies an HTTP request and `Result` is an HTTP response.

Composing the response

An HTTP response, as we saw in *Chapter 7, Web APIs*, is composed of:

- the status code (such as 200 for a successful response, or 404 for a missing page)
- the response headers, a key-value list indicating metadata related to the response
- The response body. This can be HTML for web pages, or JSON, XML or plain text (or many other formats). This is generally the bit that we are really interested in.

The Play framework defines a `play.api.mvc.Result` object that symbolizes a response. The object contains a `header` attribute with the status code and the headers, and a `body` attribute containing the body.

The simplest way to generate a `Result` is to use one of the factory methods in `play.api.mvc.Results`. We have already seen the `Ok` method, which generates a response with status code 200:

```
def hello(name:String) = Action {
  Ok("hello, $name")
}
```

Let's take a step back and open a Scala console so we can understand how this works:

```
$ activator console
scala> import play.api.mvc._
import play.api.mvc._

scala> val res = Results.Ok("hello, world")
res: play.api.mvc.Result = Result(200, Map(Content-Type -> text/plain;
charset=utf-8))

scala> res.header.status
Int = 200

scala> res.header.headers
Map[String,String] = Map(Content-Type -> text/plain; charset=utf-8)

scala> res.body
play.api.libs.iteratee.Enumerator[Array[Byte]] = play.api.libs.iteratee.
Enumerator$$anon$18@5fb83873
```

We can see how the `Results.Ok(...)` creates a `Result` object with status `200` and (in this case), a single header denoting the content type. The body is a bit more complicated: it is an enumerator that can be pushed onto the output stream when needed. The enumerator contains the argument passed to `Ok`: `"hello, world"`, in this case.

There are many factory methods in `Results` for returning different status codes. Some of the more relevant ones are:

- `Action { Results.NotFound }`
- `Action { Results.BadRequest("bad request") }`
- `Action { Results.InternalServerError("error") }`
- `Action { Results.Forbidden }`
- `Action { Results.Redirect("/home") }`

For a full list of `Result` factories, consult the API documentation for Results (https://www.playframework.com/documentation/2.4.x/api/scala/index.html#play.api.mvc.Results).

We have, so far, been limiting ourselves to passing strings as the content of the `Ok` result: `Ok("hello, world")`. We are not, however, limited to passing strings. We can pass a JSON object:

```scala
scala> import play.api.libs.json._
import play.api.libs.json._


scala> val jsonObj = Json.obj("hello" -> "world")
jsonObj: play.api.libs.json.JsObject = {"hello":"world"}


scala> Results.Ok(jsonObj)
play.api.mvc.Result = Result(200, Map(Content-Type -> application/json;
charset=utf-8))
```

We will cover interacting with JSON in more detail when we start building the API. We can also pass HTML as the content. This is most commonly the case when returning a view:

```scala
scala> val htmlObj = views.html.index("hello")
htmlObj: play.twirl.api.HtmlFormat.Appendable =

<!DOCTYPE html>
```

```
<html lang="en">

    <head>

...


scala> Results.Ok(htmlObj)

play.api.mvc.Result = Result(200, Map(Content-Type -> text/html;
charset=utf-8))
```

Note how the `Content-Type` header is set based on the type of content passed to `Ok`. The `Ok` factory uses the `Writeable` type class to convert its argument to the body of the response. Thus, any content type for which a `Writeable` type class exists can be used as argument to `Ok`. If you are unfamiliar with type classes, you might want to read the *Looser coupling with type classes* section in *Chapter 5, Scala and SQL through JDBC*.

Understanding and parsing the request

We now know how to formulate (basic) responses. The other half of the equation is the HTTP request. Recall that an `Action` is just a function mapping `Request => Result`. We can access the request using:

```
def hello(name:String) = Action { request =>

    ...

}
```

One of the reasons for needing a reference to the request is to access parameters in the query string. Let's modify the `Hello, <name>` example that we wrote earlier to, optionally, include a title in the query string. Thus, a URL could be formatted as `/hello/Jim?title=Dr`. The `request` instance exposes the `getQueryString` method for accessing specific keys in the query string. This method returns `Some[String]` if the key is present in the query, or `None` otherwise. We can re-write our `hello` controller as:

```
def hello(name:String) = Action { request =>
  val title = request.getQueryString("title")
  val titleString = title.map { _ + " " }.getOrElse("")
  Ok(s"Hello, $titleString$name")
}
```

Try this out by accessing the URL `127.0.0.1:9000/hello/Odersky?title=Dr` in your browser. The browser should display `Hello, Dr Odersky`.

We have, so far, been concentrating on GET requests. These do not have a body. Other types of HTTP request, most commonly POST requests, do contain a body. Play lets the user pass *body parsers* when defining the action. The request body will be passed through the body parser, which will convert it from a byte stream to a Scala type. As a very simple example, let's define a new route that accepts POST requests:

```
POST          /hello              controllers.Application.helloPost
```

We will apply the predefined `parse.text` body parser to the incoming request body. This converts the body of the request to a string. The `helloPost` controller looks like:

```scala
def helloPost = Action(parse.text) { request =>
  Ok("Hello. You told me: " + request.body)
}
```

You cannot test POST requests easily in the browser. You can use cURL instead. cURL is a command line utility for dispatching HTTP requests. It is installed by default on Mac OS and should be available via the package manager on Linux distributions. The following will send a POST request with `"I think that Scala is great"` in the body:

```
$ curl --data "I think that Scala is great" --header
"Content-type:text/plain"  127.0.0.1:9000/hello
```

This prints the following line to the terminal:

```
Hello. You told me: I think that Scala is great
```

There are several types of built-in body parsers:

- `parse.file(new File("filename.txt"))` will save the body to a file.

- `parse.json` will parse the body as JSON (we will learn more about interacting with JSON in the next section).

- `parse.xml` will parse the body as XML.

- `parse.urlFormEncoded` will parse the body as returned by submitting an HTML form. The `request.body` attribute is a Scala map from `String` to `Seq[String]`, mapping each form element to its value(s).

For a full list of body parsers, the best source is the Scala API documentation for `play.api.mvc.BodyParsers.parse` available at: `https://www.playframework.com/documentation/2.5.x/api/scala/index.html#play.api.mvc.BodyParsers$parse$`.

Interacting with JSON

JSON, as we discovered in previous chapters, is becoming the de-facto language for communicating structured data over HTTP. If you develop a web application or a web API, it is likely that you will have to consume or emit JSON, or both.

In *Chapter 7, Web APIs*, we learned how to parse JSON through json4s. The Play framework includes its own JSON parser and emitter. Fortunately, it behaves in much the same way as json4s.

Let's imagine that we are building an API that summarizes information about GitHub repositories. Our API will emit a JSON array listing a user's repositories when queried about a specific user (much like the GitHub API, but with just a subset of fields).

Let's start by defining a model for the repository. In Play applications, models are normally stored in the folder app/models, in the models package:

```scala
// app/models/Repo.scala

package models

case class Repo (
  val name:String,
  val language:String,
  val isFork: Boolean,
  val size: Long
)
```

Let's add a route to our application that serves arrays of repos for a particular user. In conf/routes, add the following line:

```
// conf/routes
GET    /api/repos/:username          controllers.Api.repos(username)
```

Let's now implement the framework for the controller. We will create a new controller for our API, imaginatively called Api. For now, we will just have the controller return dummy data. This is what the code looks like (we will explain the details shortly):

```scala
// app/controllers/Api.scala
package controllers
import play.api._
import play.api.mvc._
```

```scala
import play.api.libs.json._

import models.Repo

class Api extends Controller {

  // Some dummy data.
  val data = List[Repo](
    Repo("dotty", "Scala", true, 14315),
    Repo("frontend", "JavaScript", true, 392)
  )

  // Typeclass for converting Repo -> JSON
  implicit val writesRepos = new Writes[Repo] {
    def writes(repo:Repo) = Json.obj(
      "name" -> repo.name,
      "language" -> repo.language,
      "is_fork" -> repo.isFork,
      "size" -> repo.size
    )
  }

  // The controller
  def repos(username:String) = Action {

    val repoArray = Json.toJson(data)
    // toJson(data) relies on existence of
    // `Writes[List[Repo]]` type class in scope

    Ok(repoArray)
  }
}
```

If you point your web browser to `127.0.0.1:9000/api/repos/odersky`, you should now see the following JSON object:

```
[{"name":"dotty","language":"Scala","is_fork":true,"size":14315},{"name":"frontend","language":"JavaScript","is_fork":true,"size":392}]
```

The only tricky part of this code is the conversion from `Repo` to JSON. We call `Json.toJson` on `data`, an instance of type `List[Repo]`. The `toJson` method relies on the existence of a type class `Writes[T]` for the type `T` passed to it.

The Play framework makes extensive use of type classes to define how to convert models to specific formats. Recall that we learnt how to write type classes in the context of SQL and MongoDB. The Play framework's expectations are very similar: for the `Json.toJson` method to work on an instance of type `Repo`, there must be a `Writes[Repo]` implementation available that specifies how to transform `Repo` objects to JSON.

In the Play framework, the `Writes[T]` type class defines a single method:

```
trait Writes[T] {
  def writes(obj:T):Json
}
```

`Writes` methods for built-in simple types and for collections are already built into the Play framework, so we do not need to worry about defining `Writes[Boolean]`, for instance.

The `Writes[Repo]` instance is commonly defined either directly in the controller, if it is just used for that controller, or in the `Repo` companion object, where it can be used across several controllers. For simplicity, we just embedded it in the controller.

Note how type-classes allow for separation of concerns. The model just defines the `Repo` type, without attaching any behavior. The `Writes[Repo]` type class just knows how to convert from a `Repo` instance to JSON, but knows nothing of the context in which it is used. Finally, the controller just knows how to create a JSON HTTP response.

Congratulations, you have just defined a web API that returns JSON! In the next section, we will learn how to fetch data from the GitHub web API to avoid constantly returning the same array.

Querying external APIs and consuming JSON

So far, we have learnt how to provide the user with a dummy JSON array of repositories in response to a request to `/api/repos/:username`. In this section, we will replace the dummy data with the user's actual repositories, dowloaded from GitHub.

In *Chapter 7*, *Web APIs*, we learned how to query the GitHub API using Scala's `Source.fromURL` method and `scalaj-http`. It should come as no surprise that the Play framework implements its own library for interacting with external web services.

Let's edit the `Api` controller to fetch information about a user's repositories from GitHub, rather than using dummy data. When called with a username as argument, the controller will:

1. Send a GET request to the GitHub API for that user's repositories.

2. Interpret the response, converting the body from a JSON object to a `List[Repo]`.

3. Convert from the `List[Repo]` to a JSON array, forming the response.

We start by giving the full code listing before explaining the thornier parts in detail:

```scala
// app/controllers/Api.scala

package controllers

import play.api._
import play.api.mvc._
import play.api.libs.ws.WS // query external APIs
import play.api.Play.current
import play.api.libs.json._ // parsing JSON
import play.api.libs.functional.syntax._
import play.api.libs.concurrent.Execution.Implicits.defaultContext

import models.Repo

class Api extends Controller {

  // type class for Repo -> Json conversion
  implicit val writesRepo = new Writes[Repo] {
    def writes(repo:Repo) = Json.obj(
      "name" -> repo.name,
      "language" -> repo.language,
      "is_fork" -> repo.isFork,
      "size" -> repo.size
    )
  }

  // type class for Github Json -> Repo conversion
  implicit val readsRepoFromGithub:Reads[Repo] = (
    (JsPath \ "name").read[String] and
    (JsPath \ "language").read[String] and
    (JsPath \ "fork").read[Boolean] and
```

```scala
    (JsPath \ "size").read[Long]
  )(Repo.apply _)

  // controller
  def repos(username:String) = Action.async {

    // GitHub URL
    val url = s"https://api.github.com/users/$username/repos"
    val response = WS.url(url).get() // compose get request

    // "response" is a Future
    response.map { r =>
      // executed when the request completes
      if (r.status == 200) {

        // extract a list of repos from the response body
        val reposOpt = Json.parse(r.body).validate[List[Repo]]
        reposOpt match {
          // if the extraction was successful:
          case JsSuccess(repos, _) => Ok(Json.toJson(repos))

          // If there was an error during the extraction
          case _ => InternalServerError
        }
      }
      else {
        // GitHub returned something other than 200
        NotFound
      }

    }
  }

}
```

If you have written all this, point your browser to, for instance, `127.0.0.1:9000/api/repos/odersky` to see the list of repositories owned by Martin Odersky:

```
[{"name":"dotty","language":"Scala","is_fork":true,"size":14653},{"name":"frontend","language":"JavaScript","is_fork":true,"size":392},...
```

This code sample is a lot to take in, so let's break it down.

Calling external web services

The first step in querying external APIs is to import the `WS` object, which defines factory methods for creating HTTP requests. These factory methods rely on a reference to an implicit Play application in the namespace. The easiest way to ensure this is the case is to import `play.api.Play.current`, a reference to the current application.

Let's ignore the `readsRepoFromGithub` type class for now and jump straight to the controller body. The URL that we want to hit with a GET request is `"https://api.github.com/users/$username/repos"`, with the appropriate value for `$username`. We create a GET request with `WS.url(url).get()`. We can also add headers to an existing request. For instance, to specify the content type, we could have written:

```
WS.url(url).withHeaders("Content-Type" ->
  "application/json").get()
```

We can use headers to pass a GitHub OAuth token using:

```
val token = "2502761d..."
WS.url(url).withHeaders("Authorization" -> s"token $token").get()
```

To formulate a POST request, rather than a GET request, replace the final `.get()` with `.post(data)`. Here, `data` can be JSON, XML or a string.

Adding `.get` or `.post` fires the request, returning a `Future[WSResponse]`. You should, by now, be familiar with futures. By writing `response.map { r => ... }`, we specify a transformation to be executed on the future result, when it returns. The transformation verifies the response's status, returning `NotFound` if the status code of the response is anything but 200.

Parsing JSON

If the status code is 200, the callback parses the response body to JSON and converts the parsed JSON to a `List[Repo]` instance. We already know how to convert from a `Repo` object to JSON using the `Writes[Repo]` type class. The converse, going from JSON to a `Repo` object, is a little more challenging, because we have to account for incorrectly formatted JSON. To this effect, the Play framework provides the `.validate[T]` method on JSON objects. This method tries to convert the JSON to an instance of type `T`, returning `JsSuccess` if the JSON is well-formatted, or `JsError` otherwise (similar to Scala's `Try` object). The `.validate` method relies on the existence of a type class `Reads[Repo]`. Let's experiment with a Scala console:

```
$ activator console


scala> import play.api.libs.json._
```

```
import play.api.libs.json._

scala> val s = """
  { "name": "dotty", "size": 150, "language": "Scala", "fork": true }
"""
s: String = "
  { "name": "dotty", "size": 150, "language": "Scala", "fork": true }
"


scala> val parsedJson = Json.parse(s)
parsedJson: play.api.libs.json.JsValue = {"name":"dotty","size":150,"lang
uage":"Scala","fork":true}
```

Using `Json.parse` converts a string to an instance of `JsValue`, the super-type for JSON instances. We can access specific fields in `parsedJson` using XPath-like syntax (if you are not familiar with XPath-like syntax, you might want to read *Chapter 6, Slick – A Functional Interface for SQL*):

```
scala> parsedJson \ "name"
play.api.libs.json.JsLookupResult = JsDefined("dotty")
```

XPath-like lookups return an instance with type `JsLookupResult`. This takes two values: either `JsDefined`, if the path is valid, or `JsUndefined` if it is not:

```
scala> parsedJson \ "age"
play.api.libs.json.JsLookupResult = JsUndefined('age' is undefined on
object: {"name":"dotty","size":150,"language":"Scala","fork":true})
```

To go from a `JsLookupResult` instance to a String in a type-safe way, we can use the `.validate[String]` method:

```
scala> (parsedJson \ "name").validate[String]
play.api.libs.json.JsResult[String] = JsSuccess(dotty,)
```

The `.validate[T]` method returns either `JsSuccess` if the `JsDefined` instance could be successfully cast to `T`, or `JsError` otherwise. To illustrate the latter, let's try validating this as an `Int`:

```
scala> (parsedJson \ "name").validate[Int]
dplay.api.libs.json.JsResult[Int] = JsError(List((,List(ValidationError(L
ist(error.expected.jsnumber),WrappedArray())))))
```

Calling `.validate` on an instance of type `JsUndefined` also returns in a `JsError`:

```
scala> (parsedJson \ "age").validate[Int]
play.api.libs.json.JsResult[Int] = JsError(List((,List(ValidationError
(List('age' is undefined on object: {"name":"dotty","size":150,
"language":"Scala","fork":true}),WrappedArray())))))
```

To convert from an instance of `JsResult[T]` to an instance of type `T`, we can use pattern matching:

```
scala> val name = (parsedJson \ "name").validate[String] match {
  case JsSuccess(n, _) => n
  case JsError(e) => throw new IllegalStateException(
    s"Error extracting name: $e")
}
name: String = dotty
```

We can now use `.validate` to cast JSON to simple types in a type-safe manner. But, in the code example, we used `.validate[Repo]`. This works provided a `Reads[Repo]` type class is implicitly available in the namespace.

The most common way of defining `Reads[T]` type classes is through a DSL provided in `import play.api.libs.functional.syntax._`. The DSL works by chaining operations returning either `JsSuccess` or `JsError` together. Discussing exactly how this DSL works is outside the scope of this chapter (see, for instance, the Play framework documentation page on JSON combinators: https://www.playframework.com/documentation/2.4.x/ScalaJsonCombinators). We will stick to discussing the syntax.

```
scala> import play.api.libs.functional.syntax._
import play.api.libs.functional.syntax._


scala> import models.Repo
import models.Repo


scala> implicit val readsRepoFromGithub:Reads[Repo] = (
  (JsPath \ "name").read[String] and
  (JsPath \ "language").read[String] and
  (JsPath \ "fork").read[Boolean] and
```

```
  (JsPath \ "size").read[Long]
)(Repo.apply _)
readsRepoFromGithub: play.api.libs.json.Reads[models.Repo] = play.api.
libs.json.Reads$$anon$8@a198ddb
```

The `Reads` type class is defined in two stages. The first chains together `read[T]` methods with `and`, combining successes and errors. The second uses the apply method of the companion object of a case class (or `Tuple` instance) to construct the object, provided the first stage completed successfully. Now that we have defined the type class, we can call `validate[Repo]` on a `JsValue` object:

```
scala> val repoOpt = parsedJson.validate[Repo]
play.api.libs.json.JsResult[models.Repo] = JsSuccess(Repo(dotty,Scala,tr
ue,150),)
```

We can then use pattern matching to extract the `Repo` object from the `JsSuccess` instance:

```
scala> val JsSuccess(repo, _) = repoOpt
repo: models.Repo = Repo(dotty,Scala,true,150)
```

We have, so far, only talked about validating single repos. The Play framework defines type classes for collection types, so, provided `Reads[Repo]` is defined, `Reads[List[Repo]]` will also be defined.

Now that we understand how to extract Scala objects from JSON, let's get back to the code. If we manage to successfully convert the repositories to a `List[Repo]`, we emit it again as JSON. Of course, converting from GitHub's JSON representation of a repository to a Scala object, and from that Scala object directly to our JSON representation of the object, might seem convoluted. However, if this were a real application, we would have additional logic. We could, for instance, store repos in a cache, and try and fetch from that cache instead of querying the GitHub API. Converting from JSON to Scala objects as early as possible decouples the code that we write from the way GitHub returns repositories.

Asynchronous actions

The last bit of the code sample that is new is the call to `Action.async`, rather than just `Action`. Recall that an `Action` instance is a thin wrapper around a `Request => Result` method. Our code, however, returns a `Future[Result]`, rather than a `Result`. When that is the case, use the `Action.async` to construct the action, rather than `Action` directly. Using `Action.async` tells the Play framework that the code creating the `Action` is asynchronous.

Creating APIs with Play: a summary

In the last section, we deployed an API that responds to GET requests. Since this is a lot to take in, let's summarize how to go about API creation:

1. Define appropriate routes in `/conf/routes`, using wildcards in the URL as needed.

2. Create Scala case classes in `/app/models` to represent the models used by the API.

3. Create `Write[T]` methods to write models to JSON or XML so that they can be returned by the API.

4. Bind the routes to controllers. If the controllers need to do more than a trivial amount a work, wrap the work in a future to avoid blocking the server.

There are many more useful components of the Play framework that you are likely to need, such as, for instance, how to use Slick to access SQL databases. We do not, unfortunately, have time to cover these in this introduction. The Play framework has extensive, well-written documentation that will fill the gaping holes in this tutorial.

Rest APIs: best practice

As the Internet matures, REST (representational state transfer) APIs are emerging as the most reliable design pattern for web APIs. An API is described as *RESTful* if it follows these guiding principles:

- The API is designed as a set of resources. For instance, the GitHub API provides information about users, repositories, followers, etc. Each user, or repository, is a specific resource. Each resource can be addressed through a different HTTP end-point.

- The URLs should be simple and should identify the resource clearly. For instance, `api.github.com/users/odersky` is simple and tells us clearly that we should expect information about the user Martin Odersky.

- There is no *world resource* that contains all the information about the system. Instead, top-level resources contain links to more specialized resources. For instance, the user resource in the GitHub API contains links to that user's repositories and that user's followers, rather than having all that information embedded in the user resource directly.

- The API should be discoverable. The response to a request for a specific resource should contain URLs for related resources. When you query the user resource on GitHub, the response contains the URL for accessing that user's followers, repositories etc. The client should use the URLs provided by the API, rather than attempting to construct them client-side. This makes the client less brittle to changes in the API.

- There should be as little state maintained on the server as possible. For instance, when querying the GitHub API, we must pass the authentication token with every request, rather than expecting our authentication status to be *remembered* on the server. Having each interaction be independent of the history provides much better scalability: if any interaction can be handled by any server, load balancing is much easier.

Summary

In this chapter, we introduced the Play framework as a tool for building web APIs. We built an API that returns a JSON array of a user's GitHub repositories. In the next chapter, we will build on this API and construct a single-page application to represent this data graphically.

References

- This Wikipedia page gives information on semantic URLs:
  `https://en.wikipedia.org/wiki/Semantic_URL` and
  `http://apiux.com/2013/04/03/url-design-restful-web-services/`.

- For a much more in depth discussion of the Play framework, I suggest *Play Framework Essentials* by *Julien Richard-Foy*.

- *REST in Practice: Hypermedia and Systems Architecture*, by *Jim Webber, Savas Parastatidis* and *Ian Robinson* describes how to architect REST APIs.

14
Visualization with D3 and the Play Framework

In the previous chapter, we learned about the Play framework, a web framework for Scala. We built an API that returns a JSON array describing a user's GitHub repositories.

In this chapter, we will construct a fully-fledged web application that displays a table and a chart describing a user's repositories. We will learn to integrate **D3.js**, a JavaScript library for building data-driven web pages, with the Play framework. This will set you on the path to building compelling interactive visualizations that showcase results obtained with machine learning.

This chapter assumes that you are familiar with HTML, CSS, and JavaScript. We present references at the end of the chapter. You should also have read the previous chapter.

GitHub user data

We will build a single-page application that uses, as its backend, the API developed in the previous chapter. The application contains a form where the user enters the login name for a GitHub account. The application queries the API to get a list of repositories for that user and displays them on the screen as both a table and a pie chart summarizing programming language use for that user:

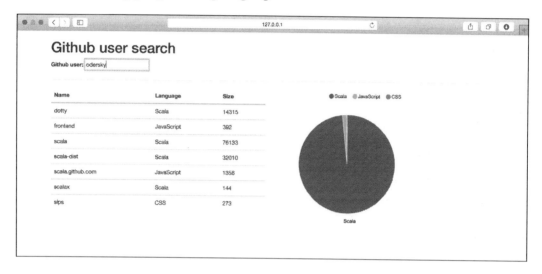

To see a live version of the application, head over to http://app.scala4datascience.com.

Do I need a backend?

In the previous chapter, we learned about the client-server model that underpins how the internet works: when you enter a website URL in your browser, the server serves HTML, CSS, and JavaScript to your browser, which then renders it in the appropriate manner.

What does this all mean for you? Arguably the second question that you should be asking yourself when building a web application is whether you need to do any server-side processing (right after "is this really going to be worth the effort?"). Could you just create an HTML web-page with some JavaScript?

You can get away without a backend if the data needed to build the whole application is small enough: typically a few megabytes. If your application is larger, you will need a backend to transfer just the data the client currently needs. Surprisingly, you can often build visualizations without a backend: while data science is accustomed to dealing with terabytes of data, the goal of the data science process is often condensing these huge data sets to a few meaningful numbers.

Having a backend also lets you include logic invisible to the client. If you need to validate a password, you clearly cannot send the code to do that to the client computer: it needs to happen out of sight, on the server.

If your application is small enough and you do not need to do any server-side processing, stop reading this chapter, brush up on your JavaScript if you have to, and forget about Scala for now. Not having to worry about building a backend will make your life easier.

Clearly, however, we do not have that freedom for the application that we want to build: the user could enter the name of anyone on GitHub. Finding information about that user requires a backend with access to tremendous storage and querying capacity (which we simulate by just forwarding the request to the GitHub API and re-interpreting the response).

JavaScript dependencies through web-jars

One of the challenges of developing web applications is that we are writing two quasi-separate programs: the server-side program and the client-side program. These generally require different technologies. In particular, for any but the most trivial application, we must keep track of JavaScript libraries, and integrate processing the JavaScript code (for instance, for minification) in the build process.

The Play framework manages JavaScript dependencies through *web-jars*. These are just JavaScript libraries packaged as jars. They are deployed on Maven Central, which means that we can just add them as dependencies to our `build.sbt` file. For this application, we will need the following JavaScript libraries:

- Require.js, a library for writing modular JavaScript
- JQuery
- Bootstrap
- Underscore.js, a library that adds many functional constructs and client-side templating.
- D3, the graph plotting library
- NVD3, a graph library built on top of D3

If you are planning on coding up the examples provided in this chapter, the easiest will be for you to start from the code for the previous chapter (You can download the code for *Chapter 13, Web APIs with Play*, from GitHub: `https://github.com/pbugnion/s4ds/tree/master/chap13`). We will assume this as a starting point here onwards.

Let's include the dependencies on the web-jars in the `build.sbt` file:

```
libraryDependencies ++= Seq(
    "org.webjars" % "requirejs" % "2.1.22",
    "org.webjars" % "jquery" % "2.1.4",
    "org.webjars" % "underscorejs" % "1.8.3",
    "org.webjars" % "nvd3" % "1.8.1",
    "org.webjars" % "d3js" % "3.5.6",
    "org.webjars" % "bootstrap" % "3.3.6"
)
```

Fetch the modules by running `activator update`. Once you have done this, you will notice the JavaScript libraries in `target/web/public/main/lib`.

Towards a web application: HTML templates

In the previous chapter, we briefly saw how to construct HTML templates by interleaving Scala snippets in an HTML file. We saw that templates are compiled to Scala functions, and we learned how to call these functions from the controllers.

In single-page applications, the majority of the logic governing what is actually displayed in the browser resides in the client-side JavaScript, not in the server. The pages served by the server contain the bare-bones HTML framework.

Let's create the HTML layout for our application. We will save this in `views/index.scala.html`. The template will just contain the layout for the application, but will not contain any information about any user's repositories. To fetch that information, the application will have to query the API developed in the previous chapter. The template does not take any parameters, since all the dynamic HTML generation will happen client-side.

We use the Bootstrap grid layout to control the HTML layout. If you are not familiar with Bootstrap layouts, consult the documentation at `http://getbootstrap.com/css/#grid-example-basic`.

```
// app/views/index.scala.html
<!DOCTYPE html>

<html lang="en">
  <head>
    <title>Github User display</title>
    <link rel="stylesheet" media="screen"
      href="@routes.Assets.versioned("stylesheets/main.css")">
    <link rel="shortcut icon" type="image/png"
      href="@routes.Assets.versioned("images/favicon.png")">
    <link rel="stylesheet" media="screen"
      href=@routes.Assets.versioned("lib/nvd3/nv.d3.css") >
    <link rel="stylesheet" media="screen"
      href=@routes.Assets.versioned(
      "lib/bootstrap/css/bootstrap.css") >
  </head>

  <body>
    <div class="container">

      <!-- Title row -->
      <div class="row">
        <h1>Github user search</h1>
      </div>

      <!-- User search row -->
      <div class="row">
        <label>Github user: </label>
        <input type="text" id="user-selection">
```

```
        <span id="searching-span"></span>
        <hr />
      </div>

      <!-- Results row -->
      <div id="response" class="row"></div>
    </div>
  </body>
</html>
```

In the HTML head, we link the CSS stylesheets that we need for the application. Instead of specifying the path explicitly, we use the `@routes.Assets.versioned(...)` function. This resolves to a URI corresponding to the location where the assets are stored post-compilation. The argument passed to the function should be the path from `target/web/public/main` to the asset you need.

We want to serve the compiled version of this view when the user accesses the route `/` on our server. We therefore need to add this route to `conf/routes`:

```
# conf/routes
GET    /        controllers.Application.index
```

The route is served by the `index` function in the `Application` controller. All this controller needs to do is serve the `index` view:

```
// app/controllers/Application.scala
package controllers

import play.api._
import play.api.mvc._

class Application extends Controller {

  def index = Action {
    Ok(views.html.index())
  }
}
```

Start the Play framework by running `activator run` in the root directory of the application and point your web browser to `127.0.0.1:9000/`. You should see the framework for our web application. Of course, the application does not do anything yet, since we have not written any of the JavaScript logic yet.

Github user search

Github user:

Modular JavaScript through RequireJS

The simplest way of injecting JavaScript libraries into the namespace is to add them to the HTML framework via `<script>...</script>` tags in the HTML header. For instance, to add JQuery, we would add the following line to the head of the document:

```
<script src=@routes.Assets.versioned("lib/jquery/jquery.js")
    type="text/javascript"></script>
```

While this works, it does not scale well to large applications, since every library gets imported into the global namespace. Modern client-side JavaScript frameworks such as AngularJS provide an alternative way of defining and loading modules that preserve encapsulation.

We will use RequireJS. In a nutshell, RequireJS lets us encapsulate JavaScript modules through functions. For instance, if we wanted to write a module `example` that contains a function for hiding a `div`, we would define the module as follows:

```
// example.js
define(["jquery", "underscore"], function($, _) {

  // hide a div
  function hide(div_name) {
    $(div_name).hide() ;
  }

  // what the module exports.
  return { "hide": hide }

}) ;
```

We encapsulate our module as a callback in a function called `define`. The `define` function takes two arguments: a list of dependencies, and a function definition. The `define` function binds the dependencies to the arguments list of the callback: in this case, functions in JQuery will be bound to `$` and functions in Underscore will be bound to `_`. This creates a module which exposes whatever the callback function returns. In this case, we export the `hide` function, binding it to the name `"hide"`. Our example module thus exposes the `hide` function.

To load this module, we pass it as a dependency to the module in which we want to use it:

```
define(["example"], function(example) {

  function hide_all() {
```

```
      example.hide("#top") ;
      example.hide("#bottom") ;
   }

   return { "hide_all": hide_all } ;
});
```

Notice how the functions in `example` are encapsulated, rather than existing in the global namespace. We call them through `example.<function-name>`. Furthermore, any functions or variables defined internally to the `example` module remain private.

Sometimes, we want JavaScript code to exist outside of modules. This is often the case for the script that bootstraps the application. For these, replace `define` with `require`:

```
require(["jquery", "example"], function($, example) {
  $(document).ready(function() {
    example.hide("#header") ;
  });
}) ;
```

Now that we have an overview of RequireJS, how do we use it in the Play framework? The first step is to add the dependency on the RequireJS web jar, which we have done. The Play framework also adds a RequireJS SBT plugin (`https://github.com/sbt/sbt-rjs`), which should be installed by default if you used the `play-scala` activator. If this is missing, it can be added with the following line in `plugins.sbt`:

```
// project/plugins.sbt

addSbtPlugin("com.typesafe.sbt" % "sbt-rjs" % "1.0.7")
```

We also need to add the plugin to the list of stages. This allows the plugin to manipulate the JavaScript assets when packaging the application as a jar. Add the following line to `build.sbt`:

```
pipelineStages := Seq(rjs)
```

You will need to restart the activator for the changes to take effect.

We are now ready to use RequireJS in our application. We can use it by adding the following line in the head section of our view:

```
// index.scala.html

<html>
  <head>
```

. . .

```
    <script
      type="text/javascript"
      src=@routes.Assets.versioned("lib/requirejs/require.js").url
      data-main=@routes.Assets.versioned("javascripts/main.js").url>
    </script>

  </head>
...
</html>
```

When the view is compiled, this is resolved to tags like:

```
<script type="text/javascript"
  data-main="/assets/javascripts/main.js"
  src="/assets/lib/requirejs/require.min.js">
</script>
```

The argument passed to `data-main` is the entry point for our application. When RequireJS loads, it will execute `main.js`. That script must therefore bootstrap our application. In particular, it should contain a configuration object for RequireJS, to make it aware of where all the libraries are.

Bootstrapping the applications

When we linked `require.js` to our application, we told it to use `main.js` as our entry point. To test that this works, let's start by entering a dummy `main.js`. JavaScript files in Play applications go in `/public/javascripts`:

```
// public/javascripts/main.js

require([], function() {
  console.log("hello, JavaScript");
});
```

To verify that this worked, head to `127.0.0.1:9000` and open the browser console. You should see `"hello, JavaScript"` in the console.

Let's now write a more useful `main.js`. We will start by configuring RequireJS, giving it the location of modules we will use in our application. Unfortunately, NVD3, the graph library that we use, does not play very well with RequireJS so we have to use an ugly hack to make it work. This complicates our `main.js` file somewhat:

```
// public/javascripts/main.js

(function (requirejs) {
  'use strict';

  // -- RequireJS config --
  requirejs.config({
    // path to the web jars. These definitions allow us
    // to use "jquery", rather than "../lib/jquery/jquery",
    // when defining module dependencies.
    paths: {
      "jquery": "../lib/jquery/jquery",
      "underscore": "../lib/underscorejs/underscore",
      "d3": "../lib/d3js/d3",
      "nvd3": "../lib/nvd3/nv.d3",
      "bootstrap": "../lib/bootstrap/js/bootstrap"
    },

    shim: {
      // hack to get nvd3 to work with requirejs.
      // see this so question:
      // http://stackoverflow.com/questions/13157704/how-to-integrate-
d3-with-require-js#comment32647365_13171592
      nvd3: {
        deps: ["d3.global"],
        exports: "nv"
      },
      bootstrap : { deps :['jquery'] }
    }

  }) ;
})(requirejs) ;

// hack to get nvd3 to work with requirejs.
// see this so question on Stack Overflow:
```

```
// http://stackoverflow.com/questions/13157704/how-to-integrate-d3-
with-require-js#comment32647365_13171592
define("d3.global", ["d3"], function(d3global) {
  d3 = d3global;
});

require([], function() {
  // Our application
  console.log("hello, JavaScript");
}) ;
```

Now that we have the configuration in place, we can dig into the JavaScript part of
the application.

Client-side program architecture

The basic idea is simple: the user searches for the name of someone on GitHub in
the input box. When he enters a name, we fire a request to the API designed earlier
in this chapter. When the response from the API returns, the program binds that
response to a model and emits an event notifying that the model has been changed.
The views listen for this event and refresh from the model in response.

Designing the model

Let's start by defining the client-side model. The model holds information regarding
the repos of the user currently displayed. It gets filled in after the first search.

```
// public/javascripts/model.js

define([], function(){
   return {
     ghubUser: "", // last name that was searched for
     exists: true, // does that person exist on github?
     repos: [] // list of repos
   } ;
});
```

To see a populated value of the model, head to the complete application example on app.scala4datascience.com, open a JavaScript console in your browser, search for a user (for example, odersky) in the application and type the following in the console:

```
> require(["model"], function(model) { console.log(model) ; })
{ghubUser: "odersky", exists: true, repos: Array}


> require(["model"], function(model) {
  console.log(model.repos[0]);
})
{name: "dotty", language: "Scala", is_fork: true, size: 14653}
```

These import the `"model"` module, bind it to the variable model, and then print information to the console.

The event bus

We need a mechanism for informing the views when the model is updated, since the views need to refresh from the new model. This is commonly handled through *events* in web applications. JQuery lets us bind callbacks to specific events. The callback is executed when that event occurs.

For instance, to bind a callback to the event `"custom-event"`, enter the following in a JavaScript console:

```
> $(window).on("custom-event", function() {
  console.log("custom event received") ;
});
```

We can fire the event using:

```
> $(window).trigger("custom-event");
custom event received
```

Events in JQuery require an *event* bus, a DOM element on which the event is registered. In this case, we used the `window` DOM element as our event bus, but any JQuery element would have served. Centralizing event definitions to a single module is helpful. We will, therefore, create an `events` module containing two functions: `trigger`, which triggers an event (specified by a string) and `on`, which binds a callback to a specific event:

```
// public/javascripts/events.js

define(["jquery"], function($) {

  var bus = $(window) ; // widget to use as an event bus

  function trigger(eventType) {
    $(bus).trigger(eventType) ;
  }

  function on(eventType, f) {
    $(bus).on(eventType, f) ;
  }

  return {
    "trigger": trigger,
    "on": on
  } ;
});
```

We can now emit and receive events using the `events` module. You can test this out in a JavaScript console on the live version of the application (at `app.scala4datascience.com`). Let's start by registering a listener:

```
> require(["events"], function(events) {
  // register event listener
  events.on("hello_event", function() {
    console.log("Received event") ;
  }) ;
}) ;
```

If we now trigger the event `"hello_event"`, the listener prints `"Received event"`:

```
> require(["events"], function(events) {
  // trigger the event
  events.trigger("hello_event") ;
}) ;
```

Using events allows us to decouple the controller from the views. The controller does not need to know anything about the views, and vice-versa. The controller just needs to emit a `"model_updated"` event when the model is updated, and the views need to refresh from the model when they receive that event.

AJAX calls through JQuery

We can now write the controller for our application. When the user enters a name in the text input, we query the API, update the model and trigger a `model_updated` event.

We use JQuery's `$.getJSON` function to query our API. This function takes a URL as its first argument, and a callback as its second argument. The API call is asynchronous: `$.getJSON` returns immediately after execution. All request processing must, therefore, be done in the callback. The callback is called if the request is successful, but we can define additional handlers that are always called, or called on failure. Let's try this out in the browser console (either your own, if you are running the API developed in the previous chapter, or on `app.scala4datascience.com`). Recall that the API is listening to the end-point `/api/repos/:user`:

```
> $.getJSON("/api/repos/odersky", function(data) {
  console.log("API response:");
  console.log(data);
  console.log(data[0]);
}) ;
{readyState: 1, getResponseHeader: function, ...}


API response:
[Object, Object, Object, Object, Object, ...]
{name: "dotty", language: "Scala", is_fork: true, size: 14653}
```

`getJSON` returns immediately. A few tenths of a second later, the API responds, at which point the response gets fed through the callback.

The callback only gets executed on success. It takes, as its argument, the JSON object returned by the API. To bind a callback that is executed when the API request fails, call the `.fail` method on the return value of `getJSON`:

```
> $.getJSON("/api/repos/junk123456", function(data) {
  console.log("called on success");
}).fail(function() {
  console.log("called on failure") ;
```

```
}) ;
{readyState: 1, getResponseHeader: function, ...}
```

called on failure

We can also use the `.always` method on the return value of `getJSON` to specify a callback that is executed, whether the API query was successful or not.

Now that we know how to use `$.getJSON` to query our API, we can write the controller. The controller listens for changes to the `#user-selection` input field. When a change occurs, it fires an AJAX request to the API for information on that user. It binds a callback which updates the model when the API replies with a list of repositories. We will define a `controller` module that exports a single function, `initialize`, that creates the event listeners:

```javascript
// public/javascripts/controller.js
define(["jquery", "events", "model"], function($, events, model) {

    function initialize() {
        $("#user-selection").change(function() {

            var user = $("#user-selection").val() ;
            console.log("Fetching information for " + user) ;

            // Change cursor to a 'wait' symbol
            // while we wait for the API to respond
            $("*").css({"cursor": "wait"}) ;

            $.getJSON("/api/repos/" + user, function(data) {
                // Executed on success
                model.exists = true ;
                model.repos = data ;
            }).fail(function() {
                // Executed on failure
                model.exists = false ;
                model.repos = [] ;
            }).always(function() {
                // Always executed
                model.ghubUser = user ;

                // Restore cursor
                $("*").css({"cursor": "initial"}) ;

                // Tell the rest of the application
```

```
      // that the model has been updated.
      events.trigger("model_updated") ;
    });
  }) ;
} ;


return { "initialize": initialize };


});
```

Our controller module just exposes the `initialize` method. Once the initialization is performed, the controller interacts with the rest of the application through event listeners. We will call the controller's `initialize` method in `main.js`. Currently, the last lines of that file are just an empty `require` block. Let's import our controller and initialize it:

```
// public/javascripts/main.js

require(["controller"], function(controller) {
  controller.initialize();
});
```

To test that this works, we can bind a dummy listener to the `"model_updated"` event. For instance, we could log the current model to the browser JavaScript console with the following snippet (which you can write directly in the JavaScript console):

```
> require(["events", "model"],
function(events, model) {
  events.on("model_updated", function () {
    console.log("model_updated event received");
    console.log(model);
  });
});
```

If you then search for a user, the model will be printed to the console. We now have the controller in place. The last step is writing the views.

Response views

If the request fails, we just display **Not found** in the response div. This part is the easiest to code up, so let's do that first. We define an `initialize` method that generates the view. The view then listens for the `"model_updated"` event, which is fired by the controller after it updates the model. Once the initialization is complete, the only way to interact with the response view is through `"model_updated"` events:

```javascript
// public/javascripts/responseView.js

define(["jquery", "model", "events"],
function($, model, events) {

  var failedResponseHtml =
    "<div class='col-md-12'>Not found</div>" ;

  function initialize() {
    events.on("model_updated", function() {
      if (model.exists) {
        // success - we will fill this in later.
        console.log("model exists")
      }
      else {
        // failure - the user entered
        // is not a valid GitHub login
        $("#response").html(failedResponseHtml) ;
      }
    }) ;
  }

  return { "initialize": initialize } ;

});
```

To bootstrap the view, we must call the initialize function from `main.js`. Just add a dependency on `responseView` in the require block, and call `responseView.initialize()`. With these modifications, the final `require` block in `main.js` is:

```javascript
// public/javascripts/main.js

require(["controller", "responseView"],
function(controller, responseView) {
  controller.initialize();
  responseView.initialize() ;
}) ;
```

You can check that this all works by entering junk in the user input to deliberately cause the API request to fail.

When the user enters a valid GitHub login name and the API returns a list of repos, we must display those on the screen. We display a table and a pie chart that aggregates the repository sizes by language. We will define the pie chart and the table in two separate modules, called `repoGraph.js` and `repoTable.js`. Let's assume those exist for now and that they expose a `build` method that accepts a `model` and the name of a `div` in which to appear.

Let's update the code for `responseView` to accommodate the user entering a valid GitHub user name:

```javascript
// public/javascripts/responseView.js

define(["jquery", "model", "events", "repoTable", "repoGraph"],
function($, model, events, repoTable, repoGraph) {

  // HTHML to inject when the model represents a valid user
  var successfulResponseHtml =
    "<div class='col-md-6' id='response-table'></div>" +
    "<div class='col-md-6' id='response-graph'></div>" ;

  // HTML to inject when the model is for a non-existent user
  var failedResponseHtml =
    "<div class='col-md-12'>Not found</div>" ;

  function initialize() {
    events.on("model_updated", function() {
      if (model.exists) {
        $("#response").html(successfulResponseHtml) ;
        repoTable.build(model, "#response-table") ;
        repoGraph.build(model, "#response-graph") ;
      }
      else {
        $("#response").html(failedResponseHtml) ;
      }
    }) ;
  }

  return { "initialize": initialize } ;

});
```

Let's walk through what happens in the event of a successful API call. We inject the following bit of HTML in the #response div:

```
var successfulResponseHtml =
    "<div class='col-md-6' id='response-table'></div>" +
    "<div class='col-md-6' id='response-graph'></div>" ;
```

This adds two HTML divs, one for the table of repositories, and the other for the graph. We use Bootstrap classes to split the response div vertically.

Let's now turn our attention to the table view, which needs to expose a single `build` method, as described in the previous section. We will just display the repositories in an HTML table. We will use *Underscore templates* to build the table dynamically. Underscore templates work much like string interpolation in Scala: we define a template with placeholders. Let's try this in a browser console:

```
> require(["underscore"], function(_) {
    var myTemplate = _.template(
      "Hello, <%= title %> <%= name %>!"
    ) ;
});
```

This creates a `myTemplate` function which accepts an object with attributes `title` and `name`:

```
> require(["underscore"], function(_) {
    var myTemplate = _.template( ... );
    var person = { title: "Dr.", name: "Odersky" } ;
    console.log(myTemplate(person)) ;
});
```

Underscore templates thus provide a convenient mechanism for formatting an object as a string. We will create a template for each row in our table, and pass the model for each repository to the template:

```
// public/javascripts/repoTable.js

define(["underscore", "jquery"], function(_, $) {

  // Underscore template for each row
  var rowTemplate = _.template("<tr>" +
    "<td><%= name %></td>" +
    "<td><%= language %></td>" +
    "<td><%= size %></td>" +
    "</tr>") ;

  // template for the table
```

```
var repoTable = _.template(
  "<table id='repo-table' class='table'>" +
    "<thead>" +
      "<tr>" +
        "<th>Name</th><th>Language</th><th>Size</th>" +
      "</tr>" +
    "</thead>" +
    "<tbody>" +
      "<%= tbody %>" +
    "</tbody>" +
  "</table>") ;

// Builds a table for a model
function build(model, divName) {
  var tbody = "" ;
  _.each(model.repos, function(repo) {
    tbody += rowTemplate(repo) ;
  }) ;
  var table = repoTable({tbody: tbody}) ;
  $(divName).html(table) ;
}

return { "build": build } ;
}) ;
```

Drawing plots with NVD3

D3 is a library that offers low-level components for building interactive visualizations in JavaScript. By offering the low-level components, it gives a huge degree of flexibility to the developer. The learning curve can, however, be quite steep. In this example, we will use NVD3, a library which provides pre-made graphs for D3. This can greatly speed up initial development. We will place the code in the file repoGraph.js and expose a single method, build, which takes, as arguments, a model and a div and draws a pie chart in that div. The pie chart will aggregate language use across all the user's repositories.

The code for generating a pie chart is nearly identical to the example given in the NVD3 documentation, available at http://nvd3.org/examples/pie.html. The data passed to the graph must be available as an array of objects. Each object must contain a `label` field and a `size` field. The `label` field identifies the language, and the `size` field is the total size of all the repositories for that user written in that language. The following would be a valid data array:

```
[
  { label: "Scala", size: 1234 },
  { label: "Python", size: 4567 }
]
```

To get the data in this format, we must aggregate sizes across the repositories written in a particular language in our model. We write the `generateDataFromModel` function to transform the `repos` array in the model to an array suitable for NVD3. The crux of the aggregation is performed by a call to Underscore's `groupBy` method, to group repositories by language. This method works exactly like Scala's `groupBy` method. With this in mind, the `generateDataFromModel` function is:

```
// public/javascripts/repoGraph.js

define(["underscore", "d3", "nvd3"],
function(_, d3, nv) {

  // Aggregate the repo size by language.
  // Returns an array of objects like:
  // [ { label: "Scala", size: 1245},
  //   { label: "Python", size: 432 } ]
  function generateDataFromModel(model) {

    // Build an initial object mapping each
    // language to the repositories written in it
    var language2Repos = _.groupBy(model.repos,
      function(repo) { return repo.language ; }) ;

    // Map each { "language": [ list of repos ], ...}
    // pairs to a single document { "language": totalSize }
    // where totalSize is the sum of the individual repos.
    var plotObjects = _.map(language2Repos,
      function(repos, language) {
        var sizes = _.map(repos, function(repo) {
          return repo.size;
        });
        // Sum over the sizes using 'reduce'
        var totalSize = _.reduce(sizes,
```

```
            function(memo, size) { return memo + size; },
        0) ;
        return { label: language, size: totalSize } ;
    }) ;


    return plotObjects;
}
```

We can now build the pie chart, using NVD3's `addGraph` method:

```
// Build the chart.
function build(model, divName) {
    var transformedModel = generateDataFromModel(model) ;
    nv.addGraph(function() {

        var height = 350;
        var width = 350;

        var chart = nv.models.pieChart()
            .x(function (d) { return d.label ; })
            .y(function (d) { return d.size ;})
            .width(width)
            .height(height) ;

        d3.select(divName).append("svg")
            .datum(transformedModel)
            .transition()
            .duration(350)
            .attr('width', width)
            .attr('height', height)
            .call(chart) ;

        return chart ;
    });
}

return { "build" : build } ;

});
```

This was the last component of our application. Point your browser to `127.0.0.1:9000` and you should see the application running.

Congratulations! We have built a fully-functioning single-page web application.

Summary

In this chapter, we learned how to write a fully-featured web application with the Play framework. Congratulations on making it this far. Building web applications are likely to push many data scientists beyond their comfort zone, but knowing enough about the web to build basic applications will allow you to share your results in a compelling, engaging manner, as well as facilitate communications with software engineers and web developers.

This concludes our whistle stop tour of Scala libraries. Over the course of this book, we have learned how to tackle linear algebra and optimization problems efficiently using Breeze, how to insert and query data in SQL databases in a functional manner, and both how to interact with web APIs and how to create them. We have reviewed some of tools available to the data scientist for writing concurrent or parallel applications, from parallel collections and futures to Spark via Akka. We have seen how pervasive these constructs are in Scala libraries, from futures in the Play framework to Akka as the backbone of Spark. If you have read this far, pat yourself on the back.

This books gives you the briefest of introduction to the libraries it covers, hopefully just enough to give you a taste of what each tool is good for, what you could accomplish with it, and how it fits in the wider Scala ecosystem. If you decide to use any of these in your data science pipeline, you will need to read the documentation in more detail, or a more complete reference book. The references listed at the end of each chapter should provide a good starting point.

Both Scala and data science are evolving rapidly. Do not stay wedded to a particular toolkit or concept. Remain on top of current developments and, above all, remain pragmatic: find the right tool for the right job. Scala and the libraries discussed here will often be that tool, but not always: sometimes, a shell command or a short Python script will be more effective. Remember also that programming skills are but one aspect of the data scientist's body of knowledge. Even if you want to specialize in the engineering side of data science, learn about the problem domain and the mathematical underpinnings of machine learning.

Most importantly, if you have taken the time to read this book, it is likely that you view programming and data science as more than a day job. Coding in Scala can be satisfying and rewarding, so have fun and be awesome!

References

There are thousands of HTML and CSS tutorials dotted around the web. A simple Google search will give you a much better idea of the resources available than any list of references I can provide.

Mike Bostock's website has a wealth of beautiful D3 visualizations: `http://bost. ocks.org/mike/`. To understand a bit more about D3, I recommend *Scott Murray's Interactive Data Visualization for the Web*.

You may also wish to consult the references given in the previous chapter for reference books on the Play framework and designing REST APIs.

Pattern Matching and Extractors

Pattern matching is a powerful tool for control flow in Scala. It is often underused and under-estimated by people coming to Scala from imperative languages.

Let's start with a few examples of pattern matching before diving into the theory. We start by defining a tuple:

```scala
scala> val names = ("Pascal", "Bugnion")
names: (String, String) = (Pascal,Bugnion)
```

We can use pattern matching to extract the elements of this tuple and bind them to variables:

```scala
scala> val (firstName, lastName) = names
firstName: String = Pascal
lastName: String = Bugnion
```

We just extracted the two elements of the `names` tuple, binding them to the variables `firstName` and `lastName`. Notice how the left-hand side defines a pattern that the right-hand side must match: we are declaring that the variable `names` must be a two-element tuple. To make the pattern more specific, we could also have specified the expected types of the elements in the tuple:

```scala
scala> val (firstName:String, lastName:String) = names
firstName: String = Pascal
lastName: String = Bugnion
```

What happens if the pattern on the left-hand side does not match the right-hand side?

```
scala> val (firstName, middleName, lastName) = names
<console>:13: error: constructor cannot be instantiated to expected type;
found    : (T1, T2, T3)
required: (String, String)
   val (firstName, middleName, lastName) = names
```

This results in a compile error. Other types of pattern matching failures result in runtime errors.

Pattern matching is very expressive. To achieve the same behavior without pattern matching, you would have to do the following explicitly:

- Verify that the variable `names` is a two-element tuple
- Extract the first element and bind it to `firstName`
- Extract the second element and bind it to `lastName`

If we expect certain elements in the tuple to have specific values, we can verify this as part of the pattern match. For instance, we can verify that the first element of the `names` tuple matches `"Pascal"`:

```
scala> val ("Pascal", lastName) = names
lastName: String = Bugnion
```

Besides tuples, we can also match on Scala collections:

```
scala> val point = Array(1, 2, 3)
point: Array[Int] = Array(1, 2, 3)


scala> val Array(x, y, z) = point
x: Int = 1
y: Int = 2
z: Int = 3
```

Notice the similarity between this pattern matching and array construction:

```
scala> val point = Array(x, y, z)
point: Array[Int] = Array(1, 2, 3)
```

Syntactically, Scala expresses pattern matching as the reverse process to instance construction. We can think of pattern matching as the deconstruction of an object, binding the object's constituent parts to variables.

When matching against collections, one is sometimes only interested in matching the first element, or the first few elements, and discarding the rest of the collection, whatever its length. The operator _* will match against any number of elements:

```
scala> val Array(x, _*) = point
x: Int = 1
```

By default, the part of the pattern matched by the _* operator is not bound to a variable. We can capture it as follows:

```
scala> val Array(x, xs @ _*) = point
x: Int = 1
xs: Seq[Int] = Vector(2, 3)
```

Besides tuples and collections, we can also match against case classes. Let's start by defining a case representing a name:

```
scala> case class Name(first: String, last: String)
defined class Name


scala> val name = Name("Martin", "Odersky")
name: Name = Name(Martin,Odersky)
```

We can match against instances of Name in much the same way we matched against tuples:

```
scala> val Name(firstName, lastName) = name
firstName: String = Martin
lastName: String = Odersky
```

All these patterns can also be used in match statements:

```
scala> def greet(name:Name) = name match {
  case Name("Martin", "Odersky") => "An honor to meet you"
  case Name(first, "Bugnion") => "Wow! A family member!"
  case Name(first, last) => s"Hello, $first"
}
greet: (name: Name)String
```

Pattern matching in for comprehensions

Pattern matching is useful in *for* comprehensions for extracting items from a collection that match a specific pattern. Let's build a collection of Name instances:

```
scala> val names = List(Name("Martin", "Odersky"),
  Name("Derek", "Wyatt"))
names: List[Name] = List(Name(Martin,Odersky), Name(Derek,Wyatt))
```

We can use pattern matching to extract the internals of the class in a for-comprehension:

```
scala> for { Name(first, last) <- names } yield first
List[String] = List(Martin, Derek)
```

So far, nothing terribly ground-breaking. But what if we wanted to extract the surname of everyone whose first name is "Martin"?

```
scala> for { Name("Martin", last) <- names } yield last
List[String] = List(Odersky)
```

Writing Name("Martin", last) <- names extracts the elements of names that match the pattern. You might think that this is a contrived example, and it is, but the examples in *Chapter 7, Web APIs* demonstrate the usefulness and versatility of this language pattern, for instance, for extracting specific fields from JSON objects.

Pattern matching internals

If you define a case class, as we saw with Name, you get pattern matching against the constructor *for free*. You should be using case classes to represent your data as much as possible, thus reducing the need to implement your own pattern matching. It is nevertheless useful to understand how pattern matching works.

When you create a case class, Scala automatically builds a companion object:

```
scala> case class Name(first: String, last: String)
defined class Name


scala> Name.<tab>
apply    asInstanceOf    curried    isInstanceOf    toString    tupled
unapply
```

The method used (internally) for pattern matching is `unapply`. This method takes, as argument, an object and returns `Option[T]`, where T is a tuple of the values of the case class.

```
scala> val name = Name("Martin", "Odersky")
name: Name = Name(Martin,Odersky)
```

```
scala> Name.unapply(name)
Option[(String, String)] = Some((Martin,Odersky))
```

The `unapply` method is an *extractor*. It plays the opposite role of the constructor: it takes an object and extracts the list of parameters needed to construct that object. When you write `val Name(firstName, lastName)`, or when you use `Name` as a case in a match statement, Scala calls `Name.unapply` on what you are matching against. A value of `Some[(String, String)]` implies a pattern match, while a value of `None` implies that the pattern fails.

To write custom extractors, you just need an object with an `unapply` method. While `unapply` normally resides in the companion object of a class that you are deconstructing, this need not be the case. In fact, it does not need to correspond to an existing class at all. For instance, let's define a `NonZeroDouble` extractor that matches any non-zero double:

```
scala> object NonZeroDouble {
  def unapply(d:Double):Option[Double] = {
    if (d == 0.0) { None } else { Some(d) }
  }
}
defined object NonZeroDouble
```

```
scala> val NonZeroDouble(denominator) = 5.5
denominator: Double = 5.5
```

```
scala> val NonZeroDouble(denominator) = 0.0
scala.MatchError: 0.0 (of class java.lang.Double)
  ... 43 elided
```

We defined an extractor for `NonZeroDouble`, despite the absence of a corresponding `NonZeroDouble` class.

This `NonZeroDouble` extractor would be useful in a match object. For instance, let's define a `safeDivision` function that returns a default value when the denominator is zero:

```scala
scala> def safeDivision(numerator:Double,
  denominator:Double, fallBack:Double) =
    denominator match {
      case NonZeroDouble(d) => numerator / d
      case _ => fallBack
    }
safeDivision: (numerator: Double, denominator: Double, fallBack: Double)
Double

scala> safeDivision(5.0, 2.0, 100.0)
Double = 2.5

scala> safeDivision(5.0, 0.0, 100.0)
Double = 100.0
```

This is a trivial example because the `NonZeroDouble.unapply` method is so simple, but you can hopefully see the usefulness and expressiveness, if we were to define a more complex test. Defining custom extractors lets you define powerful control flow constructs to leverage `match` statements. More importantly, they enable the client using the extractors to think about control flow declaratively: the client can declare that they need a `NonZeroDouble`, rather than instructing the compiler to check whether the value is zero.

Extracting sequences

The previous section explains extraction from case classes, and how to write custom extractors, but it does not explain how extraction works on sequences:

```scala
scala> val Array(a, b) = Array(1, 2)
a: Int = 1
b: Int = 2
```

Rather than relying on an `unapply` method, sequences rely on an `unapplySeq` method defined in the companion object. This is expected to return an `Option[Seq[A]]`:

```scala
scala> Array.unapplySeq(Array(1, 2))
Option[IndexedSeq[Int]] = Some(Vector(1, 2))
```

Let's write an example. We will write an extractor for Breeze vectors (which do not currently support pattern matching). To avoid clashing with the `DenseVector` companion object, we will write our `unapplySeq` in a separate object, called `DV`. All our `unapplySeq` method needs to do is convert its argument to a Scala `Vector` instance. To avoid muddying the concepts with generics, we will write this implementation for `[Double]` vectors only:

```
scala> import breeze.linalg._
import breeze.linalg._

scala> object DV {
  // Just need to convert to a Scala vector.
  def unapplySeq(v:DenseVector[Double]) = Some(v.toScalaVector)
}
defined object DV
```

Let's try our new extractor implementation:

```
scala> val vec = DenseVector(1.0, 2.0, 3.0)
vec: breeze.linalg.DenseVector[Double] = DenseVector(1.0, 2.0, 3.0)

scala> val DV(x, y, z) = vec
x: Double = 1.0
y: Double = 2.0
z: Double = 3.0
```

Summary

Pattern matching is a powerful tool for control flow. It encourages the programmer to think declaratively: declare that you expect a variable to match a certain pattern, rather than explicitly tell the computer how to check that it matches this pattern. This can save many lines of code and enhance clarity.

Reference

For an overview of pattern matching in Scala, there is no better reference than *Programming in Scala,* by *Martin Odersky, Bill Venners,* and *Lex Spoon.* An online version of the first edition is available at: `https://www.artima.com/pins1ed/case-classes-and-pattern-matching.html`.

Daniel Westheide's blog covers slightly more advanced Scala constructs, and is a very useful read: `http://danielwestheide.com/blog/2012/11/21/the-neophytes-guide-to-scala-part-1-extractors.html`.

Index

futures
about 83-86
blocking until completion 88, 89
concurrency and exception
handling 156-158
parallel execution, controlling with execution contexts 89, 90
result, using 86-88
stock price fetchers example 90-92
URL 84

G

GitHub
follower's graph 187-189
URL 348
GitHub API
URL 144
GitHub servers
URL 316
GitHub user data
about 346
URL 346
Group by
aggregations with 138, 139

H

HashingTF 293
headers
adding, to HTTP requests in Scala 159-162
Hello world
with Akka 191-193
HTML templates 348-350
HTTP 159
HTTP headers
adding 158

I

indexing 22-24
invokers 135

J

JavaScript dependencies
through web-jars 347, 348

java.sql.Types package
API documentation, URL 105
JDBC
about 96
API documentation, URL 120
connections enriching, with pimp my
library pattern 108-111
connections, with loan pattern 106-108
database server, connecting to 97
data, inserting 98-100
data, reading 100-103
first steps 96, 97
functional wrappers 105
result sets in stream, wrapping 111-113
summary 104, 105
tables, creating 97, 98
versus Slick 141
JFreeChart 47
JFreeChart documentation
URL 52
JSON
about 143-145
consuming 335-337
external APIs, querying 335-337
interacting with 333-335
parsing 338-341
JSON4S types 149
JSON files 280, 281
JSON in Scala
about 146-149
fields extracting, XPath used 150-152
JSON4S types 149

K

k-fold cross-validation 309

L

LAPACK library 17
lazy computation 43, 44
L-BFGS method 33
life-cycle hooks 220-224
line type
customizing 53-57
Ling-Spam dataset
URL 261

Thank you for buying
Scala for Data Science

About Packt Publishing

Packt, pronounced 'packed', published its first book, *Mastering phpMyAdmin for Effective MySQL Management*, in April 2004, and subsequently continued to specialize in publishing highly focused books on specific technologies and solutions.

Our books and publications share the experiences of your fellow IT professionals in adapting and customizing today's systems, applications, and frameworks. Our solution-based books give you the knowledge and power to customize the software and technologies you're using to get the job done. Packt books are more specific and less general than the IT books you have seen in the past. Our unique business model allows us to bring you more focused information, giving you more of what you need to know, and less of what you don't.

Packt is a modern yet unique publishing company that focuses on producing quality, cutting-edge books for communities of developers, administrators, and newbies alike. For more information, please visit our website at www.packtpub.com.

About Packt Open Source

In 2010, Packt launched two new brands, Packt Open Source and Packt Enterprise, in order to continue its focus on specialization. This book is part of the Packt Open Source brand, home to books published on software built around open source licenses, and offering information to anybody from advanced developers to budding web designers. The Open Source brand also runs Packt's Open Source Royalty Scheme, by which Packt gives a royalty to each open source project about whose software a book is sold.

Writing for Packt

We welcome all inquiries from people who are interested in authoring. Book proposals should be sent to author@packtpub.com. If your book idea is still at an early stage and you would like to discuss it first before writing a formal book proposal, then please contact us; one of our commissioning editors will get in touch with you.

We're not just looking for published authors; if you have strong technical skills but no writing experience, our experienced editors can help you develop a writing career, or simply get some additional reward for your expertise.

[PACKT] **open source**
PUBLISHING   community experience distilled

Python Data Science Essentials

ISBN: 978-1-78528-042-9   Paperback: 258 pages

Become an efficient data science practitioner by thoroughly understanding the key concepts of Python

1. Quickly get familiar with data science using Python.

2. Save tons of time through this reference book with all the essential tools illustrated and explained.

3. Create effective data science projects and avoid common pitfalls with the help of examples and hints dictated by experience.

R for Data Science

ISBN: 978-1-78439-086-0   Paperback: 364 pages

Learn and explore the fundamentals of data science with R

1. Familiarize yourself with R programming packages and learn how to utilize them effectively.

2. Learn how to detect different types of data mining sequences.

3. A step-by-step guide to understanding R scripts and the ramifications of your changes.

Please check **www.PacktPub.com** for information on our titles

Scala for Machine Learning

ISBN: 978-1-78355-874-2   Paperback: 520 pages

Leverage Scala and Machine Learning to construct and study systems that can learn from data

1. Explore a broad variety of data processing, machine learning, and genetic algorithms through diagrams, mathematical formulation, and source code.

2. Leverage your expertise in Scala programming to create and customize AI applications with your own scalable machine learning algorithms.

3. Experiment with different techniques, and evaluate their benefits and limitations using real-world financial applications, in a tutorial style.

Practical Data Science Cookbook

ISBN: 978-1-78398-024-6   Paperback: 396 pages

89 hands-on recipes to help you complete real-world data science numerical projects in R and Python

1. Learn about the data science pipeline and use it to acquire, clean, analyze, and visualize data.

2. Understand critical concepts in data science in the context of multiple projects.

3. Expand your numerical programming skills through step-by-step code examples and learn more about the robust features of R and Python.

Please check **www.PacktPub.com** for information on our titles